LEAN MANAGEMENT OF GLOBAL SUPPLY CHAIN

Japanese Management and International Studies
(ISSN: 2010-4448)

Editor-in-Chief: Yasuhiro Monden *(University of Tsukuba, Japan)*

Published

Vol. 1   Value-Based Management of the Rising Sun
         edited by Yasuhiro Monden, Kanji Miyamoto, Kazuki Hamada,
         Gunyung Lee & Takayuki Asada

Vol. 2   Japanese Management Accounting Today
         edited by Yasuhiro Monden, Masanobu Kosuga,
         Yoshiyuki Nagasaka, Shufuku Hiraoka & Noriko Hoshi

Vol. 3   Japanese Project Management:
         KPM — Innovation, Development and Improvement
         edited by Shigenobu Ohara & Takayuki Asada

Vol. 4   International Management Accounting in Japan:
         Current Status of Electronics Companies
         edited by Kanji Miyamoto

Vol. 5   Business Process Management of Japanese and Korean Companies
         edited by Gunyung Lee, Masanobu Kosuga, Yoshiyuki Nagasaka &
         Byungkyu Sohn

Vol. 6   M&A for Value Creation in Japan
         edited by Yasuyoshi Kurokawa

Vol. 7   Business Group Management in Japan
         edited by Kazuki Hamada

Vol. 8   Management of an Inter-Firm Network
         edited by Yasuhiro Monden

Vol. 9   Management of Service Businesses in Japan
         edited by Yasuhiro Monden, Noriyuki Imai, Takami Matsuo &
         Naoya Yamaguchi

Vol. 10   Management of Enterprise Crises in Japan
         edited by Yasuhiro Monden

Vol. 11   Entrepreneurship in Asia: Social Enterprise, Network and Grossroots
         Case Studies
         edited by Stephen Dun-Hou Tsai, Ted Yu-Chung Liu, Jersan Hu &
         Shang-Jen Li

Vol. 12   Lean Management of Global Supply Chain
         edited by Yasuhiro Monden & Yoshiteru Minagawa

Japanese Management and International Studies – Vol. 12

LEAN MANAGEMENT OF GLOBAL SUPPLY CHAIN

editors

Yasuhiro Monden
University of Tsukuba, Japan

Yoshiteru Minagawa
Nagoya Gakuin University, Japan

 World Scientific

EW JERSEY · LONDON · SINGAPORE · BEIJING · SHANGHAI · HONG KONG · TAIPEI · CHENNAI · TOKYO

Published by

World Scientific Publishing Co. Pte. Ltd.

5 Toh Tuck Link, Singapore 596224

USA office: 27 Warren Street, Suite 401-402, Hackensack, NJ 07601

UK office: 57 Shelton Street, Covent Garden, London WC2H 9HE

Library of Congress Cataloging-in-Publication Data
Lean management of global supply chain / [edited by] Yasuhiro Monden & Yoshiteru Minagawa.
    pages cm. -- (Japanese management and international studies ; vol. 12)
    ISBN 978-9814630702
    1. Lean manufacturing. 2. Production control. 3. Business logistics. 4. Quality control.
5. Cost control. I. Monden, Yasuhiro. II. Minagawa, Yoshiteru
    TS155.L3276 2015
    658.5'62--dc23
                                                2015007460

British Library Cataloguing-in-Publication Data
A catalogue record for this book is available from the British Library.

In-house Editors: Lum Pui Yee/Chandrima Maitra

Typeset by Stallion Press
Email: enquiries@stallionpress.com

Printed in Singapore

Japan Society of Organization and Accounting (JSOA)

Mission of JSOA and Editorial Information

For the purpose of making a contribution to the business and academic communities, the Japan Society of Organization and Accounting (JSOA), is committed to publishing the book series, entitled *Japanese Management and International Studies* (JMIS), with a refereed system.

Focusing on Japan and Japan-related issues, the series is designed to inform the world about research outcomes of the new "Japanese-style management system" developed in Japan. However, as the series title suggests, it also promotes *"International Studies"* on the interface of managerial competencies between Japan and other countries that include Asian countries as well as Western countries under the globalized business activities of Japanese companies.

Research topics included in this series are management of organizations in a broad sense (including the business group or networks) and the accounting that supports the organizations. More specifically, topics include business strategy, business models, organizational restoration, corporate finance, M&A, environmental management, operations management, managerial & financial accounting, manager performance evaluation, and reward systems. The research approach is interdisciplinary, which includes case studies, theoretical studies, normative studies and empirical studies, but emphasizes real world business.

Each volume contains the series title and a book title which reflects the volume's special theme.

Our JSOA's board of directors has established an editorial board of international standing. In each volume, guest editors who are experts on the volume's special theme serve as the volume editors. The details of JSOA is shown in its bylaws contained in the home-page: http://jsoa.sakura.ne.jp/english/index.html.

Editorial Board

Contents

Japan Society of Organization and Accounting (JSOA)   v

Editorial Board   vii

Preface   xiii

About the Editors   xix

List of Contributors   xxi

PART I: Lean Management of Global Supply
         Chain Management   1

1. Lean Management of Global Supply Chain:
    Dynamic Combination Model of Market, Product
    Life-Cycle, Product Design, and Supply Chain   3
    Yasuhiro Monden

2. How to Facilitate Inter-Firm Cooperation
    in a Fabless Global Supply Chain   47
    Yoshiteru Minagawa

3. Ikea's Almost Fabless Global Supply Chain — A
    Rightsourcing Strategy for Profit, Planet, and People   65
    Rolf G. Larsson

4. Effects of Transfer Pricing Taxation on the
    Performance Control of Japanese Foreign
    Subsidiaries   83
    Makoto Tomo and Anson Yoshiharu Matsuoka

5. Innovation of Eco-Cars Based on
    the Global Inter-Firm Collaboration   101
    Yasuhiro Monden

6. Communization Strategy and Performance
    Management in the Japanese Automobile Industry   133
    Noriyuki Imai

PART II: Lean Management and
          Performance Evaluation
          in the Business Operations   145

7. Financial Performance Measures for the Lean
    Production System   147
    Zhi Wang and Yasuhiro Monden

8. Management Control Systems for Lean
    Management in Medical Services — A Case
    Study at Lund and Kameda   161
    Rolf G. Larsson, Yoshinobu Shima, and Chiyuki Kurisu

9. Management Control for Horizontal Network
    Organizations of SMEs — In the View Point of
    Profit Allocation Mechanism of Joint
    Manufacturing on Order   189
    Yoko Ogushi

10. Measuring the Performance of Lean
    Implementation at a Commercial Printing
    Company — An Action Research Approach   205
    Khodayar Sadeghi and Mohammad Aghdasi

PART III: Related Topics in Managerial
           & Cost Accounting   229

11. Mechanisms for Lowering Budgetary
    Slack in Japanese Companies   231
    Ken Lee, Naoki Fukuda, and Satoko Matsugi

12. Influence of Decision-Making Goal and Accurate Product-Costing Goal on the Design of Sophisticated Costing Systems: Proposal of Multi-Goal Coordination Approach 251
Nikhil Chandra Shil, Mahfuzul Hoque, and Mahmuda Akter

Index 283

Preface

This volume will explore the **Lean Management of Global Supply Chain** by extending the ways of approaching lean management originated by Japanese Just-in-Time production system.

The book will especially provide the readers on how to select the best global supply chain out of inter-firm network, fabless system or market firms, etc.

This book will explain how the global supply chain (GSC) could be organized by considering causal relationships of the stage differences in (1) market needs, (2) product design architecture, and (3) product life-cycle, for the purpose of reducing the total costs of GSC. The readers can study the cases of Apple, Toyota, BMW, IKEA, and Taiwan TSMC, etc.

For exploring the above purpose we will provide the following three areas as our research themes to the readers:

PART I: Lean Management of Global Supply Chain Management
PART II: Lean Management and Performance Evaluation in the Business Operations
PART III: Related Topics in Managerial & Cost Accounting

PART I. Lean Management of Global Supply Chain Management

Supply chain stands for the flows of goods and services from outsourcing the materials and parts, and manufacturing the in-house parts and assembling them for final products, thus selling them to the final customers. How to manage such supply chain "rationally or effectively" in a global perspective is called "global supply chain management" in this book. Here the "rational or effective" management intends to realize the cost effectiveness, and the system with such cost competitiveness is called the "lean management of the global supply chain" in the title of this book.

In this preface the editor-in-chief (Monden) will state roughly how the differences in cost competitiveness will appear depending on the differences in the grade of the complexity or simplicity of the product design structure. When the grade of complexity (or differentiation) of product architecture (design structure) will change from its higher level to the lower level, then the organizational forms of the supply chain will be moved from the hierarchical vertical-integration or inter-firm network ("Keiretsu") to the fabless network or market firms structure. The typical cases will be as follows:

(A) The supply chain of an automobile, for example, can make the lowest cost per unit of the product if it has the vertically integrated organization, whose typical one is the holding company that has many layers of subsidiary and related controlling companies.

(B) The supply chain of a flat-panel TV or smartphone, for example, which has the middle level of modular grade, can achieve the lowest cost per unit of the product if it has the Fabless network or alliance network organization.

(C) The supply chain of a personal computer, for example, which is the highest in the modular grade (or the lowest in the complexity of products design architecture), can achieve the lowest cost per unit of the product if it purchases most of the parts from the market.

The above described relationships will further be extended and elaborated in detail by the following four factors:

(1) Market needs: This will mainly vary depending on how wealthy people are (i.e., from the low-end or less-wealthy market to the high-end or wealthy market through the middle class market.

(2) Product life cycle or the cycle of business domain or industry: That is from the infancy stage to the decline stage via the growth and maturity periods. According to the well-known Boston Consulting Group's idea, the cycle will move through the business categories of "question mark", "star", "cash cow", and "dog".

(3) Product architecture: That is from the complex or integral type product to the common modular type product through various "hybrid" products composed of both integral parts and modular parts. Here the grade of hybridization between complex and modular parts will be mainly determined by the differences in income levels of the customer in each market. The top management will make decision on the weights of the mixture between complex and simple (modular) parts, which correspond to the priority of the customer.

(4) **Supply chain organization**: As described earlier, that is from the vertically integrated organization to the market through the Keiretsu network and the fabless network.

The different stages in each of the above four factors will have some correlations among factors, but the directions of movement through the various stages will differ depending on the regional difference of the markets. That is the difference between the markets of the emerging countries and the advanced countries. The correlations among four factors also differ depending on the difference in the time-length of the product "life cycle" in question.

Such elaborated propositions will be verified by the various practical cases presented in many chapters of this book.

The main theme of this volume is to explore the above global value-chain, and it will be studied in the following 6 chapters of PART I:

1. Lean Management of Global Supply Chain: Dynamic Combination Model of Market, Product Life-Cycle, Product Design, and Supply Chain
2. How to Facilitate Inter-Firm Cooperation in a Fabless Global Supply Chain
3. Ikea's Almost Fabless Global Supply-Chain — A Rightsourcing Strategy for Profit, Planet, and People
4. Effects of Transfer Pricing Taxation on the Performance Control of Japanese Foreign Subsidiaries
5. Innovation of Eco-Cars Based on the Global Inter-Firm Collaboration
6. Communization Strategy and Performance Management in the Japanese Automobile Industry

PART II. Lean Management and Performance Evaluation in the Business Operations

How efficiently the operations process of a company is going will be measured by the performance evaluation system or the management control system. For this control purpose the performance of the manufacturing process has long been measured by the physical metrics such as the lead-time (i.e., operation's time), inventory levels at each process, defect rate, number of actual workforce of each process, etc. However, it is not necessarily clear what kinds of *financial* measure or metrics should be used to assess the performance of (1) each team or department, (2) the company as a whole and (3) the consolidated business group as a whole, respectively. Thus, PART II will investigate and propose the solutions for such management control problems.

This problem will be investigated under the following topics of chapters:

7. Financial Performance Measures for the Lean Production System
8. Management Control Systems for Lean Management in Medical Services — A Case Study at Lund and Kameda
9. Management Control for Horizontal Network Organizations of SMEs — In the View Point of Profit Allocation Mechanism of Joint Manufacturing on Order
10. Measuring the Performance of Lean Implementation at a Commercial Printing Company — An Action Research Approach

PART III. Related Topics in Managerial & Cost Accounting

Finally PART III of this book contains the following two chapters as special interesting papers related to the themes of PARTS I & II.

The first chapter conducts the budgetary control system as another management control system discussed in PART II. The implicit "slack" as a kind of allowance for attaining the severer budget target is often introduced into the budgetary target figure. This study explores what background may exist in the Japanese firms for not introducing the budgetary slack.

The second chapter proposes the design method of appropriate cost accounting system. There are two goals of accounting system; one is to have variety of systems for measuring "different costs for different decision purposes." The other is to have the "activity-based costing" to measure the right amount of costs as precise as possible. How to balance these two goals in designing the costing system will be proposed.

Thus, the following chapters will be presented:

11. Mechanisms for Lowering Budgetary Slack in Japanese Companies
12. Influence of Decision-Making Goal and Accurate Product-Costing Goal on the Design of Sophisticated Costing Systems: Proposal of Multi-Goal Coordination Approach

Acknowledgments

I am very grateful to Ms. Juliet Lee Ley Chin, the senior consulting editor of Social Sciences in the World Scientific Publishing Company for her invaluable advice to make this volume a reality. Also her long-term support to this book series is sincerely appreciated. Further, Ms. Lum Pui Yee and Ms. Chandrima Maitra, the desk editors on the publisher's side, are acknowledged for taking care of the marketing and manuscripts. The contributing authors of this volume are also amply rewarded for their new ideas or knowledge that contribute to the business management and managerial accounting, thereby, being of some use to people around the world.

Principal Volume Editor
Yasuhiro Monden
March 31, 2015

About the Editors

 **Yasuhiro Monden** is Professor Emeritus of the University of Tsukuba and currently serving as Visiting Professor at MBA Program of the Nagoya University of Commerce and Business (NUCB), both in Japan. He is also currently the president of Japan Society of Organization and Accounting (JSOA). He has been majoring in production management and managerial accounting. He received his PhD from the University of Tsukuba, where he also served as Chairperson of the Institute and Dean of the Graduate Program of Management Sciences and Public Policy Studies. Monden has gained valuable practical knowledge and experience from his research and related activities in the Japanese automobile industry. He was instrumental in introducing the Just-In-Time (JIT) production system to the United States. His book, *Toyota Production System* (Engineering and Management Press: IIE, 1983, 1993, 1998 and 2012 from Taylor & Francis Group) published in English, is recognized as a JIT classic; it was awarded the 1984 Nikkei Prize by the *Nikkei Economic Journal*.

Dr. Monden's academic research includes papers in *Journal of Management Accounting Research* (AAA), *Advances in Management Accounting*, *International Journal of Production Economics*, and numerous articles in *International Journal of Production Research*. Monden was a Visiting Professor at the State University of New York at Buffalo in 1980–1981, and at Stockholm School of Economics, Sweden in 1996. He has also professionally guided on lean management system and strategic cost management in Singapore and Thailand as an expert of Japan International Cooperation Agency (JICA), an agency of the Japanese Ministry of Foreign Affairs, and his service as a committee member of the second examination of Certified Public Accountant in Japan.

Yoshiteru Minagawa is a Professor in the Faculty of Commerce at Nagoya Gakuin University in Japan. He has been majoring in management accounting. He received his PhD from Nagoya University. He was a Visiting Scholar at the Berkeley Roundtable on the International Economy at the University of California, Berkeley in 1999–2000, and at the College of Business at San José State University in 2012–2013.

His current research interests focus on the role of management accounting in supply chains, and customer value-based pricing strategies. His main publications include Profit allocation rules to motivate inter-firm network partners to reduce overall costs, in Y. Monden (ed.) *Management of An Inter-Firm Network*, Singapore: World Scientific Publishing Co., pp. 61–76 (2011); Management of humanitarian supply chains in times of disaster, in Y. Monden (ed.) *Management of Enterprises Crises in Japan*, Singapore: World Scientific Publishing Co., pp. 149–164 (2014).

List of Contributors

Mohammad Aghdasi
Industrial Engineering Department, Engineering Faculty
Tarbiat Modares University, Iran

Mahmuda Akter
Department of Accounting & Information Systems
University of Dhaka, Bangladesh

Naoki Fukuda
Graduate School of Business
University of Hyogo, Japan

Mahfuzul Hoque
Department of Accounting & Information Systems
University of Dhaka, Bangladesh

Noriyuki Imai
Graduate School of Business
Meijo University, Japan

Chiyuki Kurisu
School of Nursing
Kameda College of Health Sciences, Japan

Rolf G. Larsson
School of Economics and Management
Lund University, Sweden

Ken Lee
Faculty of Management
Otemon Gakuin University, Japan

Satoko Matsugi
Faculty of Business Administration
Tezukayama University, Japan

Anson Yoshiharu Matsuoka
Graduate School of Economics
Seijo University, Japan

Yoshiteru Minagawa
Faculty of Commerce
Nagoya Gakuin University, Japan

Yasuhiro Monden
The University of Tsukuba, Japan
The NUCB Business School, Japan

Yoko Ogushi
Faculty of Economics
Niigata University, Japan

Khodayar Sadeghi
Industrial Engineering Department, Engineering Faculty
Tarbiat Modares University, Iran

Nikhil Chandra Shil
Department of Business Administration
East West University, Bangladesh

Yoshinobu Shima
Faculty of Business Administration
Kinki University, Japan

Makoto Tomo
Faculty of Economics
Seijo University, Japan

Zhi Wang
Faculty of Commerce
Nagoya University of Commerce and Business, Japan

Part I

Lean Management of Global Supply Chain Management

1
Lean Management of Global Supply Chain: Dynamic Combination Model of Market, Product Life-Cycle, Product Design, and Supply Chain

Yasuhiro Monden
University of Tsukuba

1. Theme of the Study

1.1. *Proposition for building the optimal supply chain: Causal relations among market needs, product life-cycle, product architectures, and supply organizations*

In this chapter the author will explore what kind of open inter-firm networks (open supply chain) will be cost-efficient (or "lean") for formulating the global supply chain. The chapter uses the knowledge of production and operations management, managerial and cost accounting, organization theory, and the institutional economics to explicate the causal relationships among (i) market needs, (ii) product life-cycle (PLC), (iii) product design architectures, (iv) supply organizations, and (v) production costs. Since each of these five factors has various levels and dynamically varies depending on the environmental changes, the author coins the scheme of system selection in each environmental condition as the "Dynamic Combination Model" of supply chain.

The structure of this chapter is as follows: the author assumes a general proposition that the optimal forms of the open inter-firm network or the global supply chain will be determined based on the causal relationships above-mentioned. After the theoretical and logical analysis is done, the author will verify such proposition based on the various case studies about the IT industry and the automotive industry. The optimality will be judged based on the cost minimization criterion per unit of the product, but this cost efficiency criterion will be re-examined in the final conclusion section. Now when each of the above-mentioned four factors (or dimensions) is divided into only two main levels for simplicity, though each of the factors usually has more than two levels, then it follows that:

(1) Market needs or wants entail the differences in the high-end market M_1 for the wealthy customers or the low-end market M_2 for the less-wealthy customers.
(2) Product design structures include product made of complex, custom-order parts A_1 or product made of simpler, standardized modular parts A_2.
(3) PLCs are the different stages of life period that transit mainly from the growth stage L_1, to the maturity stage L_2.
(4) Organizational forms of the global supply chain will be identified as various forms from the hierarchical vertical-integration S_1 to the pure market-firms network S_2 via the *Keiretsu* network or the fabless network.

Since these factors are directly correlated with other factors one by one, let us consider the causal relationships, step by step, to construct the general causal theory among all factors in order to configure the optimal supply chain.

The result will be the author's proposition that the best form of the global supply chain structure in terms of cost efficiency will be the optimal combination between the various levels in the aforestated four factors (or four dimensions), and its brief summary is as follows:

(1) The **hierarchical vertical-integration or *Keiretsu* network (i.e., inter-firm network), S_1,** is best suited for the stage of the complex-type product A_1, for the wealthy customers' market M_1, and the growing stage of the PLC L_1. That is, the optimal point or vector (M_1, A_1, L_1, S_1) in the four dimensional space as depicted in Fig. 1.
(2) The **pure market network S_2** is best suited for the simpler, modular-type product A_2, for the less-wealthy customers' market M_2, and in the maturity or declining stage of PLC L_2, in the advanced countries (while the market S_2 is suited well for the growing stage of PLC L_1 of the emerging countries). That is the optimal point or

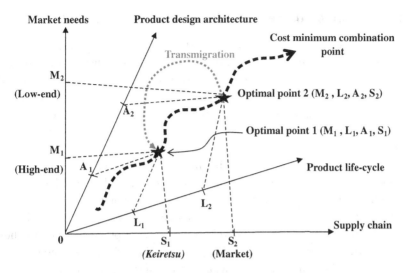

Fig. 1.   Dynamic Combination Model of the cost minimum combination points in the four dimensional space in the advanced countries.

vector (M_2, A_2, L_2, S_2) in the four dimensional space in the advanced countries as depicted in Fig. 1.

Since the top management of the firm should transit the position of **the best business model** (or the vector in the optimal point in the Euclidean space of four dimensions in Fig. 1) to some optimal balance, the role of top management must be to shorten, as much as possible, the distance between the optimal point and the actual point because if the distance became longer the acquisition cost of unit product would be higher.

The optimal combination points may not be on the *linear* line that starts from the origin point ($M_0 = 0$, $M_0 = 0$, $M_0 = 0$, $M_0 = 0$). **The direction suggested by the dotted-arrow tip in Fig. 1 is of the firms of the wealthy market (or advanced countries)**, where the optimal point will transit toward the north-eastern direction from the optimal point 1 to the optimal point 2, with the assumption that even the firms of advance country must provide the modular product to the less-wealthy market when their industry cycle matured, whereas the optimal point of **the firms of the less-wealthy market (or emerging countries)** will transit reversely from the point 2 to the point 1.

1.2. *Dynamic business model for lean management*

The "business model" in this chapter stands for the combination of four factors (or dimensions) that can minimize the unit production or purchase cost of product or service. However, since each business model consists of such four factors, the author will use the specific form of supply chain or specific form of organizations (including even the network of the independent firms in the competitive market) in order to represent the concrete business model.[1]

Further the actual optimal point must be the "zone" rather than the "point", because the growth period of PLC, for example, must have a certain length of the period rather than a single time point.

In case of the firms of the advanced countries, Sony and Panasonic, for example, have experienced relatively longer period of growth before they got into the maturity. When did their transition of PLC happen in the past? It was the time when the firms of the emerging or middle-advanced countries, such as Samsung and LG Electronics have made their **disruptive innovation** in the Chrystal panel television or semi-conductor in terms of their sales prices. For the zones of other factors see Fig. 3.

Because the earlier proposition is a *general theory of the causal relationships* the author will first make a theoretical analysis (see Sec. 2) and then make verifications (see Sec. 3) of this proposition through the case studies on the IT industry (especially the smartphone of Apple and Asian brand-makers) and the automotive industry (European, Japanese, and American automakers).

---

[1]The "**Business Model**" in this chapter stands for the mechanism or process for the business manager under a certain environment (consumers' market needs, and wants) to transform the business resources (fund, labors, materials, facilities, and information) to the valuable product or service with a certain product-architecture under the certain supply chain (including the independent firms network in the suppliers market). It can also be rephrased as the mechanism of earning the maximum profits with the least costs and satisfying the stakeholders' requirements. It could be summarized as a mechanism of transforming the inputs (or production resources) to the outputs (goods or services), which is the production process in the traditional micro economics.

"**Business innovation**" includes the change of the earlier defined business model, but the author will not concretely specify what kind of product or service could be introduced in the new business model of a concrete company in this chapter.

2. Reasons of the Causal Relations among Various Factors

2.1. *Several concepts in the Dynamic Combination Model*

Before getting into the verification of the earlier proposition on the Dynamic Combination Model, let us first clarify several concepts in the proposition in detail.

2.1.1. *Concepts of the "production or purchase costs per unit" of product or service*

2.1.1.1. "Make of buy" decision should be made by the "unit production cost" and the "unit purchase cost": A case study of Toshiba

Toshiba has once been manufacturing the standard Alkaline Battery in their group's subsidiary company called Toshiba Battery Inc. But since the global price of the "rare metal" as main materials of the battery has doubled during three years from 2005 to the end of 2007, Toshiba decided to sell their manufacturing facilities of Toshiba Battery to FDK of Fujitsu group, and to procure all of the volume out of FDK and to sell them with Toshibha brand (*The Nikkei*, 2008).

In this way Toshiba decided to "Buy" the battery instead of "Make" in their own house. However, this decision was not made based on the reason why Coase's "transaction costs" (which is the cost of *"purchase management"* for buying the battery from the market) became cheaper than the in-house "managerial cost" for making them at home.[2]

---

[2]**Concept of the "transaction costs" by Coase and Williamson:** According to Williamson (1991, p. 284) the "transaction cost" (or governance costs) in a broad sense includes not only (i) the transaction costs in the market (i.e., costs for managing the market transaction), but also includes (ii) transaction costs between the inter-firm allied firms (or Williamson's "Hybrid") (i.e., managerial costs for inter-firm coordination), and (iii) transaction costs within the hierarchically integrated organization (i.e., managerial costs for internal coordination). This is because the transaction of merchandise includes not only transaction in the market, but also the inter-firm or intra-firm transactions within the inter-firm or hierarchical organization.

criterion for this "make or buy" decision was that the "unit purchase cost" (= market price) from the FDK became cheaper than the "unit manufacturing cost" at Toshiba plant (i.e., Toshiba Battery Inc.). The real reason was that the (incremental) **unit manufacturing cost** of a battery (= **direct material cost** + **processing costs**) at Toshiba plant became more expensive than the unit purchase cost from FDK, under the increased material purchase costs of "rare metals". Right now all of the Japanese Alkaline Battery makers (Mitsubishi electricity, Fujitsu, Toshiba, and Sony) except Panasonic and Hitachi are all paying just a commission as a fabless commissionaire (i.e., original equipment manufacturer or OEM manufacturing).

2.1.2.   Concept of the "product design architecture"

The product design architecture is the basic design idea about how the product designer will consider the basic design about the following two matters (Fujimoto, 2004, pp. 124–126):

(1) The way of matching between various *functions* of the product demanded by customers and the various *structural components* of the product.

The only use the (ii) managerial costs to be spent for adjusting the transaction within the firm. Williamson has broadened the concept of transaction costs by using the term: the *governance costs* so as to include the marginal costs to be spent for additional transaction within the firm or inter-firm, which include various managerial costs for transferring the goods and services between the departments or inter-firm. The broader concept of transaction costs include the incremental costs which will be spent for motivating the people working in the intra-firm or inter-firm organization. However, both Coase and Williamson neglected the (incremental) unit production or purchase costs per product or service itself (for more details see Monden, 2001).

In the cost accounting system the transaction costs of Coase should be charged on the purchase cost itself or allocated to it based on the predetermined allocation base for the purpose of measuring the direct material costs, but the major portion of the (incremental) direct material costs is of course the purchase costs *per se.*

Notwithstanding the earlier-mentioned difference of the governance costs and the author's unit cost of purchase or manufacturing, both of the analysis is similar in the viewpoint that considers only the "cost" in selecting the supply chain.

(2) The connection (interface) rules between the various structural components. In other words, the architecture implies (i) the way of connection between functions and structures, and (ii) the way of connection between various components (or parts).

In case of an automobile, each function of a car is supported by many components while each component is also contributing to the various functions. Such product like an automobile is called an **"integral"** **type product**. However, in case of a personal computer, for example, the correspondence between functions and components is almost "one to one matching". Such product is called a **"modular" type product**.[3]

However, since the above-mentioned two types of products are merely conceptual dichotomy and the real product contains both types of parts (output of suppliers or in-house manufacturing processes) as its composing parts, it would be practically useful to consider the architecture of any product as a **"hybrid" architecture product**. Thus, the grade of hybridity depends on the grade of product complexity or simplicity in their hybrid design architectures (Monden & Larsson, 2014).

2.1.3. Concept of the "supply chain structures"

2.1.3.1. Two concepts of parts from the product design architectures: Specialized parts (or custom-made parts) and common parts

From the viewpoint of product design architecture there are two concepts of parts.

(1) Group of specialized exclusive-use parts for a specific model of a certain company, which is called an "integral" type. The example is a kind of specific part to be utilized only for a certain car-model (such as the hybrid car of "Prius") of Toyota Motors.

(2) Group of common parts (commonly usable parts, or standard parts), which is called a "modular" type. For example, a printer of various printer-makers can be utilized for almost any company's personal computer system such as Dell, Lenovo, etc.

---

[3]In Fig. 3 the product architecture dimension could be considered as similar to the "asset specificity".

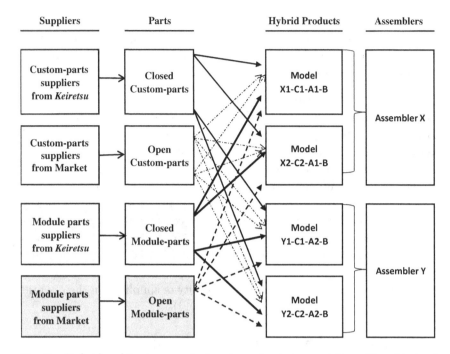

Fig. 2.   Hybrid architecture product and supply chain consisting of four kinds of suppliers.

2.1.3.2. The suppliers from the inter-firm network and the suppliers from the market

Since both kinds of the parts are supplied by a certain firm of *Keiretsu* network or by a firm in the competitive market, they will be classified into the four groups supplied by the following four different types of suppliers (see Fig. 2):

(1) "Closed" custom-parts suppliers from inter-firm network (or called *Keiretsu*);
(2) "Open" custom-parts suppliers from market;
(3) "Closed" module-parts suppliers from inter-firm network (or called *Keiretsu*);
(4) "Open" module-parts suppliers from market.

Here the "Keiretsu" is a group of firms in the inter-firm network, which are formed and controlled by a core company and has a long-term transaction relationship with the core company. They are allied with the core company in terms of capital ownership, managerial directors, or inter-firm transaction as major suppliers, etc.

As an example of the (2) "Open" custom-parts suppliers from market, the case of Apple's iPhone is raised. As will be explained in detail in Sub-sec. 5.1, the characteristic of iPhone's development method is based on the approach for the "integral" type product architecture. Apple coordinated the interfaces of various specifications of many functional components such as panel, graphic processing unit (GPU), communication system, camera, battery, and external-style design, etc. Therefore, the interface between the various components is fully coordinated during this design phase. As a result they can procure various components out of many suppliers in the market, who satisfy iPhone's specification, but they are not the suppliers of Apple's *Keiretsu*.

2.1.3.3. "Hybrid Supply Chain" that uses both market and inter-firm network (*Keiretsu*)

Note that the concept of "Hybrid", which Williamson (1991) used is entirely different from my concept of "Hybrid" that I initially used in my earlier chapter on "Robust Supply Chain" (Monden & Larsson, 2014, in its Fig. 1). Williamson's concept of "Hybrid" is the inter-firm network organization, which is positioned as a unique transaction form placed between the market transaction and the hierarchy transaction. However, the author's concept of Hybrid implies the "Hybrid network of market and inter-firm network". That is why I introduced the concept of "Pareto Optimum" to describe the optimal balance of procurements from both the market and the *Keiretsu* or inter-firm network.

Also any kind of product has both integral parts and modular parts at the time though their proportions would differ from each product, such that the author proposed the concept of *hybrid product* that has *hybrid product architectures*.

2.1.3.4. "Fabless" supply chain as the hybrid of market and inter-firm network

The "fabless" supply chain in which the core company has no manufacturing plants and consigns their fabrication functions to the outside firms.

Such cases can be seen in the relation between Apple and Taiwan Hon Hai (called electronic manufaturing service or EMS) and in the relation between Qualcomm (fabless semiconductor firm in USA) and Taiwan

TSMC (foundry). In these cases the consigned firms such as Hon Hai and TSMC are independant companies in the market and so Apple's fabless supply chain is essentially the "Hybrid network" of market and inter-firm network. If the consigned company is strong in their technology, they can be an independent firm in the market and could supply their manufactured parts to many other brand companies too.

In the other cases, however, the "fabless" supply chain will be included in the category of the inter-firm nework (i.e., *Keiretsu*) only, because the "operational alliance" that has no capital alliance can be contracted within the inter-firm network, though such contract is usually short-term during the model-life of the product. In this case the parts supplier in question is relatively weak in their technology and has to be involved only in the manufacturing function under the control of core firm.

2.1.3.5. Cost-reduction efficiency versus attractiveness by differentiation

The modular-based parts are usually good for cost-reduction efficiency, since they can enjoy both scale-merit and scope-merit thanks to the wider uses of these parts in a variety of models. On the other hand, the specialized parts have a benefit of differentiating the products for quality attractiveness to individual customer's preferences. As the author see it, the mixture of larger use of modular-based parts and the less but effective use of specialized parts could yield both efficiency and attractiveness.

2.2. Autonomously evolving factors

2.2.1. The reason why the "market needs or wants" will transit from low-end products to the high-end products in the emerging countries and reverse in the advanced countries

For considering this reason let us divide the markets into two categories: market for the wealthy people (major market in the advanced countries) and market for the less-wealthy people (major market in the emerging countries).

(1) In the emerging countries the GDP and the income per capita will grow rapidly and thus the preference of majority of the people will transit

from the low-end products to the high-end products in proportion to their income growth.

(2) In the advanced countries the situation is somewhat complicated. When the new attractive branded product such as Apple's iPhone was developed and sold to the high-end market, people's demands for such product is higher. However, sooner or later the competitors will emerge from the emerging countries that provide low-price products to the low-end market, and gradually such new products will be introduced to the market of the advanced countries, thus increasing their sales share in the global market. This will undermine the market of advanced countries and gradually decrease the sales of big firms of advanced countries. However, it is tougher for the attacked big firms to find or create some new attractive products. Also the wage rate in the advanced countries the proportion of the people of less-higher wage rate will grow when confronted the depressions. Thus, even in the advanced countries the demand for low-end products will grow. Such example could be seen in the popularity of "old" models of smartphone whose price is reduced in the market. This phenomenon is seen in the comparison between the less sales-*amount* growth rates than the sales-*units* growth rates in the smartphone business. And eventually even the firms of advanced countries have to develop and sell the low-end products as a "double brand" strategy.

2.2.2. The reason why the "PLC (or industry life-cycle)" will proceed from the growth stage to the maturity stage and finally reach the decline stage

Any creature in this planet including all animals and plants will first be born, grow up, get old and die as a rule of natural world. And even the artificial in the modern globalized world will follow the same rule and will be explained by the following reasons:

The first innovator, when they developed the new attractive product and put it into the market, could get the higher profit and thus the innovator company will grow in the market. However, sooner or later the production technology of the first runner will be copied or modified by many followers' firms, and further the more advanced technologies of the similar product will be developed by the newcomers in the market. In other words, many suppliers will participate in the same product market, and because of the competition among them the product technology will be accumulated in the industry as a whole. As a result the production costs per unit and the price will be reduced due to the furious competition and thus the initial runners' performance in the market will reach the maturity stage and finally the declining stage.

The aforementioned process could also be followed between the firms of the advanced countries (G7 or wealthy nations) and the emerging countries (Brazil, Russia, India, China, South Africa, also known as BRICS, and others) nowadays. The related explanations for this situation have been made by Vernon (1966) and the *innovator's dilemma* theory of Christensen (1997 and 2000).

2.3. *Causal relationship between two factors*

In this section the author will describe the causal relationship between four factors raised in Sec. 1. Since it would be too complicated if we would consider the simultaneous causal relations among many variables, the author will explain such causal relations among various factors by taking only two factors at a time and such relationship will be sequentially linked with one factor by another factor until all factors will be stepwise and sequentially linked.

As shown in Fig. 3, actually both the variables of the market needs and the PLC are *independent* variables and they will not be affected by any

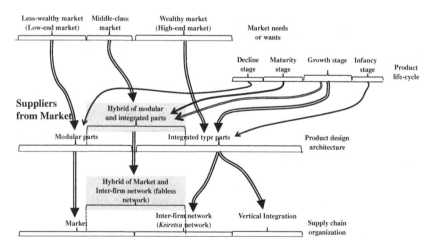

Fig. 3.   Cost-minimum combination points in the four dimensional space in the advanced countries (another expression of Fig. 1).

other variables, while the product design architectures will be affected by both market needs and PLC simultaneously. Further, the variable of the product design architectures will in turn affect the forms of supply chain structure (see Fig. 3).

2.3.1. The reason why the "market needs or wants" will determine the product architecture

Whether the supply chain will move to the market-like mechanism or reversely to the *Keiretsu*-network organization will depend on the proportion of the parts type that dominates the hybrid product structure, which is ultimately determined by the customer's preference:

(1) Market for the less-wealthy customers, where majority of the people prefer cost-efficient models that use the modular type parts.
(2) Market for the wealthy customers, where majority of the people prefer the quality-attractive models that use the integral type parts.
(3) Market for the middle class customers, where majority of the people prefer both cost-efficient and quality-attractive features that use both modular and integral parts at the same time with some optimal balance ratio.

2.3.2. The reason why the "PLC" will determine the product design architectures

While the industry is being developed, the technical knowledge about the hierarchical components of product that is vertically composed of major components and sub-parts, etc. will be accumulated and shared among many assemblers and suppliers in the industry. Then the initial need for integrating or coordinating the interface of various components will be gradually reduced, and thus the modular components will eventually appear which could be used by various kinds of product models.

This is the general reason why the stage transition of PLC from growth period to mature period will cause the change of the product architecture from the integral type to the modular type.[4]

---

[4]Although the product design architecture will change depending on the change of market needs and the stage transition of PLC, it will also change evolutionally

2.3.3. The reason why the "product design architectures" will determine the supply chain systems

2.3.3.1. The reason why the "integral type product" will be best suited for the vertically integrated firm or the inter-firm network

Integral type product requires the custom-made parts whose mutual interface must be coordinated beforehand for their assembly. Take automobile, for example, if the assembler of automobile corrals the various parts suppliers within their inter-firm network, then the automobile assembler can develop each parts together with the parts suppliers and reduce the parts costs on account of applying the "design-in" approach, in which they could allocate the product target cost to each parts as the target unit-amount of each part cost. Then both of the parties could achieve the target amount of part cost through "value-engineering" or *target costing* techniques (see Monden, 1995). Thus, **the *unit manufacturing cost* (*or unit purchase cost*) of each part will be much less expensive than the acquisition cost from the market (i.e., purchase cost of outsourced part).**

On the other hand if the final maker of the integral type of product would like to use the parts developed and manufactured by the parts-makers in the market, who can make the custom ordered parts, as seen in the relations of Apple and Sharp (crystal panel maker for the iPhone), the final product maker (Apple) must coordinate the interface among various parts in their own side. In this case **the design architecture of the purchased parts must be custom-made one, and the parts supplier must have excellent development technology** of the parts in

---

and autonomously (Shibata (2012)). The reason why the product design architecture will transit autonomously from the integral type to the modular type will be as follows:

According to Simon (1981) the human will design the artificial product as a hierarchical structured form due to the "bounded rationality" in the human cognitive ability. By designing such hierarchical structure the human can manage its complexity. In pursuing such hierarchical decomposition process and exploring the rules of mutual dependencies between the multiple hierarchy levels and between the plural components, the modular type architecture of product will be developed. This is the evolutionary interpretation for the process of transition of product architectures.

question. In such case **its procurement is done from the plural parts suppliers in the competitive market with much lower price than the manufacturing cost in the brand maker.** Thus, this is the case of such "open custom parts" as shown in the Fig. 2.

2.3.3.2. The reason why the "modular type product" is best suited for the market-based transaction

When the components of the common platform of the product became *modular* ones, then such common modules could be utilized by variety of products and as a result could be produced in a massive volume. Here the usage by variety of product can realize the *"economy of scope"*, and the mass production can achieve the reduction in the "unit production cost" of the suppliers as *"economy of scale"*. In summary, **the supplier of modular parts, thanks to both the economies of scale and scope, will reduce the *unit manufacturing costs* of the modular parts. Therefore, the product maker will purchase such cheaper modular parts from the competitive market with cheaper price.**

Since the modular parts will not necessitate coordination of the interface among various parts, they can be easily procured from the market and enjoy much reduced cost of purchase, thanks to the aforestated economies, than the manufacturing cost in the *Keiretsu* network or the vertically integrated firm.

3. Verification of the Proposition on the Optimal Supply Chain through the Case Study of the Electronics Industry (e.g., Smartphone) that has the Shorter PLC: Optimal Causal Relations in the *Growth Stage* of the iPhone's PLC

3.1. *Global supply chain of Apple's iPhone*

Supply chain of the Apple's *Smartphone* is as follows:

Five levels defined from the down-streams to the up-streams are:

(1) Sales companies;
(2) Software, system/infrastructure owners;
(3) Product providers;
(4) Component providers;
(5) Material and tool suppliers.

Overview of Silicon Wafer Foundry Business

● **Manufacturing supply chain of electronic products**

▪ Five levels are defined: (1) Material and tool suppliers; (2) Component provider; (3) Product providers; (4) Software, system/infrastructure owners; (5) End users
▪ New business model of component provider created by fabless design houses + Wafer foundries + testing/packaging houses
▪ Wafer foundry business focus on the customers from component providers

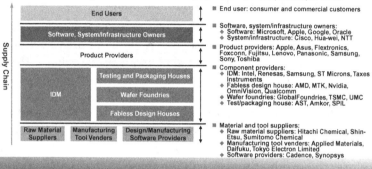

Fig. 4. Supply chain of smartphone as the open network composed from the global market (this figure was adapted from Hsieh, 2013a and 2013b).

The examples of concrete company names of each layer of the smartphone are written in the right side of Fig. 4. Note that Apple is the **product provider** of the product: smartphone as hardware, but they are focusing only on the product design for **hardware**, **soft (applies and contents)** and various **infrastructures**. The **component providers** for making the semiconductor (system LSI) of smartphone such as Qualcom and Broadcom in the US have created the new business model by concentrating on their business network of [the **fabless design houses** (such as Qualcom) + **wafer foundries** (such as TSMC in Taiwan) + testing and packaging houses]. On the other hand, the traditional **"Integrated Device Manufacturer"** (IDM) such as Intel, Renesas, Samsung, and Texas Instruments are still working as strong providers of components.

Further as a consigned manufacturer of the silicon wafers, the TSMC in Taiwan is the most successful and is regarded as world's No. 1 wafer foundry. The **silicon wafer foundry** (TSMC) focuses on the customers from the component providers (such as Qualcom in the US, who provides semiconductor to Apple's iPhone). As **materials and tool suppliers,** there are many Japanese manufacturers such as Hitachi Chemical, Shin-Etsu, Daifuku, and Tokyo Electron, etc.

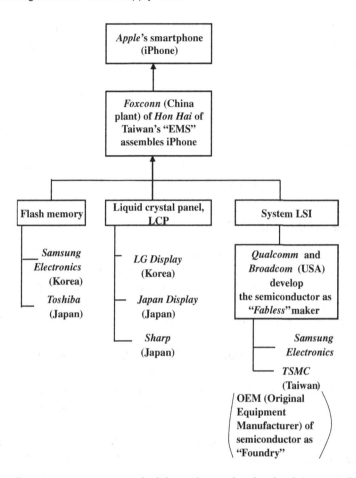

Fig. 5.   Open custom-parts supplied from the market for Apple's smartphone.

The various parts used for Apple's smartphone are the custom-made parts for the iPhone only, such as the crystal panel which Apple calls as "Retina-panel", they are not procured from the Apple's long-term *Keiretsu* suppliers, but are purchased from the open parts market, where various parts-makers are competing with each other in the same market. Therefore, this form of suppliers should be called the "Open" custom-parts suppliers from the market (See Fig. 5).

The network organization seen in Fig. 5 is changeable when the new model of iPhone is designed annually, since the specifications of each part in the new Apple model would be changed, thus, the suppliers would change in accordance with such model-change. However, since this is not the spot-purchase in the conventional market and is based on the contract that will be kept for the model-life of one year during which the member change will not occur.

In the following sub-sections the vertically divided network from the development, final assembly, and the manufacturing of various parts such as system large-scale integration (LSI), crystal panel, and flash-memory, etc. and the sales and services of iPhone will be examined step by step. Such *"vertically"* divided network is sometimes called the *"horizontally"* divided network from the viewpoint of the equal positioned partnership between suppliers and Apple.

3.2. Development of iPhone

As noted in Sub-sec. 3.1, Apple plays a role as developer of iPhone, and all manufacturing jobs are consigned to the outside firms. Thus, Apple is called a *"fabless"* firm that takes an *"asset-light"* strategy, thereby enhancing the return on asset (ROA) and also reducing the fixed capacity costs (depreciation costs) of facilities to achieve the *"lean"* *management in the global supply chain.*

The characteristic of Apple's product development method is based on the approach for the "integral" type product architecture. As mentioned earlier, Apple designs hardware, soft (OS, applies, and contents) and various infrastructures. They first make their own design for the Operating Soft (iOS) and central processing unit (CPU), and further coordinate the interfaces of various specifications of the other functions such as panel, GPU, telecommunication system, camera, battery, and external-style design, etc. (Nobeoka (2012)). In other words, Apple's design approach is for the "integral" type product that the author has explained in the Sub-sec. 2.3.3.1.

Regarding the software development, for example, **iPhone 6** which begun its sale on September 9, 2014 has a new application soft; iPhone 6 added a new function of easy payment called "**Apple-Pay**", by which the iPhone user can pay by just holding up iPhone over the iPhone reader of the retail store. For this function Apple allied with the big chain restaurants and the big department stores to be used in their 220,000 stores in the US. (Such easy payment system by smartphone was preceded by Samsung electronics a year before.) For this new function Apple also made alliances with big credit-card firms and big banks. In addition, they use the fingerprint recognition system to identify the individual payer without using the payer's credit-card number. This "Apple Pay" system is also installed in the "**Wearable Watch**" as a wearable terminal, which was again preceded by Samsung (*The Nikkei*, 2014b and 2014c).

However, it should be emphasized that the integration or coordination between the various main functions and main structural components is considered only in their design process, and also the interface between the various components is fully coordinated during the design phase. As a result they can procure various components from many suppliers of the market, who are not the suppliers of *Keiretsu*.

3.3. *Final assembly of iPhone*

Final assembly of iPhone is made by *Foxconn Technology Group*, which is the manufacturing subsidiary company in China of *Hon Hai Precision Industry Company Ltd.*, Taiwan. Hon Hai as EMS is assembling various digital parts for iPhone.

Taiwan EMS makers such as *Hon Hai* has the following cost-competitive sources (Kawakami, 2012):

(1) "Merit of the industry cluster" in the Taipei and Hsinchu Science Park;
(2) "Merit of scale" is enjoyed as the mass-production place of products and parts in China. However, this merit has decreased recently due to the increase of wage rate in China.

"Fabless" supply chain of Apple could be rephrased as the "asset-light" strategy, which has been very successful when we see the evaluation measure of "Cash Conversion Cycle" (CCC: cash collection lead-time). CCC is the number of days from purchase and sales to cash collection, as represented by the following formula:

$$CCC = (\text{Collection days of accounts receivables}$$
$$+ \text{Number of days of inventory})$$
$$- (\text{Payment days of accounts payables}).$$

Each of these days is the average figure during the period.

If such CCC days are shortened, the firm has more power of yielding the cash. Then the *free cash flow* (= operating cash flows + investment cash flows) will be ample, so that the quickly available fund for R&D and sales promotion could be increased.

The CCC of Apple became a *minus figure* since 2000, while it was more than 70 days in 1996. Apple's high performance of CCC is mainly indebted to their "fabless" manufacturing, but also due to inventory control and restructuring of products variety. On the other hand, the CCC of Asian digital firms such as SONY, Panasonic, and Samsung Electronics are about 40 days in 2010 (*The Nikkei*, 2013f).

3.4. *Semiconductor (system LSI) of iPhone*

As stated in Sub-sec. 3.1, (Figs. 4 and 5) the iPhone's semiconductor (system LSI) is supplied by American makers of Qualcomm and Broadcom, etc. utilizing the wafer foundry of TSMC of Taiwan. TSMC specializes in making the circuit on the silicon wafer (this process is called the preceding process of semiconductor manufacturing). The system LSI is used for telecommunication and image processing of smartphone.

3.4.1. *Excellent performance of TSMC*
and their business model

TSMC has earned the **operating profit ratio on sales of 35.8%** in 2013 (ended in December 2012), while Intel for memory protection unit (MPU) of personal computer (PC) was 27.4%, and Samsung Electronics for memory of PC and smartphone was 12.0% (*The Nikkei*, 2013a).

TSMC has made the facility investment of almost US$10 billion in 2013. Such huge amount of facility investment for manufacturing the semiconductor could not be continued each year by any other makers except Intel and Samsung. Thus, so many number of the fabless semiconductor makers have increased recently, and TSMC has enabled their rapid growth, thanks to this big demand, with keeping the higher capacity usage rate and the 90% share in the system LSI of 28 nm chip size in 2012 (*The Nikkei*, 2012).

Although the price of semiconductor is determined on the auction-like competitive market, TSMC can keep their higher price on account of their excellent technology in terms of the shrunk chip and enlarged wafer, thus achieving the very high operating profit ratio. This has further enabled their continuous facility investments and R&D expenditure to develop their competitive technology. Thus, the higher performance of TSMC is not due to the "small profit and quick returns".

3.4.2. Can high performance of TSMC be explained by the "smile curve" theory of electronics industry?

Richard Baldwin (2013) has applied the smile curve theory to explain the performance of each member in the global supply chain. He says that although the smile curve in the 1970s was relatively flat, it became a U letter form in the 21st century and as a result the value-added allocated to the wealthy countries has decreased in the manufacturing stage.[5]

Such change of the smile curve occurred since the globalization of 21st century has eased the transition of the manufacturing intelligent assets (such as idea and know-how or technology) from the advanced country to the emerging country. Thus, the firms of the wealthy countries (G7) will face the loss in the stage of "fabrication" of goods, while the firms of the emerging country (BRICS) will get the profit, though the wealthy countries still can get wealth in the stages before and after the stage of fabrication; they are the stages of design, marketing, management of complex supply chain, retail services, and "after-services" of the sales, etc. (the smile curve proceeds from the left side to the right side), since in these stages the services to be provided quickly and flexibly by the collective intelligent people could not be easily copied by the emerging countries.

However, he says that in the stage of fabrication the more profit or more value-added will appear in the emerging countries because they have acquired the intelligent assets in this stage of global supply chain. This part of Baldwin's analysis may seem to be well explaining the high performance of TSMC (35.8%) and Samsung Electronics (27.4%) of their operating profit ratio on sales. But actually the profit of Foxconn in China (i.e., plants of Hon Hai, Taiwan) is small and the wage rate of Foxconn has been increased due to the labor dispute (*The Nikkei*, 2013g). As I see it, the high performance of TSMC is based on their intensive R&D activities to acquire the excellent technology in terms of the shrunk chip and enlarged wafer, and so it could be regarded that they have been concentrating on the *pre-fabrication stage* of smile curve in providing the system LSI.

---

[5]The concept of smiling curve itself was first proposed by Stan Shi, the founder of Acer, an IT company headquarter in Taiwan, in 1992. Based on this theory Acer has invested intensively in R&D to develop innovative technology in PC-related products as well as its services areas.

3.4.3.   How the "IDM" such as Intel, Samsung, and Renesas are changing their business model?

The "IDM" are those semiconductor makers that have the *vertically inte-grated organization* within their own business group. It may seem that their business model has no relationship with the fabless model, which I have discussed up to this point. However, Renesas and Fujitsu are also trying to use TSMC as their consigned manufacturer. Further, Intel and Samsung are getting into the consigned maker business just like TSMC. Actually Samsung had No. 3 share as a wafer-manufacturer busi-ness even in 2013. Such changes in Samsung and Intel are based on the decline in the demand for semiconductor to be utilized in MPU of PC. The demand for such MPU was reduced on account of the growing usage of smartphone by the customers as alternative of PC (*The Nikkei*, 2013a).

3.5.   Chrystal panel and flash memory of iPhone

Chrystal panel of iPhone is what Apple calls as "Retina display", which is a custom-made component for iPhone. However, Apple will not procure this custom-order component from their *Keiretsu* suppliers unlike the cases in Japanese manufactures, but it is supplied by many independent firms such as LG Display (Korea), Japan Display (Japan), and Sharp (Japan), etc. who are competing with each other in the market. Thus, the "Retina dis-play" is the *open custom-made parts provided from the competitive market* (see Fig. 5).

The flash memory of iPhone has also been supplied by the Sam-sung Electronics and Toshiba who are competing in the open competitive market.

3.6.   Post-fabrication services of iPhone

3.6.1.   Mobile-phone telecommunication service firms (i.e., "carriers") in the final service stages of iPhone supply chain

The model "iPhone 6" (began its sale from September 2014) is now being sold worldwide by many sales companies of communication ser-vices. In Japan the telecommunication service of iPhone has been sold by

SoftBank (SoftBank mobile), au (KDDI group), NTT DoCoMo (or DoCoMo), TU-KA, and EMOBILE.[6]
These communication service companies are earning profit through the communication fee (call charges). Since they are taking roles in the service stage which is the subsequent process in the "smile curve", they can earn higher profits among all processes of the whole supply chain.

Apple has reduced the consignment ratio of manufacturing to Taiwan Hon Hai due to the wage rate increase in their China plant (Foxconn). The profit of Hon Hai was thus decreased and Hon Hai also took a license of a communication service company and began to enter the communication carrier service stage (*The Nikkei*, 2013g).

3.6.2. *Makers of the application software ("Appli") of iPhone*

The most famous made-in-Japan "application software" (Applies) for the smartphone is the LINE, which enables "free" voice communication, email, and chat and was developed and managed by Japanese team of Korean company (currently called NHN Play Art). This is currently widely used not only in Japan but also in Middle East and south-eastern Asia.

Such communication "Applies" of LINE and Skype, etc. are accelerating many people to leave the cellular (portable) phone and the wired (cable) telephone and invading the revenue sources of these telephone business (*The Nikkei*, 2013e).

3.6.3. *"Multi-layer strategy" by the smartphone maker for the "business ecosystem" and selection by the customer*

As explained in the Sub-sec. 3.2 (development of iPhone), the smartphone business has **many layers of firms** in its final stage (services stage) of the whole value chain. Especially important service providers are the telecommunication service providers (carriers), the **"Appli"** suppliers, and the contents suppliers. The companies surrounding this stage should first select

---

[6] Also there are companies called Mobile Virtual Network Operation (MVNO) who borrows the cable from the carrier (i.e., NTT DoCoMo) and sells cheaper communication service to the customers. If a customer uses both tablet and smartphone at the same time, two contracts must be made, which double the communication costs. Thus, MVNO can provide less expensive services to such users.

what layer they should participate in and then to what extent their product or service could be provided as "open" business to their rivals.

For example, Amazon is selling its electronic book via their "Kindle" terminal (Tablet PC), and the Kindle users can access the "Kindle-store" freely via this terminal and the Kindle Appli. However, Amazon is also openly providing this Kindle-store to the rival's terminals such as Apple iPhone or "iPad", by which these rival terminal users can also use not only Apple's "iBooks" Appli but also Amazon's Kindle Appli to access the Kindle store, thereby they buy the Amazon's electronic books (Negoro, 2014).

Such situation is called as the "**business ecosystem**" (ecological system) where varieties of firms are providing the application softs and its stores, and the contents and its stores to the final customers, thus, these Applies providers and contents providers are competing each other as well as co-existing through mutually complementary relations. Such system is analogous to the biological ecology system (for business-ecosystem see Iansiti & Levien, 2004). In case of Apple, they are preparing the App Store and iTunes Store for the providers and developers of application softs and contents. Thus, Apple established the ecosystem surrounding the iOS and the iPhone, iPad, and Apple TV, such that Apple can be one of "**platform leaders**" in the mobile industry, though Apple's eco-system is not so "open" compared to the Android OS related ecosystem led by Google (Yasumoto, 2013, pp. 226–227). See Fig. 6 for the inter-firm network of the business ecosystem.

As another example Google provides "Android OS" as an open OS to the automobile companies such as Honda and General Motors, and tries to develop vehicle information system using big-data of automobiles, whose drivers' car-driving data could be absorbed into Google's server via Android OS (Negoro, 2014).

3.6.4.   *Apple Sales International in Ireland: "Base Erosion and Profit Shifting" of the international taxation problem*

Unlike the fabless system for manufacturing of iPhone, Apple holds their own wholesale company in their consolidated business group. Apple established the wholesale company of iPhone in Ireland, called Apple Sales International (ASI) that purchases the iPhone from Hon Hai in China (Foxconn) and sells them to Apple retail companies in many overseas countries which receive only the sales commissions. Thus, most of the group's

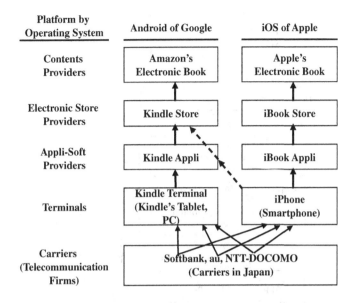

Fig. 6.   Multi-layers inter-firm network of business ecosystem.

profit (joint profits) earned outside the USA could be absorbed by the Ireland ASI (see Fig. 7).

3.6.4.1.   Double avoidance of taxes

This is what the Organization for Economic Cooperation and Development (OECD) calls as Base Erosion and Profit Shifting (BEPS) of the international taxation problem. Because of the aforestated scheme Apple could hardly be taxed by either the USA or Ireland tax authorities. The Internal Revenue Service (IRS) of the US will tax only the *corporations* who were established in the USA, while the Ireland will tax only the firms whose central managerial functions are located in Ireland. Thus, Apple is a typical case of the "double avoidance of taxes".

3.6.4.2.   "Check-the-box Classification Regulations"

US firms can select either the *corporation* (object to be taxed in the US) or the *members or branch* of the firm (object not to be taxed in the US) when they establish the firm in overseas. The firm can make a check on the blank box of the questionnaire sheet when they select such alternatives.

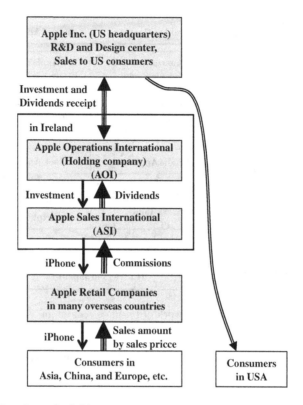

Fig. 7.   Sales channel of iPhone.

The overseas firm such as Apple's ASI could be legally exempted from taxation by IRS if ASI became a subsidiary company (i.e., a "grandchild" firm of Apple in the US), based on the "check-the-box classification regulations", because such subsidiary firm can be regarded as Apple's *branch* in overseas. For this purpose Apple established the holding company called *Apple Operational International* (AOI) in Ireland, under which ASI became as subsidiary company of AOI and was regarded as Apple's branch or member constituting the Apple. Thus, ASI will not be taxed by the US tax authority. Also the dividends, which AOI as parent company of ASI will receive from the ASI, could not be legally taxed by the US tax-authority because AOI is the overseas firm of Apple (see Fig. 7).

As a result of the above-mentioned tax-saving actions most of Apple's profit after tax will be saved in the overseas sales company (ASI) located in Ireland, and the cash balance of Apple also could be saved in ASI (*The Nikkei*, 2013b).

4. Low-Price Smartphone: Its New Product Development Method, New market, New Global Supply Chain, and PLC Stage

4.1. *Causal relations of the low-price smartphone*

In this section the author will present how the *disruptive* innovation of business model has appeared in the smartphone industry. This innovation in business model has effects on the following aspects:

(1) The **product development method** was changed from the development and design method for the integral-type product architecture to the one of the modular type product architecture.

(2) The **new market** has emerged for the low-end smartphone in the emerging countries, and this low-price smartphone begun to expel the high-price smartphone in the world market. In other words, the bipolarization of markets has appeared (see Fig. 8).

(3) The **new global supply chain** for low-end product has appeared as a strong tag of Chinese brand makers and Taiwanese component maker (Media Tek) and also Taiwanese foundry (TSMC), while the high-end product supply chain between Apple, Qualcomm, etc. and TSMC is still active.

(4) The **PLC** of iPhone seems to be gradually transiting from the growing stage to the maturity stage. Though Apple's financial performance of both the sales amounts and sales units in their global iPhone segment is still growing as of the year 2014 compared to the previous years, but both of their growth rate are gradually declining.

The aforementioned four changes will be explained one by one in the flowing sub-sections.

4.2. *Product development method of the low-price smartphone by Chinese brand makers*

The product development method (or product architecture) of iPhone was explained in the Sub-sec. 3.2.

Semiconductor fabless-maker in Taiwan called *Media Tek* provides the product *design blueprint* itself as a "Reference" for finding the various assembling components of the smartphone itself and the operating system (OS) as well as the system LSI, etc. to the Chinese smartphone makers ("brand" makers) who sell the low-price (US$110) smartphones to the

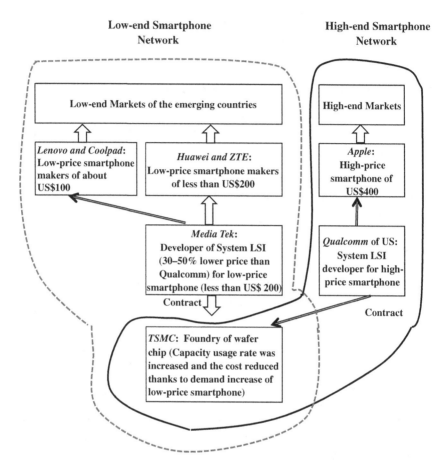

Fig. 8.   "China + Taiwan" network for the low-price smartphone, compared with the high-price smartphone network.

customers of China and the emerging countries (see Fig. 8). Therefore, these final product makers for low-end market will not be actually involved in the product development phase that requires complicated integration of various functional components. Thus, since the product makers who are inferior in their development technology also could easily enter the smartphone production, their participation in the smartphone business is very vigorous. Therefore, they can avoid or reduce their development costs for the final product (*The Nikkei*, 2013c and 2013d).

This point is entirely different from the development method of iPhone by Apple, who conducts their own original custom-made product that is necessary to coordinate various custom-made components through the merchandize planning, product planning, and designing activities. The Chinese mobile-phone makers are rather adding the simpler and tiny functions to be loved by customers, such as mechanism of inserting the two SIM cards for possible utilization of plural communication-service companies or by attaching the magnet showing the geographical directions (Watanabe, 2013).

4.2.1. *Chinese smartphone makers use the "common module parts" from the market, unlike the Apple who uses the "custom-made parts" from the market*

In China there are many suppliers who provide the ***common module parts*** for smartphone. All of the brand product makers can purchase these common modular parts from the market. For example, the core semiconductor (system LSI) is also supplied as a chip-set, which is provided by Taiwanese *Media Tek* and others (Watanabe, 2013).

4.3. *Transition from the custom-made smartphone to the modular smartphone: The low-end product is expelling the high-end product from the market*

In the world of smartphone market, the sales of the high-price smartphones of US$400 of Apple, Samsung, and Sony are declining in their growth rate. This is because the low-price smartphone below US$200 and middle-price smartphone of US$200–400 are growing rapidly since 2013. This is because *Media Tek* (supplier of less expensive system LSI) and *TSMC* (foundry of wafer chip) tagged with China smartphone makers have well succeeded in supplying the low-price smartphone to the low-end markets of emerging countries (see Fig. 8) (*The Nikkei*, 2013b and 2013c).

4.4. *Bipolarization of markets and the "double-brands" strategy*

This is the same phenomena of the flat panel TV of Japanese electronics makers that suffered from modularization of product architecture. In Figs. 1 and 3, the smartphone business of Apple and Samsung is positioning on the integral type product-architecture and on the high-end market, while the smartphone of China is positioned on the modular type architecture and on the low-end market. In order to cope with such trend Apple began to introduce the *reasonable-price* iPhone 5c as well as the high-price iPhone 5s since September 2013. This must be called the "double-brands" strategy (or "two-sword fencer"). In the iPhone 5s the fingerprint recognition system was introduced while iPhone 5c has simpler functions and designs.

Google has renewed their operating system soft (OS): "Android 4.4" which could be installed even into the smartphone for the users of emerging countries. Google reduced the unnecessary functions for this new OS, so that it could also be installed in the low-price smartphone (below US$100) popular in the emerging countries like the "Nexus 5" which was jointly developed by Google and LG Electronics (Korea) (*The Nikkei*, 2013h).

Since there are the markets for wealthy, middle-class, and less-wealthy customers both in the advanced market and in the emerging market, the "double brands" (or "hybrid") strategy must be applied to both of the countries, but it must also be considered what customers are majority in each country.

5. Verification of the Proposition through the Automobile Industry that has Longer Product Life-Cycle

5.1. *Hybrid of hierarchy and inter-firm network (Keiretsu) of Toyota group*

In the USA there were many vertically integrated big companies during late 19th century and early 20th century as depicted by A. Chandler (1977) as "visible hand", such as Standard Oil, US Steel, AT&T, Ford Motors, etc. though many of them were divided by the antitrust law.

In Japan, on the other hand, there are many business groups consisting of the multi-layers of firms, which are linked by the hierarchical capital ownership.[7]

---

[7]There are three tiers or layers of firms constituting the Toyota Business group (Noguchi, 2012, pp. 129–134).

The **Tier 1 group** is the consolidated subsidiary companies. For each of them Toyota owns more than 50% voting rights as their parent company. Toyota owns about 500 subsidiary firms, whose total employees are 320,000 people. Excepting

As I see it the "Keiretsu" network or the vertically integrated business group of Japanese automobile industry as illustrated for Toyota group in Fig. 9 is so strong and still well-fitted to the product architecture of its "integrated" type, which was explained in Sec. 1. This is because each automobile has to use 20,000 or 30,000 of parts, and the interface of most of the parts must still be configured not only in the design phase but also in the manufacturing phase since most of them are still custom-made parts rather than the modular parts. This point is entirely different from the small-sized products of the consumer electronics or home appliances such as TV and smartphone.

For such supply chain between Toyota, sales dealers and parts suppliers, the Toyota's information system (or "Order Entry System") has been developed and still used very well (for more details on such information system see Monden, 2012).

The optimal combination point for such Japanese automobile network of four dimensions in Fig. 1 has long been the point 1 (M_1, A_1, L_1, S_1) rather than the point 2 (M_2, A_2, L_2, S_2). That is why there still exist Japanese advocators who strongly and consistently suggest the integrated architecture (i.e., complicated product design) and the group network organization (*Keiretsu* supply chain) as recommendable future polices of Japanese manufacturing industries.

However, we should also consider the following changing trends in the global market needs, the product architecture and the supply chain network,

---

Hino Motors and Daihatsu Motors, these firms are mainly domestic and overseas assemblers of Toyota cars.

The **Tier 2 group** is Toyota's consolidated affiliated firms. For each of them Toyota owns the voting rights of not-less-than 20% or less than 50%. However, more than 50% of the voting shares of each of these companies are owned by the leagues of Toyota, its group firms of Fig. 9 and the related banks. Toyota Motor Corporation applies the so-called "equity method" for their simplified consolidation. These companies are called "Keiretsu" firms that mainly include the major components makers such as Denso and Aisin Seiki, etc. Most of these companies were once split out of Toyota Motors or Toyota Industries Corporation, as shown by the dotted lines in Fig. 9.

Each of the Tier 2 firms has many subsidiary companies, which could be called as the **Tier 3 firms**. They are not shown in Fig. 9, and most of them are unlisted in the stock market, because the stocks of most of Tier 3 firms are completely (100%) owned by Tier 2 and Tier 1 companies.

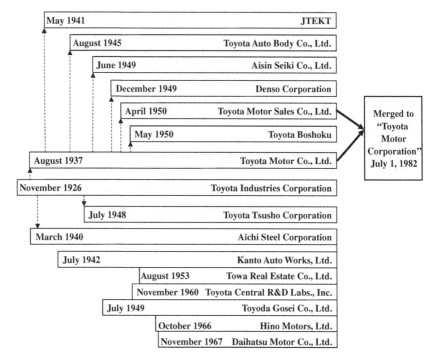

Fig. 9.   Formation of Toyota group: *"Hybrid of Hierarchy and Inter-firm Network (Keiretsu)"* (Quoted from Monden, 2012, p. 78).

etc. in the Japanese automobile industry:

(1) **Market needs or wants** in the emerging countries are mainly for the less-wealthy customers in the low-end market (M_2). For this situation the author has written the chapter (Monden & Larsson, (2014): Sub-sec. 5.2 on "Optimal balance of hybrid supply chain that comprises cost efficiency and attractiveness").

(2) Unlike the electronics or digital products industry, the automobile industry has a much longer **PLC** and is still under the growing stage of its PLC. This is due to their continuous innovations for de-maturing or rejuvenation for developing the electric vehicles, IT technologies, etc. depicted as "Transmigration" in Fig. 1. So they are in the middle of point 1 and 2 meanwhile the automakers in the emerging countries are beginning to grow just after taking off the infancy stage.

(3) **Product design structures** begun to include the simpler, standardized modular parts (A_2). For this situation refer to the Sub-sec. 5.2.

(4) **Supply chain** begun to include the "**firms in the market**" (S_2) rather than *Keiretsu* network, especially in the suppliers of the electric vehicle components. For this situation refer to the paper entitled: "Innovation of Eco-Cars Based on the global Inter-Firm Collaboration" by Monden (2015).

(5) **Supply chain** begun to also include the **contracted manufactures** in the global chain. In other words, the automobile manufacture itself begun to include the "fabless" system by using the OEM manufactures (positioned **in the midst of S_2 and S_1**). Sub-sec. 5.3 will describe this situation.

5.2. *Emergence of the modular design architecture in the auto-industry*

Even in the automobile industry the product design architecture has been moving from the integral-type to the modular-type, and the supply chain is also changing because the **fabless auto-makers** have emerged together with the **consigned manufacturers of automobile** that are similar to the EMS in the flat-panel TV and the smartphone manufacturing. Let us examine these two phenomena in the following sections.

5.2.1. *"Hybrid" network of the market and the inter-firm network*

The details of how Toyota and Nissan have been adopting the common modules system for the components of their common platform (i.e., the running functional mechanism) were written in Monden & Larsson (2014). As is seen in the common modules system of Toyota (called *"Toyota New Global Architecture"*; TNGA) and of Nissan (called *"Common Module Family"*; CMF), the various major components such as (i) engine component, (ii) front underbody, (iii) cockpit, and (iv) rear underbody of the common platform will be used as *common module* components for variety of car models for a longer period of time. On the other hand, the other supplementary groups of parts positioned above the platform are unique to each model and subject to frequent change as *custom-made* components of each model.

In Japanese auto-makers the common modular components will still be purchased from the *Keiretsu* suppliers so that such components should be called the "closed" module parts as depicted in Fig. 2, while the custom-made components of each model should be called the "closed" custom parts in Fig. 2. However, when the "closed" module parts will become the "open" module parts to be procured from the market suppliers, their procurement costs per unit will be much reduced thanks to economies of scope and scales. In this case it follows that the "Hybrid network of the market and the inter-firm network" is used.

5.2.2. *Modularization of Volkswagen cars as "MQB"*

The current Japanese auto-makers modular system is merely applied to the narrow platforms for the same sized cars. However, VW's modular concept is one step advanced; it crosses the common platforms of all Front-engine Front-wheel drive (FF) cars of the previous five varieties of sizes communized to the one transverse "mega-module" called Modular Querbaukasten (MQB) in Germany; or Modular transverse kit in English (see Fig. 9).

Volkswagen has four different "modular transverse kits" for:

(1) Cars called NSF of small horizontal engines;
(2) Cars called MQB;
(3) Cars called MLB of vertical engines; and
(4) Cars called MSB of big and high-grade ones.

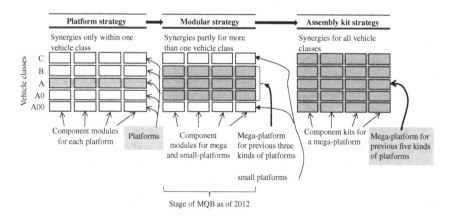

Fig. 10.   MQB of Volkswagen as of 2012.

Source: Adapted from Volkswagen homepage (May 2, 2012) with the author's modification.

Such product architecture strategy for the mega-platforms is linked to the multi-brands strategy of Volkswagen. They are going to reduce costs through mega-platform strategy and also increase profits from the high-end brands setting the higher prices. Such approach is similar to the Toyota's double-brands strategy as explained earlier.

5.2.3. *Mega-suppliers*

Under the mega-platforms strategy of Volkswagen, Renault and most of the European automobile manufacturers are procuring their core components from Robert Bosch SG, Continental AG, AG (German tire and brake manufacturer), Valeo (French powertrain manufacturer), and Michelin, etc. Since these mega-suppliers are supplying their parts to most of the auto-makers throughout the world, they are not the solid allied suppliers (*Keiretsu*) of a certain specific auto-manufacturers, but are independent from the specific auto-makers, thus being the independent firms of the open markets.

While the auto-assemblers are using such common parts as the commodities that are subject to the price competition in the parts market, they also have their own differentiated "black-boxed" parts (or custom parts) as sources of earning their profits. This approach is similar to Toyota's one. Therefore, the automobile makers have the hybrid network consisting of both the markets and the inter-firm organization (*Keiretsu*).

Toyota also tries to change their hitherto "keiretsu" suppliers into the *mega suppliers* who could sell their products (parts) to not only Toyota but also to many other (rival) auto-makers, so that their engineering protocol could be global standards (*The Nikkei*, 2014e). Examples are: Denso for electronic safety technologies, Aisin AI for manual transmission, Shiroki for door-frame, Advics for brake-system, Toyota Industries Corp. for diesel-engine, and Toyota Boshoku for sheets.

5.2.4. *The full-lineup strategy (or double brands strategy) of big automobile companies*

(1) The Japanese mini-car manufactures such as Daihatsu and Suzuki will take the strategy of focusing on the less-wealthy market.
(2) But the big auto-makers such as Toyota, Nissan, and Honda will have a so-called full-lineup strategy and sell their cars to all of the (a) wealthy market, (b) middle-class market and (c) less-wealthy market at the same time, and thus they seem to have three types of supply-chains at the same time.

5.3. *Contract manufacturer and OEM manufactures in the automobile industry*

In the United States the contract manufacturers (or manufacturing on assignment or OEM) in the automobile industry are increasing, who manufacture the various kinds of automobile parts or assemble the final components.

Such manufacturers are different from the traditional parts-makers for the auto assemblers. A single contract manufacturer will make any kind of components such as engine, tire, suspension, etc. at the same time in the same plant. Each major component is assembled on the individual lines of the same plant, while the traditional parts-maker manufactures each of these parts in the separate part-maker individually, or otherwise the final auto-maker has made or assembled such parts in their own plant. The consignee can make any kind of parts with the same method that uses a kind of cell, on which each part is set for its assembly, instead of using a conveyer line. Such line can be changed in its cell shape or in its cell length.

5.3.1. *Android Industries, Magna International and Nedcar as commissioned companies*

The most famous commissioned company is **Android Industries,** founded in 1988, and 33.4% of stockholders' capital is held by Mitsui & Co., Ltd. (Japanese trading company). Android has customers of the Big three in the US, and especially 85% manufacturing processes of the full-sized Sport Utility Vehicle (SUV) of General Motors (GM). Android makes their own facilities before they propose the commissionaire contract to the new customers. Although the demand for Big three have increased after the economic crisis in 2008, they have not added their new plants in the US, but have increased their OEM production volume.

Others are **Magna International** (Canada) and **VDL Nedcar** (Netherlands). Magna Steyer (Austria), which is a subsidiary company of Magna International, has been manufacturing "G-class" for Mercedes-Benz, "X3" for BMW, and "Jeep Grand Cherokee" for Chrysler, as their manufacturer on assignment. VDL Nedcar produces the model "MINI" for BMW in their Netherlands plant.

Such consignee companies are similar to the EMS such as Taiwan Hon Hai or the foundry (as semi-conductor manufacturing firm such as Taiwan TSMC).

Behind the growth of the contract manufacturers in the automobile industry there must be the spreading trend of communization of components in the broader platforms in auto-industry. Under such modularization trend the fabless business model has been rapidly spreading in the US and European auto-industries. This may mean that the automobile also is getting into the "commoditization" under severe price competition (*The Nikkei*, 2014d).

5.3.2.   *Mitsubishi Motors supplies the pickup truck to Fiat-Chrysler Group as OEM*

Mitsubishi Motors Corporation will supply the Sport Utility Truck (SUT) to Fiat in Italy and Chrysler in America as OEM with the brand names of Fiat and Chrysler, respectively. This SUT is called Triton in Mitsubishi and it was newly developed and will be manufactured in Mitsubishi's Thailand plant. The pickup truck is popular in the US and the emerging countries, but Fiat has supply shortage of pickup and wishes to satisfy the demand by OEM of Mitsubishi, while Mitsubishi's Thailand plant has demand shortage due to the political struggle, thus tries to assure the high capacity usage rate of plant through OEM (*The Nikkei*, 2014d).[8]

6.   Conclusion

6.1.   *Summary*

In this chapter the author explored what kind of combination among market, PLC, product design, and supply chain should be made as the **best Business Model**. In other words, the author made a general proposition that the optimal forms of the open inter-firm network or the global supply chain will be determined based on the causal relationships among the market needs, the PLC, the product architectures, and the unit costs.

Starting from or depending on the market needs or wants and the PLC in question to which the company is facing, the top management of the firm should configure the combination of four dimensions in Fig. 1 toward some optimal point. In determining such optimal balance, the role of top

---

[8]Italian automaker Fiat has completely (100%) acquired the Chrysler group on January 1, 2014. The SUT is a combined vehicle of SUV and pickup truck. Mitsubishi developed the new model called "Triton" that has four door cabin with open head and uses 4WD in their SUV called "Pajero".

management is to shorten the distance between the optimal point and the actual point as much as possible, because if this distance became longer the acquisition costs (i.e., manufacturing or purchase costs) per unit product would be higher and the better profits could not be earned.

Then the author further verified this proposition through the case studies on the IT industry (smart phone as a shorter life-cycle product) and the automotive industry as a longer life-cycle product.

First, let us briefly summarize the case of smartphone business models. As I said in the earlier paragraphs, the market needs will come first and it determines the following various factors' levels. From this view point there are two different kinds of products in the smartphone business. Those are (a) high-grade or high-price product (i.e., smartphones made by Apple and Samsung, etc.) and (b) low-grade or low-price product (i.e., smartphones made by Lenovo and Coolpad, etc. in China). For each of these two kinds of products the best combination among market needs, PLC, product design architecture, and supply chain form would be different.

(1) Smartphone for high-end market should be (i) high-grade or high-price product, (ii) product life-stage of the growing *with declining speed*, (iii) integral (complex) architecture, and (iv) fabless network although the product development phase of complex architecture is most important.

(2) Smartphone for low-end market should be (i) low-grade or low-price product, (ii) product life-stage of the growing *with increasing speed*, (iii) modular (simple) architecture, (iv) mainly market-based network including the product development phase.

Next, let us briefly summarize the case of automobile business models. Again the market needs or wants will come first and it determines the following factor levels. From this view point there are two different kinds of products in the automobile business.

(1) High-end market cars should be (i) high-grade or high-price product, (ii) product life-stage of the *growing*, (iii) integral (complex) architecture, and (iv) vertical integrated network or inter-firm network.

(2) Low-end market cars should be (i) low-grade or relatively low-price product, (ii) product life-stage of the growing with increasing speed, (iii) modular (simplex) architecture, and (iv) fabless network or market-based network. In this category the electric automobiles (Electric Vehicles (EV), Hybrid Vehicles (HV), Plug-in Hybrid Vehicles (PHV), and Fuel Cell Vehicles (FCV)) can be included, though the prices of

these electricity-related cars are still high, but they will follow similar characteristics as (2) of smartphone.

Further, for the big company the full-lineup strategy (or double-brand strategy) would be necessary that has both (1) type and (2) type products at the same time.

6.1.1. *Business model and the creation of value-added product or service*

So far we have discussed what kind of combination among market needs, PLC, product architectures, and supply chain is appropriate as a **lean (cost-efficient) business model**. However, even though such combination itself may bring the efficient low-cost production, it must be just a mechanical structure as a business system. The much more important element for earning the positive revenue must be how to create the customer value of the merchandise itself.

The customer value of the merchandise is the added value by which the customer will be pleased to have it. In other words, there must be something attractive by which the product could be well accepted by the customer. That is, the product must have such attractive flavor to be loved by the customer as Steve Job's has created by iPhone.

6.1.2. *Transmigration of the PLC: How can we rejuvenate the PLC?*

The PLC emphasized by Vernon (1966) and Abeggren and Boston Consulting Group (1978) is that a product will progress through the stages of infancy, growth, maturity, and finally decline, etc. However, Abernathy *et al.* (1983) says that the manufacturing industries can indeed arrest — and in some circumstances even reverse — the maturation process and we would argue for the possibility of industrial "de-maturity". Since any prosperous product or industry is destined to decline at last, this de-maturity concept or idea seems to be attractive.

As I see it, however, the concept of "de-maturity" assumes that the matured (or declined) business could be reversed to the younger and growing business (or anti-aged). But, in the real business world the declined business usually will be *removed* out of the company in question, and the new business will be *introduced* as a "regeneration", or "transmigration", or "re-incarnation", or "turnover" of the ailing company. So the term "re-generation" or "transmigration" would be more appropriate than the term "de-maturity". Such transmigration is equivalent to the innovation. Thus, we have to explore the following topics to make the "transmigration" before the PLC get into the decline stage.

6.1.3. *How we could create the customer-value from now on*

In Sub-sec. 4.1, the author said that "the low-end product is expelling the high-end product from the market." Certainly the iPhone's "unit sales" are still growing even though its growth rate is decreasing. But, sooner or later iPhone's price will go down just like the fact that the price of crystal panel TV has decreased with 30% per year. Then where will Apple earn their profits from now?

According to the Apple's consolidated balance sheet as of March 29, 2014, their **cash on hand** is $41,350 million (= cash and cash equivalents $18,949 million + short-term marketable securities $22,401 million: note that this amount is after they have paid for the "repurchase of common stock" $23,000 million in 2014), which is **41%** of the retained earnings $98,934 million.

Thus, Apple is now a *cash-rich* company, but unfortunately **Apple could not yet find any other prospective fields for their future investment.**

Similar situation can be seen in almost half (1,800 firms) of Japanese listed company (on a stock exchange) as of 2014. They are also called "cash-rich" companies or in many cases the "net-cash" companies, so that the easy monetary policy and/or reduction of corporate tax rate could have no positive effect on their effective investment in the real business. Such policy may just drive people to seek for capital gain out of the bubbly increase of asset prices.

6.1.4. *The extension of the Business Model of the cost minimum combination to the profit maximization*

Although the Business Model of this chapter considered various factors that will ultimately affect the global supply chain, it assumed the market needs and the PLC as environmental premises. However, such markets needs and PLC could be changed by the efforts of the company. The new market of the newly introduced product or service could be created even in the nearby fields of the existing business of the firm in question, and the PLC itself could be changed or reversed when the new product or service is introduced through the "blue ocean strategy" advocated by Kim & Mauborgne (2004).

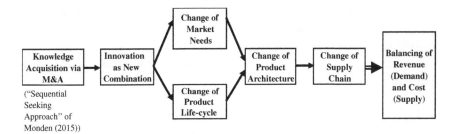

Fig. 11. Expanded Business Model to change the structure of supply-chain.

Further this chapter considered only the cost-efficiency goal of the Business Model for the reorganization of the supply chain in terms of the unit production or procurement costs. The cost reduction is vitally necessary for any business, but it is not sufficient. The real business must also consider the revenue or profit aspects and eventually must enhance the business value or the shareholder value through creating the customer value and employees' value. Thus, the business model proposed in this chapter must be expanded or connected to such business-value creation model that also considers social welfare and sustainability (for considering the sustainability in global supply chain see Matsuo (2014) and Larrson (2015)). Actually in the business combination decisions through Merger and Acquisitions (M&A) the valuation models of business value considers not only the cost reduction effect but also the revenue expansion effect caused by the business combination in question. This is another problem which was not considered by Coase and Williamson's transaction costs theory (this problem was pointed out by Monden (2001), and Dekker (2004) also pointed that the inter-firm transactions would not minimize the transaction costs only).

Our "causal relation" model for building the optimal supply chain depicted in this chapter could be expanded by connecting it to the creation of innovation through the knowledge acquisition via M&A as the following Fig. 11.

Acknowledgment

This chapter was presented at the 11th International Industrial Engineering Conference on January 7, 2015 held by the Department of Industrial Engineering, Tarbiat Modarres University, Iran, and the Iranian Institute of Industrial Engineering, which was sponsored by Asian Productivity Organization. The author, Monden, is grateful to Professors Mohammad

Reza Amin-Naser, Amir Albadvy, Seyed Hesamedin Zegordi, Mohammad Aghdassi, and Ehsan Nikbakhsh of Tarbiat Modarres University for their invitation to this conference and fruitful comments, and also for their arrangement for my visit to Iranian automobile company Iran Khodro Industrial Group (IKCO).

References

Abernathy, W. J., Clark, K. B., & Kantrow, A. M. (1983). *Industrial Renaissance*: *Producing a Competitive Future for America*. New York: Basic Books.

Abeggren, J. & Boston Consulting Group (1978). *Portfolio Strategy*. Tokyo: President (in Japanese).

Baldwin, R. (2013). Misthinking globalization. Retrieved from www. ide. go.jp/.../pdf/2013WTO_Keynote1_Baldwin_paper_en.p. (search date September 1, 2013).

Chandler, A. D. Jr. (1977). *The Visible Hand: The Managerial Revolution in American Business*. Boston: The Belknap Press of Harvard University Press.

Christensen, C. M. (1997). *The Innovator's Dilemma: When New Technologies Cause Great Firms to Fall*, (2000, revised edn.). Boston: Harvard Business School Press.

Coase, R. (1937). The Nature of the Firm, *Economica*, 4, pp. 386–405.

Dekker, H. C. (2004). Control of Inter-Organizational Relations: Evidence on Appropriation Concerns and Coordination Requirements, *Accounting, Organizations and Society*, 29(1), pp. 27–49.

Fujimoto, T. (2004). *Philosophy of Japanese Manufacturing*. Tokyo: Nikkei Inc. (in Japanese).

Hsieh, D. (2013a). *Silicon Wafer Foundry Business*, June 21 (unpublished).

Hsieh, D. (2013b). *TSMC* 2013, November (unpublished).

Iansiti, M. & Levien, R. (2004). *The Keystone Advantage: What the New Dynamics in Business Ecosystem Mean for Strategy, Innovation, and Sustainability*. Boston: Harvard Business School Press.

Kawakami, M. (2012). Utilize the Information of Taiwan Companies: Positive Outsourcing for Collaboration, *The Nikkei*, November 6. "Economic Seminar" (in Japanese).

Kim, C. & Mauborgne, R. (2004). Blue Ocean Strategy, *Harvard Business Review*, 82(10), pp. 76–84.

Larrson, R. (2015). Ikea's almost fabless global supply-chain — A rightsourcing strategy for profit, planet, and people, in Y. Monden *et al.* & Y. Minagawa (ed.), *Lean Management of Global Supply Chain*, Singapore: World Scientific Publishing Co. Pte. Ltd.

Matsuo, H. (2014). Global supply chain should be reexamined from the viewpoint of social welfare and sustainability. *The Nikkei*, October 31 (in Japanese).

Monden, Y. (1995). Concurrent target costing by parts manufactures and product manufactures, in Y. Monden (ed.), *Cost Reduction Systems: Target Costing and Kaizen Costing*, Portland: Productivity Press. Chapter 18, pp. 191–203.

Monden, Y. (2001). Integration of Organization Economics and Corporate Finance for the Business Reorganization, *JICPA Journal*, 13(4), pp. 41–47 (in Japanese).

Monden, Y. (2012). *Toyota Production System: An Integrated Approach to Just-In-Time* (4th edn.). Boca Raton: Taylor & Francis Group.

Monden, Y. & Larsson, R. (2014). Robust supply-chain management for the disasters: Based on the product design architectures, in Y. Monden (ed.), *Management of Enterprise Crises in Japan*, Singapore: World Scientific Publishing Company, pp. 125–148.

Monden, Y. (2015). Innovation of eco-cars based on the global inter-firm collaboration, in Y. Monden *et al.* (ed.), *Lean Management of the Global Supply Chain*, Singapore: World Scientific Publishing Co Pte. Ltd.

Negoro, T. (2014). Multiple Layers Structure of Industry to be Selected by the Customers, *The Nikkei*, September 29. "Economic Seminar" (in Japanese).

Nobeoka, K. (2012). Regeneration of Manufacturing: Value-Creation for Pleasing the Customer Using the Strength of the Integrated Design, *The Nikkei*, May 28. "Economic Seminar" (in Japanese).

Noguchi, Y. (2012). *Reason of Japanese Defeated Manufacturing*. Tokyo: Toyo Keizai Inc. (in Japanese).

Picot, A., Dietl, H., & Frank, E. (2005). *Organization: Eine Ökonomische Perspective* (4th edn.). Stuttgart: Schäffer-Poeschel Verlag GmbH.

Shibata, T. (2012). Lesson from the Depression of Home Electronics: Strategy Corresponding to the Industry Life-Cycle, *The Nikkei*, November 30. "Economic Seminar" (in Japanese).

Simon, H. A. (1981). *The Siences of the Artificial* (2nd edn.). Cambridge: The MIT Press.

The Nikkei (2008). Reorganization of battery production: Toshiba consigned the total battery production to other company and Panasonic reduced to the half, January 26 (in Japanese).

The Nikkei (2012). Taiwan TSMC invested 430 billion yen to the new plant: Only one winner of the foundry of semi-conductor, December 16 (in Japanese).

The Nikkei (2013a). TSMC earns the operating profit ratio on sales of 35.8%; Samsung and Intel chase after TSMC in the foundry business, April 23.

The Nikkei (2013b). Tax-saving strategy of Apple: Double avoidance of tax as a matter of fact, June 3.

The Nikkei (2013c). Taiwan is boosting the low-price smartphone: Contracted design and production using the common modules accelerate the low-price, August 20 (in Japanese).

The Nikkei (2013d). 100 dollar smartphone increases in the emerging countries: The duopoly by Apple and Samsung was crumbled, August 24 (in Japanese).

The Nikkei (2013e). NTT DoCoMo lost telephone revenue down to 1/4 due to the increase of communication Applies, August 24 (in Japanese).

The Nikkei (2013f). Big electronics firms challenge the smartphone risk: Improvement of the fund cycle efficiency by inventory reduction, etc. for the demand change and the shorter demand cycle, October 11 (in Japanese).

The Nikkei (2013g). Hon Hai participates in communication carrier service, October 31.

The Nikkei (2013h). Google "Andriod" OS was renewed for the low-price smartphone of the emerging countries, November 1.

The Nikkei (2014a). Acceleration of contract manufacturing of automobile in the USA: Android plants increased up to 20 in five years, August 5 (in Japanese).

The Nikkei (2014b). Wearable watch to be sold from next year, September 10 (in Japanese).

The Nikkei (2014c). iPhone as a wallet: Alliances with banks, etc., September 10 (in Japanese).

The Nikkei (2014d). Mitsubishi Motors supplies SUT to Fiat Chrysler group as OEM, September 20.

The Nikkei (2014e). Toyota's reorganization of Keiretsu: Release hidden power to the world, December 15 (in Japanese)

Vernon, R. (1966). International Investment and International Trade in the Product Cycle, *Quarterly Journal of Economics*, 80(2), pp. 190–207.

Volkswagen (2012). Homepage. Retrieved from http://jp.motorq.org/page/mqb-platform-volkswagen-3302.html (search date May 2, 2012).

Watanabe, M. (2013). China Makers' Vigorous Participation in Smartphone: Success on Account of the "Vertical Division" of Supply Chain and the Progress of Common Modular-Parts Market, *The Nikkei*, May 3. "Economic Seminar" (in Japanese).

Williamson, O. E. (1991). Comparative Economic Organization: The Analysis of Discrete Structural Alternatives, *Administrative Science Quarterly*, 36, pp. 269–296.

Yasumoto, M. (2013). IT industry: Cases of Google and IBM, in Yoshihara *et al.* (ed.), Chapter 10, pp. 218–239 (in Japanese).

2

How to Facilitate Inter-Firm Cooperation in a Fabless Global Supply Chain

Yoshiteru Minagawa*
Nagoya Gakuin University

1. Introduction

Vertical integration is a business model wherein one firm is completely responsible for executing a whole range of functional business operations from new product development to the production and distribution of consumer products. A vertically integrated firm, which engages itself in the entire process of generating value for customers, can ultimately control the value chain.

However, because a vertically integrated firm is responsible for upstream, midstream, and downstream business functions, it must face the demanding challenge of increased capital requirements. This study addresses capital investments in new product development. New products are in the growth stage of the technology life cycle, in which there is particularly huge potential for product innovation. Increased product innovation on the supply side can further increase market demand for the release of new products. Hence, growing products can facilitate product technology breakthroughs. At the same time, markets for growing products regularly generate an increase in the demand for new products, making it impossible for firms to survive unless they continue to release new products. This competitive environment inevitably mandates increase in capital investment.

---

*I would like to express my sincere and deep appreciation to Professor Yasuhiro Monden (University of Tsukuba). His comments and suggestions on my research were very helpful.

Therefore, firms that serve growing product markets, face the problem of raising sufficient funds to survive product innovation races. Implementing a fabless supply chain is one solution to fulfilling the enhanced capital requirements needed for R&D.

New popular technology products are indicative of the growth cycle of technological development; this cycle is unique as it holds huge potential for product innovation. The increased emphasis on product innovation on the supply side has further raised market demand for new products. Consequently, industries that supply new popular products enforce strategic rules, whereby their supply chain companies cannot survive unless they constantly keep on supplying such products. This competitive environment inevitably mandates that companies increase their capital investments. As such, getting new products to market at the lowest cost is the most important competitive advantage to be achieved.

A fabless business strategy benefits consumers by enabling them with speedier acquisition of new products. Fabless firms (i.e., firms without fabrication facilities) utilize their time and resources on the development and marketing of innovative products while outsourcing manufacturing to electronics manufacturing services (EMSs).

Likewise, EMSs must make investments in the development of new products and new production techniques.[1] The EMS innovations are brought into use not only to satisfy the requirements of fabless firms but also to launch new businesses.

Because each of the participants in a fabless supply chain is a legally independent firm, it may act only according to its own interests and without regard for others' interests. Therefore, in order to enhance cooperation between firms in fabless supply chains, participants need to solve the problem of opportunistic behaviors. Opportunistic behavior refers to "self-interest seeking with guile" (Williamson, 1985, p. 47). The problem of opportunism arises mainly due to asymmetric information (Perloff, 2008, p. 637). Opportunistic behavior is categorized into two

---

[1] Asnuma's studies on supplier–buyer relationships in the Japanese automobile industry succeeded in clarifying the following two types of part suppliers: "Drawing supplied" suppliers are engaged in manufacturing parts according to the drawings supplied by core firms. "Drawing approved" suppliers manufacture parts according to the drawings that are made by the respective suppliers themselves and approved by core firms. The study principally considers EMSs categorized as "Drawing supplied" (Asanuma, 1988).

types: adverse selection and moral hazard (Perloff, 2008, p. 637). Adverse selection refers to the market failure that can occur when actors have asymmetric information (Perloff, 2008, p. 637). In such a market, better-informed market actors may exploit less-informed ones. When less-informed market actors understand well-informed actors' incentives to exploit actors with less information, they can underestimate the value of the traded goods and thereby refrain from agreeing to transactions with the well-informed market actors. Therefore, asymmetric information results in market failure by preventing desirable transactions. Moral hazard is related to the problem of how to induce market actors to act properly when their actions cannot be observed directly and, therefore, contracted upon (Holmström, 1982, p. 324).

This study examines the most valuable administrative practices for enhancing cooperation in a fabless supply chain.

2. Incentive Alignment-Driven Cooperation Enhancement in Fabless Supply Chains

2.1. *Facilitating cooperation between fabless firms and EMSs*

Among supply chain integration implementation practices is power-centric coercion, in which the most powerful focal firms rely on the imbalance of bargaining power to extract favorable behavior from those participants with less bargaining power. Opinions are divided as to the merits and demerits of supply chain integration driven by power-centric coercion.

This study explores the source of power influences to integrate all participants in inter-firm networks within collaborative processes according to the work of Maloni & Benton (2000). Maloni & Benton (2000, p. 54) showed the following six bases of inter-firm power: first, focal firms offer pecuniary rewards and additional business accompanied by additional pecuniary rewards for the partners. This positively influences the integration of inter-firm networks. Second, partners can establish rules regarding the imposition of penalties for engaging in opportunistic behavior, ultimately generating inter-firm power. Third, when participants have access to the knowledge and skills they desire, it can enhance their dependence on the supply chains. Fourth, if firms highly value being part of certain supply chains, they desire association with the supply chains. Fifth, creating parent–subsidiary relationships can drive tight control of supply chains. Sixth, the focal firms of supply chains rely on their judiciary right to influence participants in order to promote supply chain integration.

This study extracts the three primal types of inter-firm power found in supply chains, as established by Maloni & Benton (2000). The first is coercive power, wherein the source (i.e., the most powerful firms) copes with the opportunistic behavior of the targets (i.e., other participants) by imposing penalties. The second is incentive alignment, in which the source awards pecuniary rewards, desired knowledge, and skills to the targets, thereby motivating them to behave in the interest of the whole supply chain. The third is contract compliance, wherein the source imposes a contract to mandate that the targets engage in favorable behavior. This study explores the implementation of supply chain integration through the inter-firm sharing of joint profit and beneficial information aimed at incentive alignment.

The following discussion involves analysis of the sharing of information on market competition, the measurement of the switching costs incurred by fabless firms and EMSs, and the allocation of joint profit across supply chains.

2.2.   *Sharing information about new product development performance*

Fabless firms (i.e., firms without fabrication facilities) utilize their time and resources on the development and marketing of innovative products while relying on the global outsourcing of manufacturing to EMSs. EMSs need to successfully achieve innovation of product and production technology. As such, EMSs are well positioned to build inter-firm relationships with highly competitive fabless firms.

In a fabless supply chain, taking a very aggressive approach to new product development is crucial to maintaining the inter-firm network's highly competitive advantage and the participants' enhanced profitability. Successful new product development in fabless supply chains cannot be achieved without a strong, reliable commitment between a fabless firm and EMSs. According to Monteverde (1995), inter-firm technical dialog in vertical integration benefits technological innovation on new product development and new manufacturing technology.

Fabless firms and EMSs collaborate to develop and sell innovative finished products. If fabless supply chains follow through on supplying attractive new products, they boost profitability for both the fabless firms and EMSs. The most important strategic agendas in the fastest-growing industries involve developing strong competitive advantages through new product development. Therefore, it is mandatory for both fabless firms and EMSs to place a high level of importance on ensuring that new products have a competitive position in the market. One of the most significant issues facing fabless firms and EMSs is to select and ally themselves with technologically competitive suppliers or buyers, thereby collectively and collaboratively delivering new finished products into emerging markets.

Regarding fabless supply chain strategy, one beneficial managerial practice involves the measurement of a new product's competitiveness. This approach helps to determine the extent to which the fabless firms and EMSs are achieving their aims of building and participating in fabless supply chains. The managerial metrics include the new sales ratio, which is measured as the ratio of current annual sales of new products to total annual sales (Whiteley *et al.*, 1998, p. 20). Whiteley *et al.* (1998) studied the usefulness of the new sales ratio in measuring R&D performance. It can be applied to inter-firm management to help achieve cooperation in new product development across the fabless supply chain. It is important for fabless supply chain partners to determine the target of the new sales ratio and to control the actual performance across the fabless supply chain.

2.3. *Sharing time-to-market information across fabless supply chains*

When it comes to growing product markets, the essence of competitive strategy is to effectively and efficiently offer newly emerging products to consumers. Capital investment in the development and supply of new products is, therefore, crucial to a supply chain's competitive advantage over others. Growing market environments force supply chain participants to accelerate the time-to-market (TTM) for new products at the lowest possible costs, to gain crucial competitive advantage. Break-even time (BET), which Hewlett-Packard utilizes for each new product development project, is an effective performance metric for managerially auditing the achievement of agile TTM. BET is defined as the amount of time that it takes to recoup total investment expenditures. The longer the BET, the riskier an investment will be, as it takes a longer period of time for an investor to recoup invested capital on the basis of discounted cash flow (House & Price, 1991).

In Fig. 1, the BET is the point at which the sales line and the life cycle cost (see Fig. 2) intersect. If it is assumed that the first developer of a

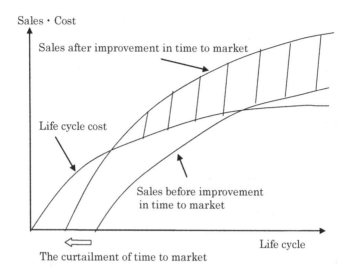

Fig. 1.   Impacts of reducing time to market on life cycle profit.

Note: The area marked by slanted lines shows the incremental increase in sales generated by a reduction in time to market without increasing life cycle cost.

Source: Impacts of reducing time to market are based on Cohen *et al.* (1996, p. 174).

new product will exclusively monopolize demand, then the acceleration of TTM can bring about a rise in the gradient of the sales line, as shown in Fig. 1. Effective cost management enables the acceleration of TTM-driven revenue improvement, thereby yielding a reduction in the BET. In a fabless supply chain, it is important that the TTM performance be known to all participants. This can help motivate the participants to improve TTM.

3. Relationship-Specific Investment Strategy in Fabless Supply Chains

3.1. *Effects of relationship-specific investments on competitive advantages in fabless supply chains*

Fabless firms implement strategies in which capital investments apply consistently and intensively to new product development, while strategically outsourcing the manufacturing of new products to EMSs. Likewise, EMSs need capital investments for the fabrication of excellent new finished products. Thus, fabless firms and EMSs ally to bring new products to market.

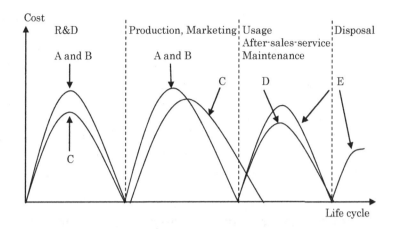

Fig. 2.   Conceptualization of supply chain life cycle costing.

Note: A. Parts manufactures; B. Finished product manufacturers; C. Marketing firms; D. Manufacturing industries; E. Consumers.

This means that the capital investments undertaken by fabless firms and EMSs are largely specialized to offer the fabless supply chains' finished products to consumers. Specialized investments are relationship-specific when they depend on both cooperating partners being dedicated to the relationship. Such investments are undertaken to support various activities undertaken by all of the participants in inter-firm networks. Relationship-specific investments can be a source of competitive advantage over rivals.

A key factor in supply chain success is reciprocal relationship-specific investments among all of the participants aimed to support customer value-generating activities occurring therein. The strategic value of tangible and intangible investments specialized to R&D is significantly greater during the growth stage of the product life cycle than it is at any other stage. Growing products are in the growth stage of the technology life cycle, in which there is particularly huge potential for product innovation. Highly progressive product innovation on the supply side can further expand the market demand for the release of new products. Hence, growing products can facilitate product technology breakthroughs. At the same time, markets for growing products regularly generate increased demand for new products, making it impossible for firms to survive unless they continue to release new products. This competitive environment inevitably mandates increase in R&D investments. Fabless supply chains are characterized by the considerable strategic value of relationship-specific investments made to satisfy fast-changing consumer demand for new products.

What is the most effective management practice for fabless supply chains to use in executing reciprocal new product development investment among partners? This study examines the switching cost incurred by fabless firms (EMSs) when they change their EMSs (fabless firms). A purpose of this study is to consider the impacts of inter-participant switching cost on a supply chain management system in which the participants use switching costs to inform their decisions regarding switching from one trading partner to another.

3.2. *Characteristics of relationship-specific investments*

Relationship-specific investments in fabless supply chains are devoted to supporting the activities occurring in fabless firms and EMSs. Such investments are a source of competitive advantages in fabless supply chains.

However, relationship-specific tangible and intangible assets are of little value when applied to other business relationships. To mitigate risk, fabless supply chains need to make relationship-specific investments based on the real options view of multi-stage investments over the whole investment life cycle (Minagawa, 2007). A multi-stage investment approach is capable of capturing the strategic flexibility to continue or discontinue projects after future cash flow uncertainty has been substantially resolved in accordance with new information that emerged (Panayi & Trigeorgis, 1998, p. 676). This study examines the effects of switching costs on managing relationship-specific investments throughout the whole life cycle.

3.3. *Switching cost*

Switching costs are incurred when a player changes from one trading partner for another. Switching cost-driven partner selection is a comparison between the switching cost incurred as a result of ending a transaction with the present partner and the profit gained from engaging in transactions with another. Accordingly, if the profit gained from engaging with the new partner is greater than the switching cost incurred due to the dissolution of a transaction with the present partner, switching from the present partner to a new one is the most profitable decision. Conversely, if terminating transactions with the present partner is ultimately more expensive, the continuation of a relationship with the present partner is most beneficial.

Jones *et al.* (2002, pp. 442–443) identified the six types of switching costs that drive consumers' replacement of service providers: (i) costs associated with the loss of benefits accrued from the pre-switching partner's trading players, (ii) extra costs incurred when post-switching goods are inferior, (iii) pre-switching search and evaluation costs, (iv) costs incurred in learning how to use a new service, (v) costs associated with the additional learning needed to facilitate customer satisfaction, and (vi) sunk costs, which are those non-recoupable costs associated with establishing and maintaining relationships. The switching cost related to (i) is an opportunity cost.

In applying the concept of switching costs set forth by Jones *et al.* (2002) to decisions on whether to switch participants in an inter-firm network, the most important trigger is dissatisfaction with business performance. Thus, this study focuses on opportunity cost-based switching costs.

3.4. *Management of relationship-specific investments from the perspective of the whole life cycle*

3.4.1. *Strategic flexibility*

The relationship duration of an inter-firm alliance influences the achievement of sustainable growth. Concurrently, inter-firm networks need effective and timely strategy reformulations to successfully cope with a change in consumer needs.

Based on Young-Ybarra & Wiersema (1999, p. 440), strategic flexibility in alliances includes the following: (i) the ability of partners to adjust their behaviors in response to changes in the environment, and (ii) the ability to exit from an alliance that no longer meets the needs of the partners (Young-Ybarra & Wiersema, 1999, p. 440). Therefore, strategic flexibility in alliances involves the timely switching of allied partners when such alliances no longer bring about excellent profitability.

3.4.2. *Strategic flexibility-driven relationship-specific investment*

This study considers how fabless supply chain participants can maintain a competitive advantage over rivals as a result of relationship-specific investments and the assets generated therein. The study divides the entire life cycle of investments into the growth, modification, and de-maturity stages.

The growth stage is characterized by enhanced product technology innovation and the resultant aggressive releases of products that are new to the industry. During the modification stage, the saturation of product innovation progresses. As a result, the firm's survival depends upon the modification of existing goods instead of marketing innovative products. During the de-maturity stage, firms need to achieve rebirth of product innovation as the top priority.

While a fabless supply chain's assets devoted to the development and fabrication of its finished products stay at the growth stage, the excellent profitability of fabless firms and EMSs relies substantially on their new products outperforming those being developed by competitors. During the modification stage, fabless firms and EMSs must cooperate to satisfy customers through marketing modified version of existing products. After the modification stage, no fabless supply chain can survive without product innovation. Switching partners is one solution to the above-mentioned issues faced by fabless supply chains at each stage of the life cycle.

3.4.3. *Effects of market price*

According to the concept of value-based pricing (Hinterhuber, 2004, p. 769), a new product price is the total amount of the following two values: the price of the competitive product that a consumer views as the best alternative and the consumer's perceived value of all attributions that differentiate the product from its competition.

From the perspective of the value-based pricing approach, the manufactured product pricing determined by an EMS is affected by the following two factors: the extent to which new products developed by fabless firms attract consumers and the extent to which the production technology of the EMS satisfies consumers. Fabless firms' finished product pricing is likewise influenced by the following factors: EMSs' excellent production technology and fabless firms' high-powered R&D.

In fabless supply chains where EMSs offer their manufactured products to fabless firms as finished product makers, consumer price acceptance for the finished products depends on two factors: EMSs' excellent production technology and fabless firms' high-powered R&D. These factors drive the higher value assigned by customers and the innovative functionality of the finished products, thereby seducing consumers to pay the prices willingly.

3.4.4. *Switching cost-driven management for relationship-specific investments*

One type of switching cost addressed in this study is the profit from a pre-switching relations — in other words, the profit lost as a result of switching to another relationship. Such opportunity cost-oriented switching costs benefit the management of fabless supply chains for the following reasons. In the measurement of the opportunity cost-oriented switching cost, it is important to establish (i) the price that consumers are willing to pay for finished products offered by the post-switching fabless firms if EMSs quit trading with the present fabless firm and instead sell their product to another fabless firm and (ii) the price that consumers are willing to pay for products offered by EMSs that sell their products directly to the external market.

Here, the opportunity cost (i.e., forgone profit) incurred by EMSs when they maintain partnerships with the present fabless firm is calculated as follows:

> Price that consumers are willing to pay for finished products
> sold by the post-switching fabless firm if the EMS switches to
> another fabless finished product manufacturer × Sales volume
> for the present fabless firm − Incurred cost.   (1)

The opportunity cost of Eq. (1) is profit forgone, as the EMS continues a partnership with its current fabless firm without changing partnerships. As such, it is the minimum profit that the EMS can demand its current fabless partner to pay. Accordingly, if the current fabless firm willingly pays a profit higher than the opportunity cost of Eq. (1) to the EMSs, then they rationally continue to sell their product to their present fabless partner. Conversely, if the profit that the EMS can earn through transacting with its current fabless partner is lower than the opportunity cost of (1), then the EMS should switch to another fabless firm.[2]

The opportunity cost incurred by a fabless firm when it switches from its current trading fabless EMS to another is calculated as follows:

> Sales of finished products − External market price of products
> fabricated by the EMS × Fabless firms' purchase volume from
> EMS − Other costs.   (2)

---

[2]Here, the concept of individual rationality in cooperative game theory was applied successfully to switching cost-oriented analysis. I owe that suggestion entirely to Professor Monden.

If the profit that the fabless firm can earn through transacting with the post-switching EMS is greater than the opportunity cost of Eq. (2), then the fabless firm should switch EMSs.

In supply chains, change of partnership is highly valued for its strategic flexibility. If certain partners can no longer achieve product technology innovation, then the termination of the partnership is strategically important. Therefore, ensuring that switching costs are transparent throughout the entire supply chain allows for the successful replacement of less competitive partners with more competitive ones.

During the growth stage, there is huge potential for new product development. This, in turn, means that there exists a huge gap in profitability between firms that can succeed in new product development and those that fail in the creation of product innovation. Therefore, the timely switching of partners is strategically important. This increases the managerial usefulness of determining switching costs based on Eqs. (1) and (2). In other words, if you can find a promising firm that can generate greater profit for you than you are getting from the relationship with your present partner, then you should switch partners.

4. Allocation of Joint Profit in Fabless Supply Chains

4.1. *Effects of joint profit allocation*

It is important to allocate joint supply chain profit among supply chain participants as a way of motivating firms with competitive advantages to participate in the supply chain. The allocation of a supply chain's joint profit can motivate participants to behave in the interest of the supply chain as a whole, ultimately increasing their shares of the profit. Allocating a supply chain's joint profits to build cooperation depends considerably on the creation of close mutual connections between the supply chain's total profits and the participants' shares. Therefore, the appropriate allocation of a supply chain's joint profits enables participants to focus on maximizing the supply chain's total profits.

4.2. *Market price-based transfer pricing in supply chains that supply growing products*

The most important business agenda for supply chains is to achieve a growth rate that is higher than that of total market demand. While the technology embodied in a finished product stays in the growth stage of the technology life cycle, the total market demand for the finished products can grow drastically. The higher the total market demand for a finished product, the bigger the gap in profit between supply chains that can attain new product development and those that fail in commercializing emerging products. Therefore, whether a fabless supply chain can gain a competitive advantage over other chains substantially relies on its participants (i.e., via fabless firms and EMSs) outperforming their competitors in terms of commercializing new products. To be competitive in growing markets, fabless firms must create new products with sophisticated design and high customer value, and EMSs must fabricate the highest-quality products.

For a fabless supply chain to achieve the highest possible sales of a finished product, fabless firms and EMSs must surpass their competitors in terms of product innovation. How can the creation of products with high customer value boost profits drastically? This occurs when consumers are willing to pay higher prices for innovative products.

Measuring the degree of contribution that fabless firms and EMSs make toward increasing the profitability of the whole fabless supply chain should be market price oriented for the following reason: the market price is affected principally by the result of competition in the market. The core of competition in fabless supply chains, as mentioned earlier, lies in new product development. Thus, the formation of market prices manifested as the result of fabless supply chain competition is based on new product development competition in the markets. The measurement of organizational performance using market price means the application of market-based transfer pricing.

Individual fabless firms and EMSs should make an appropriate decision regarding whether to continue the present partnership or switching to another partner. They must effectively execute a study on the differences between the profit earned through continuation of transaction with the present partner and the potential profit incurred as result of switching partnerships. This can be determined through measuring the profits of fabless firms and EMSs using the market prices of EMSs' manufactured products and the market prices of the finished products offered by fabless firms. The level of market price is affected principally by competition in the market. The core of competition in fabless supply chains lies in new product development.

Transfer prices for EMSs' manufactured products refer to the value realized when firms sell the products in the external market. The transfer price can be determined using a value-based pricing approach. Assume that prices in external purchase markets and those in external selling markets are equal. The respective profits of fabless firm and EMS-based new product businesses can be calculated as follows:

> Fabless firm's profit earned from specific new product business = (Total market demand for a new product × Firm's market share for the new product) × (Finished product market price for the new product − Variable cost of goods sold per unit, including purchase cost for an EMS's manufactured product − Unit's variable selling cost) − (Direct capacity cost + Apportioned capacity cost). (3)

> EMS's profit earned from specific new product business = Quantity of products sold to a fabless firm × (Products' market prices − Variable cost of goods sold per unit − Unit's variable selling cost) − (Direct capacity cost + Apportioned capacity cost). (4)

What is the strategic value to managers of the above-mentioned market-based transfer price for EMSs' manufactured products in determining profits of supply chain partners? EMSs need to implement a strategy that ensures excellent manufacturing practices in order to enhance product quality and thus increase customer value, which in turn increases the attractiveness of fabless firms. This enables an increase in orders from fabless firms. However, if a fabless firm demands that it be able to purchase an EMS's product at a price less than the external market price for the product, then the EMS is likely to engage in transactions with another fabless firm instead of the present one. Fabless firms are willing to purchase an EMS's products at the external market price when the quality of the EMS's products is sufficiently attractive. As such, when an EMS's products fail to satisfy fabless firms, the fabless firms are likely to switch transaction partners.

4.3. *Fabless supply chains that supply mature products*

Products in the mature stage of the product life cycle can no longer be expected to increase in sales. As a result, yielding profit during the mature stage depends largely on complete reduction in profit forgone from unfulfilled orders and on cost control throughout all business operations.

Therefore, all participants in supply chains that market mature products must collaborate to reduce costs across the supply chains. Profit increases in supply chains that supply mature products cannot be achieved without effective cost reduction. It is important to allocate any additional profit gained as a result of inter-participant cooperative cost reduction among the participants; this serves to motivate the participants to reduce supply chain costs. What rules should be followed in the allocation of joint profits in mature product marketing supply chains? The most effective rule regarding the inter-participant allocation of joint profit is based on cost. Joint profit is allocated among participants based on their activity costs. Increased joint profit earned through cooperative activities by individual participants is allocated among participants according to the costs they incurred through their activities.

One practice for cost management in mature product businesses is functional shiftability. In order for supply chains to efficiently achieve customer satisfaction, it is important that they decide which performers are best suited to individual functions in the supply chain and then shift those responsible for performing specific functions as necessary. This is the role of functional shiftability (Mallen, 1973). Functional shiftability is more feasible in well-integrated, trust-based supply chains than in arms-length transactions.

However, functional shiftability in supply chains typically brings about an increase in the operational costs of the participants who have to carry out new tasks previously accomplished by other participants. Therefore, the focal firm of a supply chain must create incentives for participants to accept functional shiftability in spite of the increased costs involved. Among these incentives is the allocation of joint profits to participants across the supply chain.

Successful cooperative management across a supply chain, including functional shiftability, requires the allocation of the supply chain's joint profit in proportion to the participants' costs. A supply chain's joint profit can be determined as follows:

> Joint profit = Amount of sales for finished products sold by a fabless firm − Total variable cost in the fabless firm, except for the cost of purchasing the EMS's manufacturing products − Total variable cost in the EMS − Total sum of direct capacity cost and apportioned capacity cost in the fabless firm − Total sum of direct capacity cost and apportioned capacity cost in the EMS. (5)

The allocation of the joint profit in proportion to participants' costs generates equal shares in terms of the per-unit cost for all participants (Dudek, 2003, p. 134).

5. Conclusion

Cooperative reciprocal investments in product innovation and cost reduction across fabless supply chains drive the higher business performance of fabless firms and EMSs. This study explored useful ways to facilitate investment by fabless firms and EMSs. First, the transparency of the new sales ratio across fabless supply chains is beneficial. Second, it is important to share information related to switching costs. This study addressed the lost profit incurred as a result of switching partners. It is important for participants in fabless supply chains to examine the difference between the profit that a partner gives up by terminating a present partnership and the profit that a partner can gain by switching to another partner. Third, carrying out market-based transfer price-oriented measurement of participants' performance enables the best use of their investments.

References

Asanuma, B. (1988). Manufacturer–supplier relationships in Japan and the concept of relation-specific skill. Working Paper No. 2, Kyoto University, Faculty of Economics.

Cohen, M. A. *et al.* (1996). New Product Development: The Performance and Time-To-Market Tradeoff, *Management Science*, 42(2), pp. 173–186.

Dudek, G. (2003). *Collaborative Planning in Supply Chains*. Heidelberg: Springer-Verlag.

Hinterhuber, A. (2004). Towards Value-Based Pricing — An Integrative Framework for Decision Making, *Industrial Marketing Management*, 33, pp. 765–778.

Holmström, B. (1982). Moral Hazard in Teams, *The Bell Journal of Economics*, 13(2), pp. 324–340.

House, C. H. & Price, R. L. (1991). The Return Map: Tracking Product Teams. *Harvard Business Review*, 69(1) pp. 92–101.

Jones, M. A., Mothersbaugh, D. L., & Beatty, S. E. (2002). Why Customers Stay: Measuring the Underlying Dimensions of Services Switching Costs and Managing their Differential Strategic Outcomes, *Journal of Business Research*, 55, pp. 441–450.

Mallen, B. (1973). Functional Spin-Off: A Key to Anticipating Change in Distribution Structure, *Journal of Marketing*, 37, pp. 18–25.

Maloni, M. & Benton, W. C. (2000). Power Influences in the Supply Chain, *Journal of Business Logistics*, 21(1), pp. 49–73.

Minagawa, Y. (2007). How can supply chain risks be reduced by mutual cooperation among partner — Application of real options and throughput accounting, in Y. Monden, M. Kosuga, Y. Nagasaka, S. Hiraoka, & N. Hoshi (eds.), *Japanese Management Accounting Today*, Singapore: World Scientific Publishing Co. Pte Ltd., pp. 177–192.

Monteverde, K. (1995). Technical Dialog as an Incentive for Vertical Integration in the Semiconductor Industry, *Management Science*, 41(10), pp. 1624–1638.

Panayi, S. & Trigeorgis, L. (1998). Multi-Stage Real Options: The Cases of Information Technology Infrastructure and International Bank Expansion, *The Quarterly Review of Economics and Finance*, 38(Special Issue), pp. 675–692.

Perloff, J. M. (2008). *Microeconomics* (5th edn.). Boston: Pearson/Addison Wesley.

Whiteley, R., Parish, T., Dressler, R., & Nicholson, G. (1998). Evaluating R&D Performance: Using the New Sales Ratio, *Research Technology Management*, 41(5), pp. 20–22.

Williamson, O. E. (1985). *The Economic Institutions of Capitalism: Firms, Markets, Relational Contracting.* New York: The Free Press.

Young-Ybarra, C. & Wiersema, M. (1999). Strategic Flexibility in Information Technology Alliance: The Influence of Transaction Cost Economics and Social Exchange Theory, *Organization Science*, 10(4), pp. 439–459.

3

Ikea's Almost Fabless Global Supply Chain — A Rightsourcing Strategy for Profit, Planet, and People

Rolf G. Larsson

Lund University

1. Introduction

Fabless production, meaning manufacturing without owning fabrication facilities, has been suggested as a novelty by the semiconductor industry. However, Ikea, the global furniture company based in Sweden, has successfully been producing their furniture in a fabless fashion since 1955. This chapter explores how Ikea manage and control its almost fabless production to reach the company's targets for sustainable profit, sustainable environment, and sustainable social responsibility. The demand for a balance between economic, ecological, and social responsibilities, sometimes referred to as triple bottom lines or TBL (profit, planet, people) has been introduced over the last 25 years. As a worldwide leader in the furniture industry Ikea has to assure that these ethical, environmental, and social standards are followed throughout the global supply chain, at the same time that low cost targets are met. To guide all its activities and processes in the global supply chain, Ikea has developed an inter-organizational management control package (MCP) for the whole supply chain in contrast to the Malmi & Brown (2008) MCP that mainly has an intra-organizational focus.

2. Literature Review

To design, manage, and control a global supply chain is a complex task, including many facets of management. However, this literature review is limited to three parts that are important to understand the Ikea case study, which are; strategy, fabless supply chains, and MCP. Wherever possible, theory has been chosen that are in some way related to Ikea as to better inform the case study.

2.1. *Strategy*

Sustainable competitive advantage can be reached in several ways. Porter (1985) advocated a strategy of low cost or differentiation, and to apply that industrywide or on a particular segment only. To carry out these choices Porter (1996, p. 68) claimed that "*strategy is the creation of a unique and valuable position, involving a different set of activities,*" were the decision of what activities the company should not perform is the essence of strategy. This focus on strategy as a choice of what activities to master on your own, and what to outsource, can also be seen in the core competence and resource-based strategies (Prahalad & Hamel, 1990; Barney, 1991). However, regardless of the decision of insourced or outsourced activities, Porter particularly emphasized the need for company activities to be in harmony through the entire value system. As an example of this Porter (1996) used Ikea and its links between activities and strategy as a fundamental element of competitive strength. Strategic positioning means that a company performs other activities than its competitors or does so in a different way. In the chapter Porter presented his interpretation of the Ikea activity map where he pointed out four strategic activities as central for Ikea in its global value creation; combining its own product range with its own modular furniture design, flat packages, coordinated purchases, and catch-your-breath pricing, as illustrated in the Fig. 1.

Originally, Porter did not question the capitalistic view that the profit gained from a company's competitive advantage position should go back to the shareholders. However, together with Kramer he later proposed that the competitiveness of a company is mutually dependent on the communities around it, and introduced the idea of creating shared value (CSV) (Porter & Kramer, 2011). The authors argued that CSV requires companies to track its social and environmental impacts, and then to rethink its whole value system and the way activities are performed. They conclude that only CSV will be sustainable in the long term.

2.2. *Designing value chains and global supply chains*

Porter (1985) claimed that the road toward cost leadership start with a new design or reconfiguration of the value chain, whereby costs may be

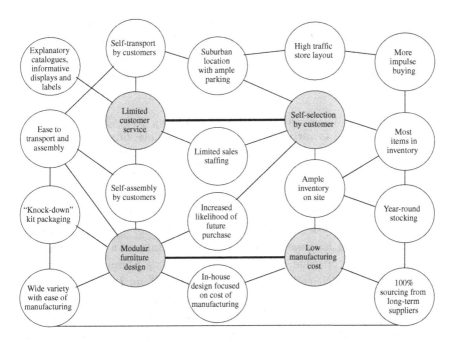

Fig. 1.   Ikea activity map.

Source: Porter, 1996, p. 71.

lowered dramatically. A new design open up for discussions of production process change, automation, direct instead of indirect sales, distribution channel change, new raw materials, changing integration backwards or forwards, new localization, and several other configuration options for a value chain. The question of reconfiguration of value chains was also discussed by Normann & Ramirez (1998), who noticed that Porter's value chain model comprised only pooled and sequential interdependence. They criticized the model for not including reciprocal interdependence, which they claimed restricts its usefulness, since relations between actors on the economic stage is no longer simple and sequential. They prefer the idea of co-production before reciprocal interdependence. Value constellation is their term for value chains and supply chains, by which they refer to the actors' co-production of a customer offer that is designed in a way so that all partners end up performing the "right" activities for them, engendering value creation on all sides. As Porter, also Normann & Ramirez used Ikea as an example of a company which co-produces customer value together with its customers and suppliers. In the catalogue Ikea writes to the customers *"we develop products, buy large quantities and process flat packages, while you help yourselves, take home and assemble."* This reconfiguration and co-production is distinguished from that of the traditional trade. The changes have also affected suppliers in cases where the company co-produces with selected partners.

> *"At least as significant is the extraordinary reconfiguration it managed to carry out with suppliers. Dealing directly with manufacturers, cutting out middlemen, and engaging many of these as long-term partners is a core part of Ikea's success"* (*Ibid.*, p. 111).

So far in the literature review, we have seen authors use the terms value chains, value systems, and value constellations for descriptions of how value is created in cooperation with others. If we take on a logistic view of the configuration of value creation the term *Supply Chain* becomes more common. In an article called *"Centralized Supply Chain Planning at Ikea"*, Jonsson *et al.* (2013) explained how Ikea manage its low cost and efficient production and distribution. They claimed that the key is that Ikea is a dominating organization with both power and competence to enforce the planning of the entire global supply chain. According to the study, Ikea's central planning of the global supply chain has improved coordination and integration, standardization, specialization, and given learning effects. To support the centralized supply chain planning Ikea uses an advanced planning and scheduling (APS) software, that all suppliers are connected to, that optimally allocate production capacity and raw materials to meet the demand. With the centralized planning model and APS, Ikea communicate with their partner suppliers and their manufacturing processes, resulting in a global supply chain dominated by Ikea without owning production facilities. This is in line with the idea of fabless production (Hurtarte *et al.*, 2007) which is to manage a business relationship where one company designs and market products that are actually manufactured by another. It is a business model that has been especially promoted by the global semiconductor industry. The business model is held together with a "shared information highway" that interconnects fabless companies with their worldwide supply chains, providing fast and reliable deliveries. According to the authors, fabless manufacturing relies on the combination of physical manufacturing processes and the global business relationships.

Quinn & Hilmer (1994) maintained that outsourcing is successful when clearly linked to strategy. However, they emphasized the need for a balance between the possibility of internally acquiring and maintaining a specific competence and the vulnerability of outsourcing. When there is a high potential for specific competence, and high vulnerability for outsourcing, their recommendation is internal manufacturing. When the situation is the opposite, purchasing is recommended. In an intermediate situation vulnerability can be handled by contracts. The authors further claimed that there exist many possible contract relations between hierarchy and market. The classical choice between make or buy, or insourcing versus outsourcing, was complemented with a hybrid of the two when Williamson (1991) introduced "hybrids" (or networks) as a third institutional form together with the ideal types of hierarchy and the classical market. In his view hybrids were more sensitive to disturbances than markets and hierarchies, since adaptation requires costly reciprocal agreements. Jacobides (2005), referring to Williamson, explained vertical disintegration as gains from trade fostering inter-firm co-specialization, which leads to standardized information and simplified coordination. These conditions may break up established value creation structures, change competitive patterns, and generate new intermediate markets, and they will also change over time. Revisions may point to reducing or increasing one's own activities, resulting in new patterns of outsourcing, insourcing, or a hybrid of the two, as Cox (2009) indicated in his suggestion of a joint venture between the supplying and the buying company.

2.3.   *Management control package for supply chains*

Management control was defined by Anthony & Govindarajan (2007) as a system of responsibility accounting, budgeting, and costing with later additions of behavioral aspects, performance indicators, reward systems, and project planning. Although it was described as a management control system, the interrelations between the different parts were not specified. In this study we follow the notion of a MCP as presented by Malmi & Brown (2008). Their "package" included a core of; strategic planning, cybernetic controls with budgets, financial- and non-financial measuring systems, and rewards. The inner core was complemented by; cultural controls, government structure, organization structure, and policies and procedures.

Management control has traditionally had an intra-organizational perspective, focusing on company activities. To be able to control the whole value system, or supply chain, both financial and non-financial information has to be shared. Inter-organizational management control widens the ambition of management control to comprise all companies in the value system. As each of the companies involved in the value system only carries out a limited set of activities in the value creation, information regarding these activities has to be shared for coordination and efficiency (Johnston & Lawrence, 1988; Cooper & Slagmulder, 2004). Further, Cooper & Yoshikawa (1994) demanded that inter-organizational management control should identify innovative ways to reduce product costs in the value system, and target costing was suggested as a suitable method. Monden & Hamada (1991) and Cooper & Chew (1996) described how Japanese companies used target costing to drive new product development processes, starting with the ultimate customers and the target price and volume, deducting the desired profit, and ending with the target for allowable costs. The companies then designed the sourcing, production, and delivery processes to reach the target cost, and in the case that they could not reach the target cost the whole process started all over again investigating new ways of combining quality, function, and price. In this design phase up to 80% of the product cost was locked for the whole life cycle of the product. Cooper & Chew (1996) highlighted that market leaders had no choice but to manage costs from the design phase and forward, and that aggressive targets focus the efforts of the design teams on creative solutions and press value engineering to its limits.

For many organizations corporate social responsibility (CSR) (Carroll, 1991 and 1999), has been the kind of policy and procedure that Malmi & Brown (2008) included as a part of the MCP. Zwetsloot (2003) suggested that CSR have a potential for businesses practices with positive impact on people, planet, and profit, in the TBL concept. Especially the external dimensions of CSR, like duties as citizens and responsibilities to social and environmental demands, have been focused due to a priority shift (Deakin & Hobbs, 2007). Elkington (2000) argued that sustainable business is a new paradigm and that companies could prove themselves to be sustainable when they lived up to the TBL mottos of economic prosperity, social justice and environmental quality. Company policies for CSR are often described as code of conducts, and Stevens (2008) emphasized that there are two primary drivers for organizational codes to be effective; cultural values and communication. As was discussed in the strategy section, Porter & Kramer (2011) suggested that CSR should be expanded to "CSV". One way of doing this is to redefine productivity in the value chain, according to the authors, as a company's value chain affects a numerous societal issues such as natural resources, working conditions and equal treatment in the workplace. Opportunities to create shared value arise when, for example, excess packaging of products and greenhouse gases in transportation are reduced, when raw material and packaging are recycled, and when new improved technology are introduced that use less resources. Such efforts will save business costs, save the environment, and add up values that can be shared. Porter & Kramer (2011) identified shared value as a policy to identifying and expanding the connections between societal and economic progress.

3. Case Study

Ikea is a well-known global furniture company based in Sweden. This case study will describe how they design and produce furniture in an almost fabless fashion in a global supply chain. The Ikea case description is presented in three parts; strategy, fabless supply chains, and MCP. The presented material comes from a longitudinal case study at Ikea, if nothing else is stated. The case study is based on interviews, documents, and homepages collected during a period of 10 years. More information from the case study was presented in Andersson & Larsson (2006).

3.1. *Ikea strategy*

Ikea was started in 1943 by the 17-year-old entrepreneur Ingvar Kamprad in the village of Elmtaryd in Agunnaryd parish in Sweden, hence the acronym Ikea. During the first years Kamprad rode around on a bicycle selling matches, pens, watches, and nylon stockings which he purchased in bulk. Later he started to advertise and deliver his goods by mail order. From 1947 furniture was included in the assortment and from 1951, the first year of the Ikea catalogue, furniture was the sole focus. In 1955, Ikea started to design its own furniture that was to be delivered in flat packages. All production was made in a fabless way by suppliers. Business went well and new stores were opened in Sweden, the Nordic countries, and abroad. The first store in the USA was opened in 1985, in China 1998, and today Ikea has about 300 stores in 26 countries.

Ikea is a low cost company with a vision *to create a better everyday life for many people*. The strategy to carry out the vision may be explained as a five-folded calibrated design. It starts with an offer to customers of "*a wide range of well designed, functional home furnishing products at prices so low that as many people as possible will be able to afford them*", consequently

Ikea start by deigning the price tag. The second phase consists of Ikea designing its own Scandinavian style, low cost, modular, ready-to-assemble furniture, all carrying Swedish names as Holme, Ivar, and Hemnes. In the third phase, Ikea design the manufacturing process for the product in its almost fabless global supply chain consisting of a network of long time partners and suppliers. Distribution is the fourth design phase where the routing of the flat packages is planned globally. The fifth design phase is to display each product in the Ikea catalogues and stores so that customers will be inspired, make their choices, and buy their furniture in a self-service model. Ikea customers are well aware that they will have to self-transport and self-assemble the furniture as this is an important part of keeping the price low.

3.2. *Ikea's almost fabless manufacturing*

Since 1955 Ikea has successfully been producing their Scandinavian design furniture in a fabless fashion together with partner suppliers in an ever growing supply chain. This makes purchasing decisions strategically important. To support these decisions Ikea has developed a purchasing matrix to get an overview of alternative geographical locations. For each material concerned the attractiveness of the regions has priority. The matrix is updated twice a year. Apart from material supply, the priorities are based on factors like the national rate of growth, risk-taking, and the UN sanction lists. The basic rule for purchasing is as always best buy. With the matrix Ikea is updated with global market prices and conditions which is an essential part of Ikea's cost leadership strategy. The choice of a supplier must be satisfactory from both the supply and the distribution point of view. It is essential to be able to effectively transport raw material and components between various processing steps and from then on to the global Ikea warehouses.

In 1992, in the aftermath of the fall of the Berlin wall, the business model slightly changed as Ikea saw a risk of supply capacity shortage. Ikea decided to start a manufacturing company, Swedwood, to ensure enough capacity, but never to exceed 10% of total production. This limitation was an important signal to the supplier network that Ikea did not intend to outcompete it. With more than 90% of their furniture produced by the network of suppliers, Ikea remains to be a global almost fabless producer. Over the years of expansion, Ikea has shifted part of their production location to the new markets in China, India, Pakistan, Bangladesh, Vietnam,

Malaysia, Thailand, and Indonesia. In 2009 the procurement balance had changed between Europe and Asia so that 40% of all production came from Poland and China.

As explained in the five-folded strategy, manufacturing is an integrated part of the value creating supply chain. In the unique almost fabless manufacturing process Ikea has taken a different approach compared to the recent trend of outsourcing. With the establishment of Swedwood, a company later merged into Ikea Industry, Ikea chose to insource up to 10% of its production and outsource more than 90%. A word that can explain this balance is "rightsourcing", which mean that in all production planning Ikea strive to optimize the balance of in- and out-sourcing. The possibility to manufacture in-house in one of Ikea Industry's plants gives Ikea an option when they cannot find a partner in the almost fabless supply chain. Jonsson *et al.* (2013), also presented in the theory section, described that Ikea's strategic planning is based on sales forecasts and sales frames on a five-year rolling horizon, updated three times per year. These plans are broken down to an 84-week rolling horizon for tactical selling and production planning for the entire global supply chain, updated weekly. Production planning is further divided into supplier capacities, a split of volumes between different suppliers and, materials requirements. For a unique supplier the effect is an 18-month commitment of volumes of selected articles, usually consisting of a spread between a guaranteed volume and a maximum. At the lowest level a weekly short-term plan levels out supplier capacities, shifting volumes from one supplier who has reached capacity limits to someone that has to fill up to the guaranteed volume. To support the centralized supply chain planning, Ikea uses APS software. With the help of the APS raw materials and production capacity is optimally allocated to meet the demand. All suppliers in the Ikea supply chain is connected to the APS, which gives the unique supplier the input data to his weekly production scheduling.

Production planning is fully integrated with distribution and deliveries to the following Ikea locations in the supply chain. Ingvar Kamprad hates wastes, and one of his favorite objects is to transport as little air as possible. Boxes has to be full, containers filled, trucks, trains and boats fully loaded, which means flat packages. The flatter, the better, an Ikea flat package allows for more than seven times as many units to fit into a shipping container compared to assembled products, which reduces transportation costs and emissions. A typical Ikea store carries a product line of 10,000 items, and to secure that these are available to customers at all time, efficient global production and distribution is a vital phase of the Ikea strategy. Ikea Distribution Services division is managing the intricate pattern of global product movements. From the current 1,200 suppliers in the almost fabless network in 55 countries, and the 44 Ikea Industry plants in 11 countries, products are shipped to distribution centers that deliver to the local stores on a just-in-time basis. As Ikea is in control of the whole process from design, production, distribution, and retail stores, they are also balancing the supply chains by placing production facilities closer to the markets and the retail stores. This is another way of reducing transportation costs and emissions.

3.3. *Ikea's management control package*

The attractiveness and competitiveness of Ikea comes from the unique mix of activities in the Ikea activity map. The modular design of furniture is a basis for Ikeas cost leadership. Ikea uses target costing for all its furniture and the first they design is the price-tag. Price minus margin gives target cost. All prices are fixed for a year, as in the Ikea catalogue, which forces Ikea to try to have production cost fixed for the same period. Ikea aims at prices at least 20% lower than competitors which means that total cost also have to be at least 20% lower. Following the target cost strategy all costs are "designed" with the modular furniture by value engineering, including design for flat package. With the knowledge from the purchasing matrix Ikea can chose to buy products and parts globally depending on market conditions. If Ikea is unable to reach target cost for a product, an assignation is made to Ikea Industry for lower manufacturing costs.

BANG mugs were for many years one of Ikea's most popular products. At its peak about 25 million mugs was sold annually in the Ikea stores all over the world. BANG is also a good example of Ikea's use of target costing for strategic purposes.

When in 1996 product developer Pia Eldin Lindstén was given the task of creating a new mug she was simultaneously told about the future price tag in the stores. In the particular case of BANG it was exceedingly low: 5 kronor (SEK). BANG was to be a price shock. Göran Björnsson, Ikea, was present at the launching of BANG. *"The first thing we designed was the price tag"*. A 5 SEK product means that the government gets 1 SEK in sales tax, one goes to Ikea and the producers and carriers get three. When BANG was launched in 1996 a good quality mug was 10 SEK. Kamprad suggested planning for a volume of one to two million BANG mugs a year.

Björnsson proposed instead a 3-year contract which guaranteed the supplier sales of 4–5 million per year. This way he was able to reduce the purchasing cost by more than 10% a piece, compared to a one-year contract of one to two million mugs. Even volume increases of this production size lead to considerable savings. This was the decision and during the first year the sales amounted to 10 million mugs.

However, product development is a process going on continuously. Last year, a new BANG mug was launched. The new mug Färgrik is lightly lower and the handle has been changed so that it will be easier to pile and will occupy less space in transports, warehouses, and stores. One of the BANG suppliers lives in Romania and has cooperated with Ikea for 15 years, so the mutual knowledge of demands and expectations is great. The products are often developed in close consultation with the suppliers and in the case of BANG the new and lower height has made manufacturing more effective by utilizing the space in the kiln better when burning, making it cost-effective and time-saving. Simple changes in the shape of the mug have reduced the cost to produce the mug significantly while creating more value for customers purchasing this simple 5 SEK coffee mug. After the redesign, Färgrik had lower production and logistical costs which enabled Ikea to reduce its prices, despite inflation to 4 SEK, as illustrated in Fig. 2.

For implementation and further development of this strategy, Ikea uses its own version of a MCP. As a large organization Ikea has a rich variety of management controls, including a core of; strategic planning, budgets, financial- and non-financial measuring systems, cultural controls, government structure, organization structure, and policies and procedures. But, target costing is a core method. The story of BANG could be repeated for most of the items in the Ikea catalogue, which annually promotes

Target costing table	BANG	and	Färgrik
Sales price	5 SEK		4 SEK
./. Sales tax	−1 SEK		−0.80 SEK
Market price(revenue)	4 SEK		3.20 SEK
./. Profit margin	−1 SEK		0.80 SEK
= Target cost	3 SEK		2.40 SEK

Fig. 2.   The mug called Färgrik, former BANG and supplementing target costing tables.

the prices for all Ikea's products. When it comes to policies and procedures in the Ikea MCP, Ikea way of purchasing home furniture products, (IWAY) plays a vital role in Ikea's demand for a balance between profit, environmental care (planet), and social responsibility (people). After its introduction in 2000, the IWAY has been a cornerstone in making global demand on suppliers for the protection of people and the environment. IWAY, also known as Ikea's code of conduct, regulates the conditions for quality, environment, and social and working conditions that all suppliers to Ikea must comply with. Long before, in 1990 Ikea decided to transform all its previous efforts regarding environmental and social issues into a sustainability action plan, which was adopted globally in 1992. The Environmental action plan was expanded over the following years and was replaced by IWAY in 2000, giving Ikea a 25 year experience of working with environmental and social issues. IWAY is based on international conventions and declarations, including the United Nations universal declaration of human rights, the International Labor Organization's declaration on fundamental principles and rights at work, and the Rio declaration on environment and development. IWAY covers working conditions, prevention of child labor, the environment, responsible forestry management and more. All suppliers in the Ikea supply chain are responsible for communicating the content of the Ikea code of conduct to co-workers and sub-suppliers and ensuring that all required measures are implemented at their own operations. However, these requirements also bring new challenges. Dahlvig (2011), former CEO of Ikea, explained that the two most difficult problems concerned labor and environmental conditions of suppliers in China. He added that the improvement of these conditions will take some time.

Ikea describe IWAY as their CSR document. With its MCP including IWAY Ikea is taking care of the economy at the same time as the ecology (green production and distribution) and the ethic side of society. With the combination of economic, ecologic, and ethic goals Ikea also meet the TBL of profit, planet, people. Actually, Ikea's sustainability strategy is called "People & Planet Positive", an extension of the original Ikea motto — helping to create a better everyday life for people. The integrated Ikea MCP, with its core of target costing and IWAY, aims to secure that Ikea continue to make a profit, at the same time as taking care of the planet and its people.

4. Case Analysis and Conclusions

In this section the case study is viewed through the lens of the literature review. Theoretical implications and practical findings are discussed and some conclusions are drawn together with a few ideas for further research.

4.1. *Ikea's updated strategy*

As was pointed out both in the literature review and in case study, Porter (1996) uses Ikea as a successful example of a low cost strategy company with good quality, function, and design. He further claims that Ikea's way of doing this is to carefully chose what activities are needed in the supply chain and decide whether the activity should be performed within the organization or outside by a partner. The strategically important activities that Ikea chose to perform in-house can be explained as core competence as in the resource-based strategy (Prahalad & Hamel, 1990; Barney, 1991). We could see that the Ikea business model changed in 1992 with the introduction of Swedwood as a fully own manufacturing company for up to 10% of all Ikea production. But the role of Swedwood, later Ikea industry, is not limited to production, the company brings knowledge of production processes and is sometimes also used as a laboratory for new ideas in production, which adds to the core competence of Ikea. With Swedwood Ikea have a possibility to bench-mark their partner suppliers with their own knowledge. Another change in the Ikea business model in 1992, identified in the case study, was the introduction of the Environmental action plan, later transformed to IWAY the Ikea code of conduct. With IWAY and the People & Planet Positive initiative, Ikea has built a cornerstone for protection of people and the environment as a complement to their low cost strategy. Ikea may be seen as a forerunner as a TBL company, they are profitable, takes good care of people and the planet. In Fig. 3, these updates in the Ikea strategy and business model are illustrated in a revised version of Porter's (1996) suggested activity map.

Compared to the lower part of the original activity map in Fig. 1 the four activities; product range, the modular furniture design, the in-house design, and manufacturing have been complemented with the People & Planet Positive demands. The fifth activity, production, was originally 100% sourcing from long-term suppliers. With the establishment of Swedwood

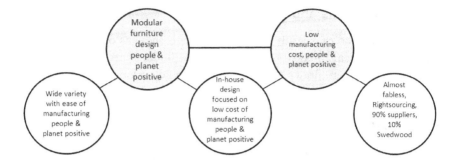

Fig. 3.   Updated Ikea activity map, lower part.

production is now "almost fabless, by rightsourcing from 90% longtime suppliers and a maximum of 10% from Swedwood." These updates in the Ikea strategy will be further discussed in the following sections.

4.2.   *Rightsourcing and almost fabless production in a global supply chain*

From 1955 to 1992, when good production facilities could be found around the world, Ikea was a typical example of fabless production, as described by Hurtarte *et al.* (2007). However, when production facilities became scarce Ikea was forced to start up Swedwood to secure production capacities. Today Ikea has a choice, as long as they can find good outsourced production they will use these partners, and when they cannot they use insourced production in Swedwood, much in the way that Quinn & Hilmer (1994) recommended. With the introduction of Swedwood and the changed business model, Ikea was able to follow the advice from Porter (1985) of reconfiguration of the value chain, whereby costs may be lowered and production processes may be changed. In the updated Ikea activity map, see Fig. 3, we describe this as almost fabless production in a global supply chain.

In this study we suggest the term "rightsourcing" for the balance between insourcing and outsourcing that is evident in the Ikea case. Rightsourcing at Ikea is an example of the hybrid pattern of outsourcing and insourcing that Jacobides (2005) discussed by referring to Williamson (1991) and his established definition of hybrids. A variant of the hybrid idea was discussed by Cox (2009), even though he suggested a joint venture between a supplying and a buying company. Another form of joint ventures and co-production with partner suppliers was suggested by Normann &

Ramirez (1998) in their description of value constellation. The rightsourcing decisions at Ikea are based on the centralized supply chain planning at Ikea that Jonsson *et al.* (2013) explained, and supported by the Ikea software for APS. As all suppliers are connected to the centralized planning model and APS, the "shared information highway" that Hurtarte *et al.* (2007) discussed, Ikea can optimize both production capacity in the supply chain (rightsource), and distribution, to meet the global demand from Ikea customers.

4.3. *Ikea's management control package for profit, people, and planet*

The case study clearly shows that Ikea applies management control systems (Anthony & Govindarajan, 2007) throughout its supply chain, the APS system is an example of this. Following the suggestions from Johnston & Lawrence (1988), Cooper & Slagmulder (2004), and Cooper & Yoshikawa (1994), Ikea control the global supply chain with shared information regarding both financial and non-financial data. As each of the companies involved in the global Ikea supply chain only carries out a limited set of the value creating activities, information regarding these activities has to be shared for coordination and efficiency. It is evident that Ikea work with a MCP, as presented by Malmi & Brown (2008). However, of all the parts of the MCP, this case study shows that for strategic decisions Ikea primarily use target costing for the low cost strategy, and IWAY for the People & Planet Positive strategy.

As demanded by Cooper & Yoshikawa (1994), inter-organizational management control should identify innovative ways to reduce product costs in the value system, and target costing was suggested as a suitable method. The Ikea strategy "*a wide range of well designed, functional home furnishing products at prices so low that as many people as possible will be able to afford them*" explains why Ikea, as a market leader, uses target costing to manage costs from the design phase and forward, as Cooper & Chew (1996) highlighted. The BANG/Färgrik mug example shows that Ikea sets aggressive market price targets for the design teams to come up with creative solutions and press value engineering to its limits to reach target costs, which is a parallel to the descriptions from Monden & Hamada (1991) and Cooper & Chew (1996) of how Japanese companies used target costing to drive new product development processes. From the case study we can conclude that target costing is a cornerstone in the Ikea MCP.

Another cornerstone in the Ikea MCP is IWAY and the People & Planet Positive strategy. Ikea has 25 year experience of working with sustainability action plans for environmental and social issues (Carroll, 1991; 1999), a program that became IWAY in 2000. IWAY is Ikea's code of conduct that regulates quality, environment, and social and working conditions that all suppliers must comply with. In this respect Ikea was an early adopter of what Elkington (2000) described as a new paradigm, companies that work with sustainability as a business model, and Deakin & Hobbs (2007) notion of new external demands for social and environmental responsibilities. As IWAY is a part of the Ikea MCP applied throughout the supply chain, Ikea have secured that IWAY is communicated to all Ikea's business partners, something that Stevens (2008) emphasized as primary drivers for organizational codes to be effective.

Further, IWAY together with target costing, are the Ikea MCP grounds for sustainability and the TBL of profit, people, and planet, as pointed out by Elkington (2000) and Zwetsloot (2003) as proofs of a company to be sustainable. The case study also show that with IWAY and the People & Planet Positive strategy, Ikea had adopted the ideas of CSV at least 10 years before the paper from Porter & Kramer (2011) was presented. Ikea and its almost fabless global supply chain may be explained as a forerunner in the TBL quest for profit, planet, and people.

5. Conclusion

Ikea has successfully been designing, producing, and marketing their furniture since 1955. This chapter has explored how Ikea manage and control its almost fabless production to reach the company's targets for sustainable profit, sustainable environment (planet), and sustainable social responsibility (people). The chapter shows that the basic Ikea strategy remains intact, it starts with an offer to customers of *"a wide range of well designed, functional home furnishing products at prices so low that as many people as possible will be able to afford them."* For carrying out the strategy Ikea follow target costing ideas and starts by deigning the price tag together with designing its own Scandinavian style, low cost, modular, ready-to-assemble furniture. When it comes to production, the Ikea strategy has been slightly changed. Rightsourcing is suggested as a term for the balance between insourced and outsourced production, resulting in an almost fabless supply chain of 90% outsourced production and 10% insourced to Swedwood/Ikea Industry. Also, the Ikea inter-organizational

MCP has been changed after IWAY became an integrated part to balance profit with people and planet in the sustainable Ikea supply chain. The result from the study points to possible implications for both research and practice. It would be interesting to see further studies of rightsourcing and its effects, and of course, case studies from other almost fabless producing companies.

References

Andersson, G. & Larsson, R. G. (2006). *Boundless Value Creation — Strategic Management Accounting in Value Systems Configuration.* Växjö: Växjö University Press.

Anthony, R. N. & Govindarajan, V. (2007). *Management Control Systems* (12th edn.). Boston: McGraw-Hill.

Barney, J. (1991). Firm Resources and Sustained Competitive Advantage, *Journal of Management,* 17(1), pp. 99–120.

Carrol, A. B. (1991). The Pyramid of Corporate Social Responsibility: Toward the Moral Management of Organizational Stakeholders, *Business Horizons,* 34(4), pp. 39–48.

Carrol, A. B. (1999). Corporate Social Responsibility: Evolution of a Definitional Construct, *Business and Society,* 38(3), pp. 268–295.

Cooper, R. & Chew, W. B. (1996). Control Tomorrow's Cost Through Today's Designs, *Harvard Business Review,* 74(1), pp. 88–99.

Cooper, R. & Slagmulder, R. (2004). Interorganizational Cost Management and Relational Context, *Accounting, Organizations and Society,* 29(1), pp. 1–26.

Cooper, R. & Yoshikawa, T. (1994). Inter-organizational Cost Management Systems: The Case of the Tokyo–Yokohama–Kamakura Supplier Chain, *International Journal of Production Economics,* 37(1), pp. 51–62.

Cox, A. (2009). Strategic management of construction procurement, Chapter 12. In *Construction Supply Chain Management Handbook,* W. J. O'Brien, C. T. Formoso, R. Vrijhoef, & K. A. London (eds.), Boca Raton: CRC Press.

Dahlvig, A. (2011). *The Ikea Edge: Building Global Growth and Social Good at the World's Most Iconic Home Store.* Boston: McGraw-Hill.

Deakin, S. & Hobbs, R. (2007). False Dawn for CSR, *Corporal Governance: An International Review,* 15(1), pp. 68–76.

Elkington, J. (2000). Cannibals with Forks: The Triple Bottom Line of 21st Century Business, *Journal of Business Ethics,* 23(2), pp. 229–231.

Hurtarte, J. S., Wolsheimer, E. A., & Tafoya, L. M. (2007). *Understanding Fabless IC Technology.* Oxford: Newnes.

Jacobides, M. G. (2005). Industry Change Through Vertical Disintegration: How and Why Markets Emerged in Mortage Banking, *Academy of Management Journal*, 48(3), pp. 465–499.

Johnston, R. & Lawrence, P. R. (1988). Beyond Vertical Integration — The Rise of the Value Adding Partnership, *Harvard Business Review*, 66(4), pp. 94–101.

Jonsson, P., Rudberg, M., & Holmberg, S. (2013). Centralised Supply Chain Planning at Ikea, *Supply Chain Management: An International Journal*, 18(3), pp. 337–350.

Malmi, T. & Brown, A. D. (2008). Management Control Systems as a Package — Opportunities, Challenges and Research Directions, *Management Accounting Research*, 19(4), pp. 287–300.

Monden, Y. & Hamada, K. (1991). Target Costing and Kaizen Costing in Japanese Automobile Companies, *Journal of Management Accounting*, 3, pp. 16–34.

Norman, R. & Ramirez, R. (1998). *Designing Interactive Strategy — From Value Chain to Value Constellation*. Chichester: Wiley & Sons Ltd.

Porter, M. E. (1985). *Competitive Advantage — Creating and Sustaining Superior Performance*. New York: The Free Press.

Porter, M. E. (1996). What is Strategy? *Harvard Business Review*, 74(6), pp. 61–78.

Porter, M. E. & Kramer, M. R. (2011). The Big Idea: Creating Shared Values, *Harvard Business Review*, 89(1–2), pp. 62–77.

Prahalad, C. K. & Hamel, G. (1990). The Core Competence of the Corporation, *Harvard Business Review*, 3, pp. 79–91.

Quinn, J. B. & Hilmer, F. G. (1994). Strategic Outsourcing. *Sloan Management Review*, 35(4), pp. 43–55.

Stevens, B. (2008). Corporate Ethical Codes: Effective Instruments for Behavior, *Journal of Business Ethics*, 78(4), pp. 601–609.

Williamson, O. E. (1991). Comparative Economic Organization: The Analysis of Discrete Structural Alternatives, *Administrative Science Quarterly*, 36(2), pp. 269–296.

Zwetsloot, G. (2003). From Management Systems to Corporate Social Responsibility, *Journal of Business Ethics*, 44(2/3), pp. 201–207.

4

Effects of Transfer Pricing Taxation on the Performance Control of Japanese Foreign Subsidiaries

Makoto Tomo
Seijo University

Anson Yoshiharu Matsuoka
Seijo University

1. Introduction

Japanese corporations have since started moving manufacturing and sales offices overseas from 1970s. It is due to location savings (cheap labor costs, securing resources), dealing with local content laws, and minimizing foreign exchange exposure. Looking at it from a financial risk perspective, if products are manufactured in the country to be sold, profit and costs would be calculated in the same currency, hence it is possible to minimize foreign exchange exposure.

In light of the globalization of companies, the Organization for Economic Co-operation and Development (OECD) tax committee has been debating about Base Erosion and Profit Shifting (BEPS) as an international taxation issue. This is the problem whereby multinational corporations transfer profits from high tax rate countries to low tax rate countries, thus countries with higher tax rates stand to lose taxation opportunities. These issues came to light and attracted attention when it was reported that companies like Starbucks, Apple, and Google were taking extreme measures in order to avoid taxes. Tax authorities tackled this problem by implementing the Transfer Pricing Taxation system (EY Foundation of Licensed Accountants, 2014, p. 13).

Additional taxes of the Transfer Pricing Taxation system is said to be considerable. According to the National Tax Agency (2013b), the average amount for each case was 700 million yen and this was six times more in comparison to the average of 119 million yen for cases which were non-Transfer Pricing related — emphasizing the impact transfer pricing has when companies are imposed with additional taxes. Also, the risk of double taxation arises whereby a company is taxed from both countries for the same income. Especially after the 1990s, Japanese companies have been relocating their manufacturing and sales bases in newly developing countries such as China. This is due to Location Savings and to capture the local markets. Thus, issues arising due to the Transfer Pricing Taxation system do not specifically occur in western countries but also in newly developing countries.

In this chapter, we shall examine the background of how tax management became necessary for Transfer Pricing Taxation system. Then we will describe the tax management methods and the effects it has on Performance Control Accounting.

2. Corporate Overseas Operations and Government Measures

2.1. *Corporate operations overseas*

As many companies relocate their manufacturing and sales offices overseas, profits that would have been generated domestically, are now transferred overseas. According to the Ministry of Economy, Trade, and Industry (2014), in 2012, the sales estimate for these overseas companies has seen a 9.2% rise year on year at 199 trillion yen, as compared to 10 years ago at 137 trillion yen, that is a 1.4 times increase. Foreign production ratio is 33.7% based on the corporations which set up operations overseas. Comparing the ordinary profit ratio between domestic and overseas subsidiaries, we can see that from 2009 to 2012, overseas subsidiaries have consistently surpassed domestic ones.

Table 1 shows the changes in numbers of overseas subsidiaries. In recent years we can observe that the numbers have seen an increase in North America and Europe. However, relatively speaking, these numbers have declined. On the other hand, looking at the Asian region in 1995, there were 4,600 companies (44%) and in 2012 there were 15,234 companies (65%). Especially in China the numbers increased dramatically from 908 companies (9%) in 1995 to 7,700 companies (33%) in 2012. Thus, we can observe that the number of companies in the Asian region, especially China, have seen a significant increase.

Table 1.   Number of Japanese subsidiaries overseas (Units: Company).

	1995		2000		2005		2010		2012	
All areas (total)	10,416	100%	14,991	100%	15,850	100%	18,559	100%	23,351	100%
North America	2,586	25%	3,316	22%	2,825	18%	2,860	15%	3,216	14%
Asia (subtotal)	4,600	44%	7,244	48%	9,174	58%	11,497	62%	15,234	65%
China	908	9%	2,530	17%	4,051	26%	5,565	30%	7,700	33%
ASEAN4	1,608	15%	2,478	17%	2,715	17%	3,027	16%	3,776	16%
NIEs3	1,965	19%	1,911	13%	2,044	13%	2,162	12%	2,605	11%
Asia others	119	1%	325	2%	364	2%	743	4%	1,153	5%
Europe	1,958	19%	2,682	18%	2,384	15%	2,536	14%	2,834	12%
Others	1,272	12%	1,749	12%	1,467	9%	1,706	9%	2,069	9%

Source: METI (2014, 2012, 2007, 2002, and 1997) ASEAN4: Malaysia, Thailand, Indonesia and the Philippines. NIEs3: Singapore, Taiwan, and South Korea.

As corporate operation overseas increases, issues regarding Transfer Pricing Taxation and International Taxation become more prevalent. Moreover, most Association of Southeast Asian Nations (ASEAN) countries involved are not members of the OECD, thus making the problem more complex.

2.2. How Japanese government deals with tax planning of companies

Although more and more companies' operations move beyond country boarders, the government still mainly depends on domestic tax revenue. As companies move their manufacturing, sales and marketing, and R&D functions overseas, profits generated by these operations likewise are being generated overseas. For the global enterprise, tax planning that aims to reduce the worldwide total amount of tax has become an issue.

In June 2012, the US raised the issue to the OECD tax committee that BEPS was decreasing tax revenues markedly. After this, the OECD has decided to address this issue by 2014–2015. It published "Addressing Base Erosion and Profit Shifting" and in June 2013, "Action Plan on Base Erosion and Profit Shifting" which indicates 15 ways to tackle BEPS. As we can see, from the following six action plans (Action 4, 8, 9, 10, 13, and 14) that are directly related to Transfer Pricing Taxation, they are taking BEPS seriously. In September 2013, the G20 leaders endorsed the OECD initiative.

3. The Need for Tax Planning and Transfer Pricing Taxation

For global companies, it is crucial to take into consideration the tax amount of their subsidiaries to maximize worldwide corporate current profit after tax. If tax management is not properly done, this increases risks of incurring additional taxes which will then possibly affect current income. Thus, as companies go global, the need for proper tax management arises.

3.1. Transfer Pricing Taxation

According to Okawara *et al.* (2002) taxation cost reduction measures can be classified into three parts: income management, cash management, and taxation risk management. Fig. 1 illustrates this.

In this chapter, we shall focus on the adjustment of transfer pricing in dealings within a company. When companies export items from a country with high tax rates to overseas subsidiaries that are located in countries with low tax rates, the lower the selling price is set, the purchasing cost is reduced for these companies. Thus, profits of these overseas subsidiaries increase.

1. Income management		
	Transfer income to low tax rate countries	
	Transfer functions and risks to low tax rate countries	
		Cost sharing contracts, commissionaire
	Usage of e-commerce	
	Reducing tariff	
		Unbundling, prior sale, warehouse, using preferential tariff, different rates for different categories of products, replacing parts.
2. Cash management		
	Loans to/from affiliates	
	Using tax havens	
	Using conduit companies	
	Using foreign tax credits	
3. Risk management for tax administration		
	Risk management for transfer price taxation	
		Transfer pricing analysis and documentation, using APAs
	Eliminating permanent establishment (PE) risk	

Fig. 1.   Tax administration cost reduction measures.

On the other hand, sales and profits of the company located in a high tax rate country decreases. By shifting profits from high tax rate countries to low tax rate countries, tax amount in high tax rate countries reduce, while tax amount at low tax rate countries increase. Although tariffs in the low tax rate countries may increase, by transferring profits overseas, companies as a whole are able to reduce their total amount of tax globally. When this kind of profit shifting is allowed, countries with higher tax rates stand to lose taxation opportunities. Transfer Pricing Taxation was implemented to prevent tax evasion of this kind.

3.2.   *Criteria for transfer pricing method*

In Performance Accounting, intra-company transfer pricing is used for department control in decentralized organizations. Criteria for these include, market price method, cost plus method (full costs + markup), price minus method.

With regards to Transfer Pricing Taxation, the "arm's length price" is a requirement as the transfer price. In Performance Accounting, the intra-company transfer price is set based on performance evaluation. However, for the Transfer Price Taxation, objectivity is required.

Table 2 shows a breakdown of methods applied in advance pricing agreement (APAs) (predetermine the method of calculation for the arm's length price with the tax authorities) for method of pre determining transfer

Table 2.   Method of determining transfer price in APAs.

	Year			
	2007		2012	
Traditional transaction methods				
Arm's length method	15	16%	8	6%
Market price method	8	9%	0	0%
Cost plus method	11	12%	3	2%
Transactional price method				
Profit split method	7	8%	16	11%
Transactional net margin method (TNMM)	50	55%	97	68%
Subtotal	57	63%	113	79%
Others	0	0%	19	13%
Total	91	100%	143	100%

Source: National Tax Agency (2008 and 2013a).

price in 2012. In the past, to determine the transfer price, the arm's length method, market price method, and cost plus methods (hereafter: the traditional transaction methods) took priority over other methods. However, in 2011 it was revised based on the OECD transfer pricing guidelines to enable the application of the best method on a case by case basis.

The number of cases for non-traditional transaction methods, which are the transactional methods, totaled 113 cases (79%) out of 143 cases. This number sees an increase from 2007. Using the methods other than the traditional transaction methods to determine the arm's length price comprises approximately 92%. This emphasizes the challenges and difficulties faced when determining transfer prices.

3.3.   *Increasing risk of additional taxes due to Transfer Pricing Taxation System in Asia*

In Asia, only the Republic of Korea and Japan are member states of the OECD. There are many countries that do not follow the OECD transfer pricing guidelines or have the proper rules in place to adhere to the model taxation treaties and it is "unforeseeable 8" of the non-OECD member states (China, India, Russia, Argentina, Brazil, Indonesia, Saudi Arabia, and South Africa), who gave an opinion regarding the BEPS action plan implementation. For newly developed countries where implementation is still in the early stages due to lack of experience and personnel, understanding and the interpretation of these systems and treaties may vary depending on who is handling it as mentioned in the Japan Business Federation (2014). As payment of royalties is deemed as "payment on profit (gained)", royalties paid may not be included as tax deductible expenses when foreign subsidiaries are in the red. Likewise, when engineers are sent to foreign subsidiaries to impart technical expertise and know-how, local tax authorities consider this as a transfer of intellectual property. Costs incurred for sending these engineers are considered royalties and withholding taxes are imposed.

At times, the tax authorities levy high tax amount without taking into account the company's business situation. Although APA systems are in place, it is actually still not functioning. Moreover, there are hundreds of administrative rulings being issued in a year, including those that are not released to the public. Tax authorities at times, impose tax based on these. Many of these administrative rulings are unclear and written abstractly, often leaving it up to the discretion of the tax assessor.

China has been a strong proponent of the "Location Specific Advantage" (LSA) concept. It brought up the fact that this has not been incorporated into the OECD Transfer Pricing Guidelines (Mori, 2014, p. 104). LSA is the concept that the source of the company's profit is not attributed to its intangible assets but rather to cheap labor costs for manufacturing (location savings) in these countries and the premium placed on these so-called brands by local consumers. However, in recent years for tax administration, many developed nations including Japan consider any profit ratio exceeding that of the compared company's profit, in fact, a valuable intangible asset. Thus, in many cases, it is said that profits are imputed to the owner of these intangible assets. (Fukushima *et al.*, 2011) Thus, even among identical transactions, arm's length prices based on both parties calculation may vary widely. Even if applying one country's calculation method to come up with the arm's length price, risk of incurring additional taxes remains.

3.4. The importance of intangible assets with regards to Transfer Pricing Taxation system

In recent years, the number of cases whereby additional taxes imposed involved cases regarding intangible assets like marketing know-how, patents, and royalties increased. OECD describes BEPS tax planning whereby transferring of intangible assets to low tax rate countries was carried out (OECD, 2013a).

In July 2013, the OECD published the "Revised Discussion Draft on Transfer Pricing Aspects of Intangibles" (OECD, 2013b). The definition of intangible assets was revised to "something which is not a physical asset or a financial asset, which is capable of being owned or controlled for use in commercial activities, and whose use or transfer, would be compensated had it occurred in a transaction between independent parties and comparable circumstances." In this chapter, location savings and market premium (benefit from local market features) is also being considered, but not as an intangible asset.

It also describes the following, "The legal owner of an intangible may initially be entitled to receive the proceeds from exploitation or transfer of the intangible." And "The right of other members of the MNE group to receive compensation for their functions performed, assets used or contributed, and risks assumed may be conceptually framed as an allocation to those other members of all or part of the return attributable to the intangible." (*Ibid.*, p. 20, para. 65)

An example of a case with regards to taxation relating to intangibles in June 2013 involved the company, HOYA Corporation in Japan. It was served with a tax notice to pay additional taxes of 90 billion yen. HOYA Corporation signed a contract to undertake the R&D of a new product for its 100% South East Asian subsidiaries. The developed technology was attributed to 100% overseas subsidiaries in Thai, Philippine, Vietnam, etc.

Hoya Corporation had signed a contract that agreed to pay a fee to their South East Asian subsidiaries whenever HOYA Corporation sold products that were manufactured using the aforementioned technology. Regarding this contract, the Tokyo Regional Taxation Bureau (TRTB) deemed that by transferring manufacturing expertise to its overseas subsidiaries, it transferred its profits and avoided taxes. HOYA Corporation insists that it carried out transactions with its overseas subsidiaries under fair and proper conditions. The payment for manufacturing expertise was also appropriately priced (*The Nikkei*, 2013, p. 17). This is an example of the taxation risks involving intangible assets.

3.5. *Avoiding additional taxation risks relating to Transfer Price Taxation system*

To avoid additional taxes due to transfer price taxation, firstly you could avail the APAs and Mutual Agreement Procedures (MAPs). However, these alone may not be sufficient. To lessen the risks of additional taxes, it is necessary for each country's tax authorities to come to an agreement with regards to determining transfer price. Although the arm's length price is regarded as the standard when determining the transfer price, this may vary between the industrialized nations and the newly developing nations. If additional taxes are imposed due to transfer pricing, tax authorities from both countries can discuss and if they reach an agreement, double taxation can be avoided. However, double taxation will be levied until the time an agreement is reached and even if there are ongoing discussions, it does not guarantee a favorable outcome.

In June 2006, Takeda Pharmaceutical Co. Ltd., was served with a tax correction notice from the Osaka Regional Tax Bureau (ORTB) with respect to its drug supply transactions with its 50:50 joint venture partner, America's Abbot Laboratories. The total six-year income amount after transfer pricing adjustment was 122.3 billion yen and Takeda Pharmaceutical Co. Ltd., received a total of 57.1 billion yen in additional taxes. This is close to half of its net income for the year 2011. In August 2006, Takeda appealed but in July 2008 this was put on hold in order to seek a MAP to resolve the double taxation issue. However, the MAP between the Japanese authorities and the US authorities did not reach an agreement. Thus, this resulted in Takeda to make a request to the ORTB to reopen the original case. In the end, the court ruled against the ORTB and Takeda won the case.

Secondly, even if an APA is not sought, it is very important to document the procedures of calculating the arm's length price. In Japan, if taxpayers do not submit proof that the transactions made between them and overseas parties are indeed made using arm's length prices in a timely manner, an estimated assessment will be imposed (or they may be taxed by estimate) and this may increase the possibility of the double taxation issue not being resolved. It is not subject to MAPs because this taxation breaches the OECD transfer pricing guideline.

Thirdly, when overseas subsidiaries negotiate with local tax authorities, these subsidiaries must be well versed with the headquarters' transfer pricing measures, etc. and the headquarters must properly communicate these to their subsidiaries.

As mentioned earlier, even without the intention of tax evasion or avoidance, there still remain risks of receiving additional taxes. Transfer Pricing Taxation system relating to intangibles often is left to the discretion of the tax authorities and are difficult to correctly anticipate. If additional taxes are imposed, the amount is relatively substantial. Moreover, the possibility of double taxation also exists. The APA systems in place also lack flexibility and not very easy to apply.

4. Tax Planning with Respect to the Transfer Pricing Taxation System

If the transfer price is adjusted in line with functions performed and risks assumed within a group of companies, profits can be reallocated without getting into conflict with the Transfer Pricing Taxation system. Typical methods for this would be cost sharing, contract manufacturing, and consignment sales (Okawara *et al.*, 2002; JETRO, 2001; Schwarz and Elina, 2006).

4.1. *Cost sharing agreement*

A cost sharing agreement is an agreement to adjust profit allocation to reflect costs shared based on anticipated benefits. Based on expected sales profits, costs to be shared means the ratio of costs of R&D for intangibles to be split between the headquarter and its overseas subsidiaries.

According to Minagawa (1993) in terms of incentive to the company's management, subsidiaries that are financially capable would merit from the cost sharing agreement. On the other hand, subsidiaries that have just started out overseas would not benefit to enter into a cost sharing agreement from a financial perspective. However, even if profits are negative, from a business performance control aspect, instead of managing through financial indicators such as being profitable for the year or cutting cumulative losses it may be more motivational to manage this through targets and budgets that are based on the actual situation.

In light of Japanese tax authorities' implementation of the Transfer Price Taxation system and focus placed on intangibles, it is effective for subsidiaries involved to enter into a cost sharing agreement for R&D activities even if their profits are negative.

4.2. *Consignment manufacturer*

Here we talk about contract manufacturer to include toll manufacturer and contract manufacturer. Based on data from Schwarz and Elina (2006) and JETRO (2001), Table 3 shows a comparison between the aforementioned contract manufacturer types and a typical full-fledged manufacturer.

Table 3. Legal rights and risks with respect to contract manufacture.

	Possess labor and equipment	Legal ownership and rights to raw materials, etc.	Manufacturing	Sales risks
Fully fledged manufacturer	√	√	√	√
			Manufacture at own risk	Sell at own risk
Contract manufacturer	√	√	√	NA
		Risk on inventory	Manufacture based on contract	Guaranteed sales of products produced
Toll manufacturer	√	NA	√	NA
		Provided by the consigner and delivered directly to the factory	Manufacture based on contract	Guaranteed sales of products produced

A full-fledged manufacturer possesses ownership and is responsible for labor costs, equipment, procurement of raw materials and parts. It manufactures and sells at its own risk. Whereby a contract manufacturer produces products based on consignment. It does not assume any risk with respect to sales of the manufactured products because sales of these are guaranteed by the consigner. Toll manufacturers manufacture based on raw materials and parts procured by the principal. Therefore, they do not hold legal ownership or title and assume no risk on inventory or procurement of materials.

4.3. *Commissionaire*

There are three types of consignment sales; commissionaire, limited-risk distributor, and commission agent as shown in Table 4. Normally when selling products overseas, the vendor (sales company) will procure products from the manufacturing company and sell these to the end user. The vendor (sales company) will purchase and market these products under their company name and sell these items to the end users while assuming risks of reputation/credibility, risk on inventory for the company.

On the other hand for consignment sales, functions performed and risks are limited. For commissionaire and commission agent, they do not assume risk on inventory because they do not purchase these. Credit risks due to bad debts are also limited. Thus as functions and risks are limited, profits to be paid will be minimized as compared to classical sales structures. Therefore, profits may be centralized to the principal. Functions such as distribution, advertising, sales promotion, and administrative work could be selectively handled by the principal. By selectively allocating these functions and their business risks within the group of companies it is possible to appropriately transfer profits.

4.4.   *The effect of consignment manufacturing, consignment sales, and integrated management*

If consignment manufacturing and consignment sales structure is adopted, integrated management for differing manufacturing and sales related operations can be done on a subsidiary basis by regional headquarter. Firstly, by concentrating inventory control, accounts receivable/accounts payable management, credit management, financing (capital procurement), and foreign exchange control redundancy can be eliminated, and costs reduced. By integrating, functions like invoicing, accounts receivable/accounts payable management, inventory management, financing and management, costs can be reduced.

Secondly, the regional headquarter can be in a position to learn things relating to intangible assets from sales activities like client lists, and contract terms with the clients. Sharing of information is also effective for the company as a whole. Information regarding orders taken and placed, inventory and funds are all gathered in one place so it is also advantageous for local management of companies.

On the other hand, if the consignment sales method is adopted, certain rights and responsibilities like inventory and deciding on sales conditions that the subsidiary sales company had, would as a result be centralized to the principal. Although partial profit centers can be adopted, the delegation of authority to subsidiary will be less.

Table 4. Legal rights and risks in consignment sales.

	Procurement	Advertising	Customer	Returning of goods, guarantee	After service	Inventory risk	Credit risk	Profit
"Classical" buy/sell distributor	✓	✓ Name value	Own company name	✓	✓	✓	✓	Gains accrued from sales of goods
Commissionaire		✓	Own company name					Sales commission
Limited-risk distributor	✓	✓	Own company name	✓	✓	Guaranteed under contract	Guaranteed under contract	Gains accrued from sales of goods
Commission agent		✓	Principal					commission

5. Consignment Sales, Consignment Manufacturing, and Issues with Regards to Business Performance Management

Since a commissioned company is an independent company in the market, it is needless to say that they are profit oriented. Should the control of a commissioned company be done through motivating them to join the network by allocating profits?

5.1. *Consignment sales and responsibility center*

For consignment sales, if you adopt the method of marking up a certain percentage on the actual selling price as the consignment fees, it will always increase in proportion to sales. Therefore, there will be too much focus only on increasing the sales figures and it will lead to cheap order taking and the profit of the consignor will be lost.

Also, accounts receivable management is a problem. Since they do not need to assume risk of sales, as long as they sell the products, they will receive a fixed amount of consignment fees. Hence they are motivated to sell even to clients who they may not be able to collect payment. Other than this, it is necessary to set rules regarding, profit ratio for sales promotions, penalties for return of goods and delayed delivery, measures to cater to specialty products, order management, credit risk management, etc.

5.2. *Consignment manufacturing and responsibility center*

For contract manufacturing, adopting a method that calculates the consignment fees based on adding a fixed percentage to standard costs has a downside. Because when production efficiency goes up, the standard costs will decrease and, the profits generated from this might not be obtained by contract manufacturer. This might weaken the incentive to reduce costs. So for example, there are cases whereby in the automobile industry, when parts manufacturers manage to succeed in cost reduction of their products, the savings made from cost reduction is split between both parties for two years. From the third year onwards the overall settlement (cost) price will be lowered. This may be a method to indirectly control an independent contract manufacturer.

Thus, when deciding on the commission fees it is possible to apply the intra-company transfer price framework. In other words, gathering information regarding the risks assumed by the consignee company, profits allocated based on contribution made by both parties including royalties for intangible assets and transfer prices will be useful. If both parties have intangible assets, profit allocation based on the ratio of intangible asset contribution is possible. If only one party has intangible assets, then deciding the commission fees based on cost ratio, or the ratio of funds invested or ratio of value to stockholders will be useful.

6. Conclusion and Further Challenges

In this chapter we have pointed out that the risks of additional taxes from transfer pricing being imposed with respect to intangibles have been surfacing for multinational enterprises. Moreover, matters are complicated due to the differing views between newly developing countries and developed countries regarding location savings and the implementation of the Transfer Pricing Taxation system concerning intangibles. Documenting the process of coming up with the transfer price, ensuring overseas subsidiaries are ready and able to cater to the demands of this system is also essential.

To tackle risks due to the Transfer Pricing Taxation system, re-organization of the company and reallocating functions is a useful method. Contract manufacturing and consignment sales are methods used for distributing functions across borders. Because, rights other than manufacturing and sales are basically centralized on the consignor (regional headquarters), the consignee (overseas subsidiary) has less autonomy. At the same time, this is also related to fundamental issues like appropriateness of income distribution that performance control accounting deals with.

For group of companies that span several different countries where accounting systems, taxation systems, rules and regulations, language, currency, and cultures differ, there is a limit in controlling these companies simply based on autonomy. Rather, adjust the whole group to adapt to different environments and by building a supply chain that includes R&D, manufacturing, sales and after service seems to be leading to a source of income for multinational enterprises.

From a tax planning perspective, when building a supply chain that includes R&D, manufacturing, sales and after service, unbundling some of the functions from the group is also another option. However, we must also bear in mind that tax planning that focuses too much on cost reduction of taxes also gives rise to new problems like BEPS.

In this chapter, we have talked about the risks of additional taxes from the perspective of transfer pricing and performance control accounting. Issues like the appropriateness of income distribution has been one of the issues that performance control accounting has been addressing in the past. What we need to further study in the future is the role of management control by looking into cases where companies reallocate functions globally, while also considering international taxation issues like Transfer Pricing Taxation system.

References

EY Foundation of Licensed Accountants (2014). A survey on BEPS measures and the effects on our companies: A survey outsourced by METI. Retrieved from http://www.meti.go.jp/meti_lib/report/2014fy/E00 4206.pdf (search date October 15, 2014) (in Japanese).

Fukushima, S., Tajima, K., & Yamada, M. (2011). Main points of issue with regards to Transfer Pricing Taxation system when setting up an Asian base: About Location Savings, *Kokuzei Sokuho*, June 20, 2011, *6179*, pp. 41–44. Retrieved from http://www.tohmatsu.com/assets/Dcom-Japan/Local%20Assets/Documents/knowledge/tax-pdf/jp_k_tax_koku zei0620_040711.pdf (search date October 15, 2014) (in Japanese).

JETRO Brussels Center (2001). Corporate Reorganization in Europe. *Euro Trend*, September 2001, pp. 2–16. Retrieved from http://www. jetro.go.jp/jfile/report/05000496/05000496_001_BUP_0.pdf (search date October 15, 2014) (in Japanese).

Minagawa, Y. (1993). *Tax Strategies of Multinational Corporations*. Aichi: The University of Nagoya Press (in Japanese).

Ministry of Economy, Trade and Industry (2014a). 43rd basic survey on overseas business activities. Retrieved from http://www.meti.go.jp/ statistics/tyo/kaigaizi/result/result_43/result_43.html_ (search date October 15, 2014) (in Japanese).

Mori, N. (2014). *The Economics of Transfer Pricing*. Tokyo: Chuokeizai-sha Inc. (in Japanese)

National Tax Agency (2008). Situations of APAs for the year 2007. Retrieved from http://www.nta.go.jp/kohyo/press/press/2008/sogo_ kyogi/pdf/01.pdf (search date October 15, 2014) (in Japanese).

National Tax Agency (2013a). Situations of APAs for the year 2012. Retrieved from https://www.nta.go.jp/kohyo/press/press/2013/sogo_ kyogi/index.htm (search date October 15, 2014) (in Japanese).

National Tax Agency (2013b). An overview of the survey achievements on corporate taxes for 2012. Retrieved from https://www.nta.go.jp/ kohyo/press/press/2013/hojin_chosa/03.htm_ (search date October 15, 2014) (in Japanese).

Organization for Economic Cooperation and Development (OECD) (2010). *Transfer Pricing Guidelines for Multinational Enterprises and Tax Administrations.* Paris: OECD.

OECD (2013a). *Addressing Base Erosion and Profit Shifting.* Paris: OECD. Retrieved from http://www.keepeek.com/Digital-Asset-Management/ oecd/taxation/addressing-base-erosion-and-profit-shifting_978926419 2744-en (search date October 15, 2014).

OECD (2013b). *Revised Discussion Draft on Transfer Pricing Aspects of Intangibles.* Paris: OECD. Retrieved from http://www.oecd.org/ctp/ transfer-pricing/revised-discussion-draft-intangibles.pdf (search date October 15, 2014).

Okawara, K., Campbell, M., & Mizuno, M. (2002). *In-depth Analysis: How to Reduce Tax Costs — Know-How for International Taxation Strategie.* Tokyo: Chuokeizai-sha, Inc. (in Japanese).

Schwarz, J. & Elina, O. (2006). Re-engineering Multinational Supply Chains, *Bulletin for International Taxation*, 60(5), pp. 187–193.

The Japan Business Federation (2014). Requests to Asian countries regarding the taxation system and implementation. Retrieved from http://www.keidanren.or.jp/policy/2014/060.html (search date October 15, 2014) (in Japanese).

The Nikkei (2013). National Tax Agency imposed additional taxes on HOYA, July 15, p. 17 (in Japanese).

5

Innovation of Eco-Cars Based on the Global Inter-Firm Collaboration

Yasuhiro Monden*

University of Tsukuba

1. Theme of this Study

This chapter will try to suggest how the innovation for eco-cars could be brought about. As Schumpeter (1926) defined the innovation as carrying out the "new combination" of various knowledge, the author will first explore how such new combination could be carried out for the eco-car development. For this purpose the writer will explore how to get the new knowledge through changing the business network organization.

In this chapter the author first defines the concept of innovation as a means of "re-birth" on the business. Then what will be the stimulus for such rebirth as innovation of automobile will be explored. The stimulus will in turn bring the inter-firm collaborations of various forms to cause the eco-car innovation.

Finally the writer will examine and propose what kind of value premises or philosophy is needed to bring about the sustainable world for the adoption of the regenerative energy for the sustainable mobility.

---

*The author is grateful to Prof. Luis E. Carretero Diaz of Complutense University of Madrid, Spain, for his invitation of my presentation of this chapter to the Conference on the *Mobility and Sustainable Human Development* directed by him, sponsored by Nissan Motor Iberica, and held at Complutense University on July 16, 2014. The comment and encouragement by Prof. Luis Carrestero for this chapter are sincerely acknowledged.

2. Innovation as "Rebirth" or "Transmigration" Stage

According to Abernathy *et al.* (1981) and (1983) the end of the maturity stage in the product cycle is not the death, but it could be reversed. Then how will the de-maturity process be caused? They explain it as follows.

The product life-cycle emphasized by Vernon (1966) and Abbegren *et al.* (1978) say that a product will progress through the stages of infancy, growth, maturity, and finally decline, etc. However, Abernathy says that "here is where the biological analogy finally breaks down, for manufacturing industries can indeed arrest — and in some circumstances even reverse the maturation process. We would argue for the possibility of industrial de-maturity."[1]

2.1. *Concepts of "re-birth" or "transmigration"*

The concept of Abernathy's "De-maturity" (or "rejuvenation") assumes that the matured (or declined) business could be reversed to the younger and growing business (or anti-aged). However, in the business world the declined business usually will be removed out of the company in question, and the new business will be introduced as a "rebirth", "transmigration", "regeneration", or "turnover" of the ailing company. So the terms "transmigration" or "re-birth" would be better than "De-mature".

3. Cause or "Stimulus" for Innovations of Eco-Cars: Five Goals

To make an innovation for eco-cars, first there must be some strong "stimulus" or cause, because the innovation needs some strong human-motivation. Among all, the strongest stimulus must be the new needs of the market or society that requires the sustainable mobility in the automobile market. When such stimulus are given, then again the new technical innovation regarding the alternative energies (i.e., non-regenerative energies (fossil energies) or regenerative energies) will emerge, which will be the most initial paradigm change.

---

[1]Unlike the criticism by Abernathy we can see such de-maturity phenomena in the biological "re-programing" (or re-starting of the cell division from the "stem cell" reproduced from any tissue portion of the matured body) as seen in the "iPS cell" or the regenerative medical treatment and the anti-aging medicines.

3.1. *Five goals of the environmental needs in the auto-market*

The following goals have appeared in time series as continuous stages or goals for environmental needs, but they still exist at the same time:

Goal 1 — Air Pollution Problem (The Clean Air Act, revised in 1970).
Goal 2 — Global Warming Problem.
Goal 3 — Fuel Consumption Problem (High-fuel efficiency; High-efficient engine).
Goal 4 — Alternative Energies Problem (Regenerative energy); This goal must be the central theme for the development of eco-cars.
Goal 5 — Cost and Price Problems of Eco-Cars' Popularization; this goal must be of immense importance to the customers.

3.1.1. (*Goal* 1) *Air pollution problem*

This is still the most important goal of the emerging countries nowadays.

In the US, the Clean Air Act as revised in 1970 (called Muskie Act) required that out of the exhaust gas of the automobile the density of carbon monoxide (CO), HO, and nitrogen oxides (NO_x) must be reduced to less than 10% of the levels of 1970 and 1971 car-models. Japanese Ministry of the Environment has also enacted the Clean Air Act of Japanese version in 1976 and 1978.

The photochemical oxidants (the smog that damages the mucous membranes in breathing organs) and the agricultural plants are damaged by the hydro carbon (HC) of gasoline or light oil (diesel oil). NO_x is also another cause of the photochemical oxidants and the acid rain. These human health problems have strongly motivated the civil movement for environmental protection (or anti-pollution) together with the strong arguments by the mass-media.

Toyota and Nissan also tried to clear the Act even by stopping their model-change for four years, spending their 36% of R&D costs to develop the methods. They developed the following two systems: the system of the so-called "***Three Way Catalyst***", which could be useful for simultaneous reduction of CO, HC, and NO_x. Toyota applied the Three Way Catalyst to the model "Crown" in June 1977.

The system called "***Electronic Fuel Injection***" (EFI), electronically controls the fuel injection in engine. In order to reduce the HC, if the ***Air/fuel ratio*** (called A/F or AFR) in the Air–Fuel Mixture is higher, then the HC can be reduced while NO_x will be increased. Thus, the control of the optimal air/fuel ratio could be done by EFI system.

Mr. Shoichiro Toyoda who was the vice president of Toyota, in charge of technology, at that time said: "The difficult situation under the severe requirement for exhaust gas became a moment or opportunity for the innovation and growth," (Toyoda, 2014).

Actually Japanese automobile manufacturers have increased their numbers of engineers in the new fields of chemistry, metallurgy, and electronics,while their previous main engineers were mostly mechanical engineers. And such inter-science approach has become useful in the later needs for lighter body, compact engines, fuel efficiency, and various electronic control technologies.

3.1.2. (*Goal 2*) *Global warming problem*

In order to prevent the global warming carbon dioxide (CO_2) in the exhaust gas must be reduced. This is the necessity for all of the human being throughout the world.

The first proposal of this need was made by the *Kyoto Protocol to the United Nations Framework Convention on Climate Change* (abbreviated as "Kyoto Protocol") in 1997, which required the target of reducing the six kinds of the warming gases by 5% compared to 1990. Japanese government has agreed to the Kyoto protocol in May 2002 and sent the approved document to the United Nations in June 2004. By this agreement Japan was obliged to fulfil the target of 6% reduction by 2008–2012.

3.1.2.1. The countermeasures for the global warming have been continuously promoted by the Intergovernmental Panel on Climate Change (IPCC)

IPCC was jointly founded by the United Nations Environment Programme (UNEP) and World Meteorological Organization (WMO) in 1988.

In April 2014 the IPCC proposed the 40–70% reduction of the warming gas (CO_2, etc.) in the air, as compared to the 2010 level, by the year 2050. This is to control the temperature increase of the earth below "2°C increase" compared to the level at the industrial revolution of 1750. For attainment of this goal the concrete countermeasures are also proposed as follows (*The Nikkei*, 2014b and 2014d):

(1) The ratio of the regenerative energy in the total electricity supply must be increased to more than 50% compared to the current level of 30%.

(2) Energy saving and the collection of CO_2 from the air.
    Unless no counter measure is undertaken the average temperature will increase by 3.7°–4.8°C by the year 2100.[2]

3.1.3. (*Goal* 3) *Fuel consumption problem (high-fuel efficiency; high-efficient engine)*

In 1975 the US government has enacted the Law for Energy Saving that required the following targets. That is, all auto-makers starting the average fuel consumption criterion of 18 miles run per 1 gallon (18 MPG) must achieve step by step the final target of **27.5 MPG** by 1985. (Note that the 27.5 MPG is equivalent to the 12 km/L.)

The reason why the Energy Saving Act was introduced to the US auto-makers was due to the oil-price increase caused by the 1st oil-crisis in 1973. At that time their popular engine displacements of big cars were 4,000 cc and 5,000 cc and the fuel consumptions were 12 MPG ($= 5.5$ km/L), which was called the "**gas-guzzler car**" by the American consumers. They have eventually cleared this requirement by 1985.

However, their fuel efficiency has not been so improved after that time. This was because they have promoted the sales of the light trucks such as pickup truck, mini-van, and sport utility vehicle (SUV) as their main

---

[2]It should be noted that this proposal report emphasized that the mentioned target could be achieved even without the nuclear electricity generation that may cause the nuclear contamination when disasters happen, though there are strong voices for the nuclear power aspect of fewer CO_2 generation (i.e., 22 g/1 kWh). The international negotiation will be made at the end of 2015 for the concrete countermeasure policy to be taken after 2020.

However, other than the warming, there are the important problems of balancing of cost allocations among various global risks of poverty, food, and energy. The poverty and food (especially in the emerging countries) will drive the strong desire for the economic growth, which in turn increases the demand for energy or demand for the electricity usage. Thus, eventually the global warming and the exhaust of the fossil fuel resources will be brought from the risks of poverty and food problems, too.

Without solving the global warming problem our descendant could not live after 100–200 years.

revenue sources, since the light trucks were not considered as passenger cars and their fuel consumption standard was about 23 MPG.

On the other hand, Japanese government has not enforced the legal fuel saving requirement, but the Japanese auto-makers themselves tried to improve the fuel efficiency because they knew that the fuel efficiency could be a strong competitive factor. The Japanese auto-makers have already achieved most of the target of the US Energy Saving Act even in 1978 because they have developed their technology during the challenging age. As of 2002, Toyota has attained the fuel efficiency of 33.6 MPG ($=$ 14.2 kg/L) and Honda has 35 MPG ($=$15 kg/L). (The above historical facts were mainly based on Shimokawa, 2009).

3.1.3.1. Current fuel efficiency of Japanese cars (*The Nikkei*, 2014c)

Compact cars as of April 2014 are about 25 km/L. Hybrid vehicle (HV) cars as of August 2014 are about 35 km/L. Gasoline lightest vehicle (called mini-car) are about 40 km/L. The readers can see that Gasoline engine cars (of mini-car) are more fuel-efficient than HV.[3]

3.1.3.2. EV, PHV, and HV that use the electricity from the oil thermal power plant are not good in view of energy efficiency

The sources of "**primary energy**" for the Electric Vehicle (EV), Plug-in Hybrid Vehicle (PHV), and HV, etc. must not be from the electricity

---

[3]Compact cars as of April 2014 are as follows:
Toyota's model "Vitz" (compact car) is 25 km/L. (1,329 cc).
Honda's model "Fit" is 24.6 km/L. (1,317 cc).
Nissan's "Note" is 24.0 km/L. (1,198 cc).
HV Cars as of August 2013
"Akua" HV (Toyota) $=$ 35.4 km/L (in 2013).
                    $=$ 37 km/L (in 2014).
Carolla "Axio" and "Fielder" HV (Toyota) $=$ 33.0 km/L.
"Prius" HV (Toyota) $=$ 32.6 km/L.
Gasoline lightest vehicle (called mini-car) in Japan as of 2014 (*Note*: Mini-car is with cubic capacity of less than 660).
Daihatsu: "Mira e:S" is 33.4 km/L as of 2014. (It will be 42 km/L in 2015).
Suzuki: "alto-eco" is 35 km/L as of 2014. (It will be 40 km/L in 2015).

Table 1.   Energy thermal efficiency and CO_2 emissions differ for each electricity generation systems.

Variations of primary energy	Energy efficiency (%)	Emitted CO_2 per 1kWh (g)
Petro-thermal power	40	742
LNG	55	52
Nuclear electricity	35	22
Hydroelectricity	80	11
Photovoltaics (Solar) (As of 2010)	10	0 (in operation of the facility)
	10	52 (in general process)
Gasoline engine	39	
Diesel engine	42	

Note: Japanese Auto makers are trying to enhance the energy efficiency of gasoline & diesel engines up to 50%.

Source: Summarized from Hirota, 2010, p. 97.

generated by non-regenerative and environment-disruptive sources such as petroleum, liquefied natural gas (LNG), and nuclear power, because the thermal efficiency of these primary energies is not good and also provide much CO_2 and/or contaminate the environment (in case of nuclear power) (see Table 1).

Thus, the primary sources of electricity energy for eco-cars must be the regenerative ones such as wind, solar, and geothermal energy and hydrogen.

3.1.3.3.   Ratio of the engine cars among various "primary" energies

More than 90% of cars sold in the global market are still the oil-engine cars, at present and even in 2020. Therefore, from the viewpoint of the market demand all auto-makers throughout the world must actually continue to develop the energy-efficient gasoline cars, as the main car in the power-train mixtures of eco-cars. Thus, for example, the "direct injection with turbo-charger in a small engine" should be developed.

3.1.4. (*Goal* 4) *Alternative energies problem (regenerative energy)*

Although Goal 2 also required that the ratio of the regenerative energy in the total electricity supply must be increased to more than 50% compared to the current level of 30%, such goal must be attained through various means of general electricity production. Goal 4 especially requires the automobile industry to promote innovative selections of the alternative energies for the power-trains.

3.1.4.1. Problem: Abernathy's view on the new selection of fuel energies

Once Abernathy *et al.* (1983) said that the initial most important functional topic for developing the power-train of automobile was to select the appropriate fuel out of *gasoline, electricity, and steam (vapor)*, etc. This was because, the core concept in developing the automobile in the initial stage was the selection of fuel as the main function (power-train function) and it became a dominant design concept for the subordinate functions of power-train.

However, as the writer see it, Abernathy's view on thinking of the alternative fuel energies is not appropriate, because they have only considered the difference in the uses of gasoline engine, electric motor, and steam engine depending on the alternative uses of various alternative fuels abovementioned. They have never recognized the difference in the prime energy. They have not seen the fact that either of gasoline engine, electric motor, or steam engine is commonly using the *identical* primary energy of the fossil fuel (i.e., petroleum or coal). As Fig. 1 shows, we should recognize the difference between the non-regenerative energies and the regenerative energies in producing EV, HV, PHV, and FCV, etc.

From Fig. 1 the author sees that the most important stimulus or goal for the human-being is to promote using the regenerative energy as "primary" energy.

3.1.4.2. Problem of the criteria for the eco-car subsidy

As the writer sees it, the subsidy criteria for the eco-cars that is set and used by the government for clearing the target of fuel efficiency is also problematic, because it evaluates only the fuel efficiency in time of driving the car, but it does not consider the fuel efficiency in time of the electricity generation at all.

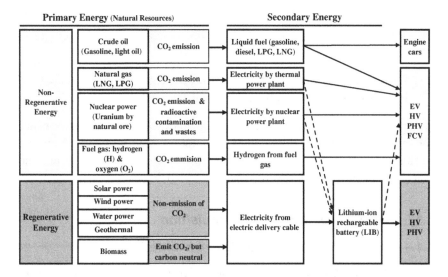

Fig. 1.   Relationship between the primary energy and the secondary energy.

3.1.5.   (*Goal* 5) *Cost and price problems of eco-car popularization*

The ultimate factor for the wider usage of eco-cars is (i) the cost and price of the vehicle itself, together with (ii) the fuel provision infrastructures. Let us see the recent prices of the popular compact HV cars of Toyota (as of April 2014) and their planned prices of Fuel Cell Vehicle (FCV).

3.1.5.1.   Comparison of prices between the gasoline-engine car (Vitz) and HV (Akua)

The Toyota's most popular gasoline car in Japan of the model "Vitz", which has the displacement of 1,329 cc and the fuel efficiency of 25 km/L, is 1,450 thousand yen (= Ca US\$ 13,200). (Note that this high fuel efficiency was achieved by applying the HV engine system that uses the high engine torque.)

On the other hand Toyota's popular compact HV car of the model "Akua", which has the displacement of 1,496 cc and the fuel efficiency of 37.0 km/L as of April 2014, is 1,860 thousand yen (= Ca US\$ 16,910).

Now why do not the readers compare the prices of these two models? The HV Akua price is more expensive than Witz by Ca US\$ 3,710 (= \$16,910 − \$13,200), which must be a **premium** on account of the benefits of fuel economy. Therefore the auto-makes should be able to provide such fuel efficiency (Nakanishi, 2013, p. 143).

4. Theories of Innovation Management through Inter-Firm Collaborations: "Ambidexterity"

How can the business firms bring about the innovation? Let us first consider the existing theories for answering this question. The summarized answer to this question is "Management by the Ambidexterity", which means the management of well usage of both right and left hands.

4.1. *Two ways of knowledge acquisition*

4.1.1. *Exploitation and exploration of knowledge*

It is well-known that Joseph Schumpeter (1926) also defined the innovation as "carrying out the new combinations" of various knowledge. Also famous James March (1991) once proposed the two different concepts in organizational learning (or organizational knowledge acquisition); regarding the acquisition of "knowledge" there are two different concepts of expansion of knowledge. First, looking for the new knowledge is called the "*Exploration* of knowledge," while utilization or exploiting and improving the existing knowledge within the own firm is called the "*Exploitation* of knowledge".

(1) The exploitation of knowledge may be interpreted as utilization of the existing strong (competitive) knowledge resources, often emphasized by the "resource-based view" for causing the innovation.
(2) The exploration of knowledge sometimes may include finding the new market needs or wants, as well as the new technological knowledge.

March further emphasized that a good balance between these two concepts was important for the firm's innovation. He contended that the company is often inclined to get only the exploitation of knowledge and thereby, neglecting the exploration of knowledge. Especially, if the company was successful in their existing business, they are declined to do the exploration of knowledge and used to get into the "competency trap".

4.2. *Knowledge portfolio between the "Keiretsu firms" and the new firms allied from market via M&A*

Another empirical research by Lavie & Rosenkopf (2006) has verified the new proposition: the *alliances with the new partners* are the knowledge exploration type and the *repetitive alliances with the same companies* are the knowledge exploitation type. Their research result suggests that good balance between "Exploration" and "Exploitation" in alliance formation, which is the knowledge portfolio," is important for the innovation. This will also tell us how to make "Ambidexterity" management.

4.2.1. *"Pareto optimal solution"*

Following the Lavie & Rosenkopf's proposition, let me introduce the "Pareto optimal solution" concept to practically induce the unique optimal balance between the *repetitive alliances with the same companies* and the *alliances with the new partners* for the effective innovation.

Here, the *repetitive alliances with the same companies* are the "Keiretsu" firms, so-called in Japanese business, while the *alliances with the new partners* are often the alliances by the new M&A, which are the real "open" alliances conducted in the free market. The operational alliances without any capital investment will also be included in the latter case.

Since having alliances of these two types are equivalent to the simultaneous seeking for two different goals (i.e., Exploitation and Exploration), it can be treated by the Pareto optimization method, and the trade-off balancing-ratio between these two goals must be predetermined by the top management as the weights to each group of collaboration goals with *Keiretsu* and market firms. As a result the optimal balancing problem in the hybrid network of the market and the inter-firm organization will be solved as shown in the next Sub-sec. 4.3.

Also in Sub-sec. 5.1, the readers can see the fact that Japanese auto-makers are mainly using the *Keiretsu* parts-makers for development and procuring of the EV battery (*Keiretsu*-type exploitation of knowledge), while European and American auto-assemblers are procuring the EV battery from the independent parts-makers in the market (market-type exploration of knowledge) (see Fig. 4), though there is an exception such as Tesla Motors.

However, the global operational alliances (without any capital investment) between Japanese mega-assemblers and overseas mega-assemblers for their joint development of EV, HV, and FCV, etc. are widely made (see Fig. 5). This could be interpreted as a hybrid-type of *Keiretsu* and market, because they made new alliance from the market but their alliance will continue for long years. So this is a hybrid-type exploration of development knowledge.

4.3. *Pareto optimum model between two goals of Exploitation and Exploration: Comparative study of Kodak and Fujifilm*

Let us apply the portfolio selection model to know the different attitudes towards knowledge acquisition between Kodak and Fujifilm. Both of the companies were confronted the ailing photo-film business under the emergence of digital camera.

In short, **Kodak** insisted on utilizing the existing strong technology within the own firm to strengthen the short-term profit of the existing film-camera. On the other hand, **Fuji** tried to acquire the new technology that requires the risky and bulky amount of investment fund. These different attitudes could be summarized as the Exploitation of the existing knowledge (Kodak) and the Exploration of future knowledge (Fuji), respectively (Furumori, 2009).

Figure 4 shows the relative positions in the "**frontier**" curve of the Pareto optimal points of the circulating life-cycles (or re-incarnation cycle) throughout (i) cradle stage, (ii) growth stage, (iii) maturity stage, and (iv) de-maturity stage, by basing on the cases of Fujifilm and Kodak. Also note that the "follower" big company will not start from the cradle stage, but from the growth stage.

4.3.1. *Multiple Pareto optimum points*

The Pareto optimal point stands for the allocation of resources, in which if another allocation is selected for improving Goal 1, then the other goal 2 will be worsened. On the other hand if some change of the current resource allocation will improve both Goals 1 and 2 at the same time, then the Pareto optimum is not yet achieved and the "Pareto improvement" could still be available.

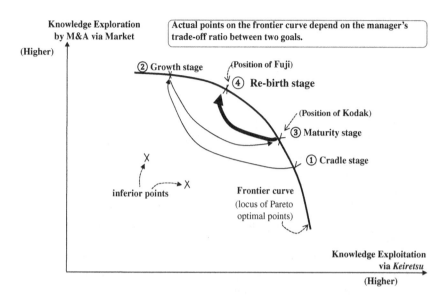

Fig. 2. Technology portfolio between the goals of knowledge Exploitation and Exploration.

We take the dimension of Knowledge Acquisition from M&A in the vertical axis and the dimension of Knowledge Acquisition from the existing *Keiretsu* in the horizontal axis (see Fig. 2). Multiple Pareto Optimum Points may be found as a set (called "Frontier") of the non-dominant solutions. Top management can apply their trade-off ratio that reflects their priority between the two goals, and get the *unique* solution point for allocating the investment fund to the existing and the new investment business projects.[4]

---

[4] Allow (1951) tried to consider if we could find some single value criteria ("Social welfare function") by integrating the subjective value criterion of various persons in a society (Allow, 1951). He proved that it would be impossible to integrate the subjective value criterion of various persons for not less than three alternatives of the social problem into a single value criterion via the democratic procedure. This proposition is often called "(general) impossibility theorem" and assumes several rational and desirable conditions.

For example, suppose there are three persons A, B, and C, and each of them has the following "ordinal" preference priority for the policies (alternative plans) X, Y, and Z:

4.3.2. *The reasons of the points at cradle, growth, maturity, and rebirth stages*

(1) In the cradle stage most of the knowledge is internal ones.

(2) In the growth stage the company will positively challenge to acquire the new knowledge from the external world.

(3) When the company became aged (old), they are inclined to increase ratio of the existing knowledge within the firm. Even when a human gets old, he lacks in adaptability to the environmental change and will not be so positive to get new knowledge, thus inclined to cling on the existing knowledge.

(4) In the rebirth or transmigration (re-incarnation) stage the attitude for challenge will vary depending on the top management's spirit. The author suggests that it will be much better for such stage company to adopt the CEO from outside (as newcomer). Because such newcomer CEO has no adherence to the past success of the company in question and also will not be constrained by the existing human relations within the company and with the existing allied firms. Good examples are Mr. Carlos Ghosn who came from Renault to Nissan for as CEO for its turnover, and Mr. Kazuo Inamori who came to Japan Airlines for its restructuring.

	A	B	C
X	100	10	1
Y	10	1	100
Z	1	100	10

Then the order of policy priority order of all three persons will be arranged as:

$$X \succcurlyeq Y \succcurlyeq Z \succcurlyeq X \succcurlyeq Y \succcurlyeq Z \succcurlyeq X,$$

where the symbols of $(X \succcurlyeq Y \succcurlyeq Z)$ stands for the priority of A, and the succeeding order of $(Z \succcurlyeq X \succcurlyeq Y)$ is the priority of B, and further the final following order of $(Y \succcurlyeq Z \succcurlyeq X)$ is the priority of C. As a result no consistent order can be achieved.

Therefore, the "decision by majority" as the democratic procedure cannot make any unique priority order (unique solution) in the society. Allow's conclusion was that only single dictator's priority order can decide the policy of the society as a whole. In the business company the CEO can make a final decision even though the board of directors could not reach the consistent agreement.

4.3.3. Emergence of innovation as a synergy effect of the inter-firm network

The author has once proposed the following *core concept of the network organization* (Monden, 2012a, pp. 18–19). The proper characteristic of a network organization is that this organization can create new *value* through the joint activities of participating companies. Such added value, created value, or premium value is equivalent to the so-called "synergy effect", which may be created by the mutual *"complementarities"*.[5]

Thus, the answer to the initial question in the outset of Sec. 1: "How can the innovation be brought about?" would be to organize the inter-firm network organization for developing the eco-cars. The concrete cases of such inter-firm network will be shown in the following Sub-secs. 5.1 and 5.2.

5. Inter-Firm Collaborations for the Eco-Car Innovation

5.1. Collaboration between the auto-maker and the parts suppliers

The modularization of EV components will be made through the closed or open networks between the auto-maker and the parts-makers as Fig. 3:

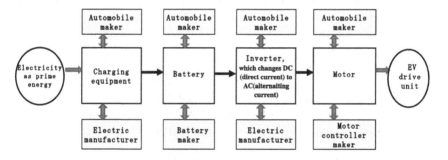

Fig. 3.   Modularizations of the EV components.

Source: Adapted and revised from Shibata, 2009.

---

[5]Such synergy effect is also interpreted as a product of the "chaos" in the theory of the complex systems, because the chaos (i.e., emergence of innovation) can emerge when various members have joined (Toko *et al.*, 1999; Hori, 1979; Nonaka, 1993 and 2013; and Monden, 2013).

5.1.1. *EV is much easier for modularization*

There are two stages for modularization of EV components.

(1) Initial Stage ("Closed" modularization):
Inter-firm network among the auto-maker, battery maker, and electric manufacture, to make the battery for car as a "closed" network. Such closed network is seen in the upper portion of Fig. 4 where all Japanese auto-assemblers such as Mitsubishi, Honda, Nissan, and Toyota are investing their capital to the battery makers. So these battery makers are the "Keiretsu" suppliers of the auto-makers.

(2) Secondary Stage ("Open" modularization):
Gradually the "open modularization" of the components will emerge for the common modules to be utilized by many auto-makers, and finally some of the parts will be of a "*de facto*" standard or a "*de jury*" standard approved by ISO, etc., as seen in Intel's memory protection unit (MPU) for the personal computer. Then the components will be procured from the market in the components industry in question. Thus, each automobile makers are forming the "**Market network**".

The examples of "open" modularization in the lower portion of Fig. 4 are as follows.

The following listed suppliers supply its lithium-ion battery (LIB) to various automakers which have no capital alliance with the supplier. Thus, they are the firms in the market, rather than the *Keiretsu* firms of a certain auto-maker (See Fig. 4).

Toshiba supplies LIB to Honda and Mitsubishi Motors.
Panasonic supplies LIB to Toyota, Audi, and Ford.
LG Cham (Korea) supplies LIB to Ford, GM, Renault, and Renault.
SB LiMotive supplies LIB to Chrysler and BMW.

It is evident that even Toyota and Honda, which have their own *Keiretsu* battery-suppliers as aforementioned, are also procuring their batteries from the market. Thus, the relations between the suppliers of Toshiba and Panasonic and the auto-assemblers of Mitsubishi, Honda, and Toyota are forming the "**Hybrid network of *keiretsu* and market**" as shown in the right side of Fig. 4.

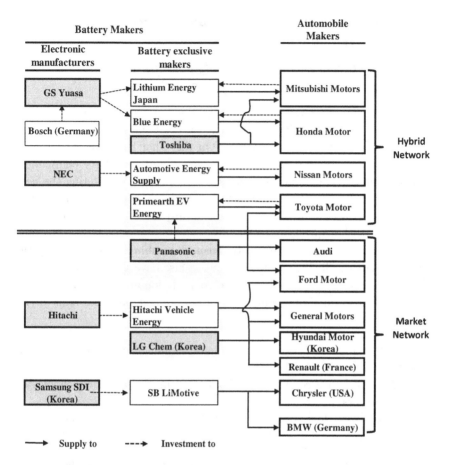

Fig. 4.   Closed and open battery makers.

Source: Adapted and revised from *The Nikkei*, 2013c.

In Fig. 4 it looks that all of the automobile makers except Japanese makers are procuring the LIB from the market, but Tesla Motors is an exception. Panasonic has invested in Tesla and they made the joint venture plant in the US, where they are jointly developing and manufacturing Tesla's battery (*The Nikkei*, 2014a). Thus, their alliance looks like *Keiretsu* relation.

5.2. *Collaboration between the auto-makers for developing the eco-cars*

5.2.1. *The global alliances of the big auto-makers for developing EV, HV, PHV, and FCV*

In the alliances of M&A, the merger is usually done between the companies of the same industry. This is a *horizontal* combination of firms for the purpose of getting the **scale merits**. On the other hand, the acquisition of stocks will make the relationship of parent and subsidiary companies. This is a *vertical* combination of firms for the purpose of entering the new business and the parent could get the new technology or knowledge of the new business. In other words the mutual "**complementarity**" is the main purpose of stock acquisition.

Seeing from the earlier purposes of business combination types the global alliances between the big automobile makers also have similar goals, though all of these alliances are the horizontal combination and also none of them in Fig. 5 has entailed any capital investment. Their purposes must be as follows:

(**Goal 1**) *Scale merit*: for reducing the development costs and increasing the sales.
(**Goal 2**) *Technical complementarity*: for getting the eco-car technologies of the partners.
(**Goal 3**) Need for "*Power-train mix*" under uncertainty and capital shortage.

Regarding Goal 3, each automobile manufacturer is developing the plural eco-cars as the power-train mix, such as HV, PHV, EV, FCV, and the highly efficient engine cars of gasoline and diesel at the same time. However, it is difficult to develop all of them by a single company due to the limitation of their R&D resources (from man-power and financial capability). Therefore, they wished to make the joint development, and thus now there are "three main groups + 1" as depicted in Fig. 5 and as a result the competition is now among the inter-groups (or competition among oligopoly). The readers should also note the time series of their alliances.

5.2.1.1. Alliance between Toyota and BMW

Let us verify the above-mentioned three goals of the big alliances by use of the case between Toyota and BMW.

Toyota and BMW (Germany) made their alliance in four steps:

(1) The first alliance contract was for environmental technologies, made on December 2011 (*The Nikkei*, 2011). Toyota began selling diesel engine cars in Europe by assembling them in their European local plan from February 2014. Thus, this alliance is for Toyota to cope with the diesel gas restriction called the "**Euro 6**", which is applied in Europe from 2014. It aims to reduce the particulate matter or particulates (PM) and NO_x in the exhaust gas of the diesel engine cars. Among all, the NO_x must be reduced down to 0.1 kg/km under the restraint of Euro 6. Toyota **needs technology for clearing Euro 6.**

(2) Then Toyota and BMW made additional agreement for exchanging the new HV technologies (from Toyota to BMW) and the weight-reduction technology of carbon fiber (from BMW to Toyota) (*The Nikkei*, 2012). This was for the **mutual complementarity of technologies.**

(3) They further expanded their alliance for joint development of HV and FCV. They have also agreed to jointly develop the lithium-ion re-chargeable battery with high-capacity. Toyota has already succeeded in developing the fuel "cell-stack" of FCV, which is the core parts of FCV, and also developed the hydrogen-storage-tank for FCV by their own. However, Toyota wishes to further reduce the price of FCV through the alliance with BMW by commonly using the core components of FCV, because Toyota began selling FCV by the price of US$70,000 from December, 2014 (*The Nikkei*, 2013a). Thus, this alliance is for **the scale merit of reducing the costs and price and increasing the sales through mass-production and mass-sales of FCV.**

Other alliances between mega-automobile makers are listed in Footnote 6.[6]

---

[6] Case of alliance of Nissan and Renault, Daimler and Ford:

The four big corporations composed of the united group of Nissan and Renault, Daimler and Ford are jointly developing the FCV. They plan to sell the FCV from the year 2017 (see Fig. 5). (*The Nikkei*, 2013b).

Case of alliance of Honda and General Motors:

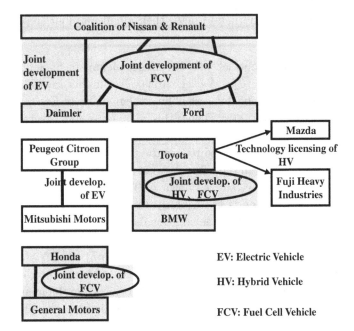

Fig. 5. The global alliances of the big auto-makers for developing EV, HV, and FCV.

Source: Adapted and revised from *The Nikkei*, 2013b and 2013c.

6. Conclusion: Short Summary and the New Philosophy for Sustainable Mobility

6.1. *Short summary*

In this chapter the author so far clarified the following points step by step (note that the key words are emphasized in italics):

(1) *"Innovation"* in the car industry must be made as a rebirth of the product life-cycle of automobile.

(2) Such innovation must be triggered by the *"stimulus"* from the environmental needs or goals.

Honda also tries to begin market sales of FCV from the year 2015 by jointly developing it with General Motors. (This alliance agreement was made in July 2, 2013 (see Fig. 5) (*The Nikkei*, 2013d).

(3) The "*necessary knowledge*" or necessary technology for the innovation could be acquired through the "*inter-firm alliances*" and the company's own knowledge.

(4) Various components of eco-cars could be procured from the "*market*" as well as the "*Keiretsu*" makers. The R&D of eco-cars could be done through the global alliances between major automobile manufacturers.

In the above step (2) the author emphasized that the most important stimulus or goal is to use the regenerative energy as an alternative energy. This will further drive us to recognize the need for changing our way of living or our philosophy for promoting the uses of regenerative energy instead of using the non-regenerative energy. Thus, the author wishes to consider the new ecological philosophy in the final section.

6.2. New philosophy

In this section let us first consider the results of pursuing the economic growth and the endless mining of natural resources, and then consider the need to develop some new philosophy for living in the modern civilized world that is confronting the environmental problems.

6.2.1. Case of Vietnamese people nowadays

Take Vietnamese people, for instance, of today (as of 2014). The individual families are all wishing to have TV, refrigerator, and washing machine, which were once called as "three kinds of divine apparatuses" by the Japanese during their highest economic growth age of 1960s. They will further wish to use the automobile and thus the motorization age will come sooner or later, and then it will be followed by the need for massive volume of petroleum. Such phenomenon is seen in China, India, Nigeria of Africa, and all over the world. Such developing route has been taken not only by the people of current advanced countries, but also will be taken by the people of the emerging countries, who have a strong desire to have more comfortable life from now.

6.2.2. Problems of the egoistic greed and the economic growth

We Japanese people have been constantly pursuing the wealth (GDP) or the economic growth as a national slogan for almost one and half century since launch of the "Meiji revolution" in 1868. This is based on the belief that if each individual or each firm, motivated by the greedy desire, pursued each one's selfish interest or profit in a competitive market, the total wealth or total income as a whole of the society could also be enhanced eventually. This was the proposition or assumption (conjecture) or the ideology (value system) of the famous "invisible hand" by the father of economics, Adam Smith.

The results would be two-fold:

(1) The environment of this planet would further be contaminated and polluted by the CO, etc., contained in the emitted gas, and the global warming would continue to aggravate due to the emitted CO_2, etc. and also the phenomena of serious big floods and landslides, etc. are occurring very often and continuously for days. As a result it follows that **human beings will not be able to live in this planet for long.**

(2) Even though new mining would continue for the shale gas in many places throughout the world for a long time, the result would be **"resource exhaust"** after hundreds of years, since there is only one mother earth in the planet, and thereby our descendants will not be able not use them and finally will cease to live any more.

In order to avoid such situations what kind of idea or "way of living" should we take? That must be to change our paradigm of "ideology" (sense of values or the philosophy) for the way of living.

6.3. *Two value-systems for the paradigm change of ideology*

(1) *Egoism (Selfishness) based value*: **"The self-interest oriented free behavior will bring the total optimum of the society as a whole."**

The neo-classical school of economics standing mainly on the general equilibrium theory for the free markets is based on the classical ideology of "invisible hand" advocated by Adam Smith's "Wealth of Nations" (Smith, 1776 and 1789). Smith says, "So long as the individual person seeks for the self-interest, then automatically the interest of the society as a whole would be enhanced, guided by the invisible hand, even though he or she did not personally intended." (quoted from Japanese translation by Okochi (1978) p. 12, originated by Smith, 1789, Chapter 2 of Part 4, p. 421.)

(2) *Sympathy* (*Altruism*) *based value*: "If people would take the cooperative behavior with a mutual sympathy, then the community life (or*symbiosis*) could be successfully maintained."

If all members of utilizing the "commons" of planet would take the "cooperative behavior" for the purpose of securing their mutual interest and be all cooperative to observe the orderly rule of the commons, then the resource would neither be drained and nor the environment be destroyed so that they all could enjoy their mutual interests perpetually. So long as such cooperative behavior exists, "the *tragedy of the commons*" (Hardin, 1968) will not happen.

6.3.1. *Cooperative behaviors*

The cooperative behaviors for the global resources are, for example, to observe the restriction by the government or the international organ, or to observe the agreement to the introduction of the "emission trading" of the greenhouse gas initiated by the Kyoto Protocol. However, the big consumer countries of energy such as the US and China have not agreed Kyoto Protocol, though there are many state governments in the US who agreed on Kyoto Protocol. It is also regrettable that there are some countries that have dropped from the agreed members. Under such situation the premises of the cooperative behavior itself is not maintained.

Therefore, the desirable paradigm change would be the transition from the isolated egoistic profit-seeking principle based on the selfish mind to the sympathy-based love-others behavior, and also the transition from the *competition* to the *cooperation or symbiosis* (in the meaning of biology or ecology). Such change will be useful for avoiding "the tragedy of the commons". The author also wishes to emphasize that the mutual cooperative behaviors include the collaborative strategic alliances and/or the inter-firm cooperative network.

6.4. *Relationship between "sympathy" and "selfish behavior" of Adam Smith*

The concept of the "sympathy" was emphasized as the most important moral concept by Adam Smith in his book on "Moral Sentiment" (Smith, 1759) as a natural feeling of pleasure to see the happiness of other people. As related to the sympathy he also raised the concept of "Pity or Compassion" to the miseries of other people. Both feelings of the sympathy and the pity or compassion are also seen in the teaching of Buddha (Bukkyo Dendo Kyokai, 1966).

Smith has tried to explore the problem of how the peaceful coexistence of individuals who have the free, equal-righted, and selfish minds could be achieved without any intervention of the central power. Smith has found that the key to solve this problem lies in the human moral sentiment of the mutual sympathy among the egoistic individuals who could live only within the society (Mizuta, 2003, p. 3).

Smith's "sympathy" in his *Moral Sentiment* should be considered as a constraint to be attached to the individual's "selfish behavior" advocated in his wealth of Nations (Doume, 2008), though Smith did not explain any relationship between these two concepts. According to this view it must be a set between Smith's sympathy and individual ego.

6.5. *"Symbiosis (coexistence) between the human-being and the nature": Philosophy in the age of regenerative energy*

Further in the age of regenerative energy the aforementioned "mutual sympathy with other people" is not enough, but the "symbiosis (coexistence) with natural world" that considers ecology" in the whole nature would be necessary, because the former idea may be still closed within the human world of a selfish greed that tries to conquer the natural world. For example, the efforts to develop the nuclear power are trials to conquer the nature by human-being, but the nuclear power plant still is continuing to contaminate the natural world, because the human-being still has no technological knowledge to stop the radioactive contamination by the nuclear wastes.

The hint for such ecology thinking in the whole natural world lies in animism (nature-based religion) that respects and observes the order of the nature as well as the order of human being. The writer sees such animism thought in the oldest cannon **"Rig Veda" of Hinduism** (religion) written in-around BC 1,200 year in Sanskrit language, in India (Monden, 2005 and 2006).

The "Rig Veda" consists of many poems of the sacred songs (hymn-book) that praise or glorify many natural gods (Tsuji, 1970 and Sacred-Text

Hinduism, 2014). The Veda (especially "Rig Veda") suggests the people to glorify and preserve the various divine fields, which are governed by **Gods of Sun, Water, Wind, Earth, River, and also various creatures** including not only animals but also plants. This idea seems to be suggesting the necessity of "symbiosis (coexistence) between the human being and the natures listed. So this is a **"nature-centered" philosophy**. Thus, for example, developing the new technology to use the regenerative energy is the movement towards the friendly coexistence between human and nature; thereby, we can have a sustainable world and prosper eternally. The coexistence between various Gods in the nature and the human being who utilizes the regenerative energies is as follows:

God of Sun will give the solar power electricity to human being.
God of Water will give the water power electricity to human being.
God of Wind will give the wind power electricity and the hydrogen gas electricity to human being.
God of Earth will give the geo-thermal power electricity to human being.
God of River will give the water power electricity to human being.
God of Creatures will give the biomass power electricity to human being.

6.5.1. *Eternal cycle of "transmigration" of nature and energy can realize sustainable mobility*

The eternal cycle of *"transmigration"* or *"rebirth"* assumes the death and rebirth of individual creature including humans, but it does not imply the "De-mature" or "Rejuvenation of the same living creature". On the other hand, in the real world the death and re-birth or "transmigration" between the parent and the child is repeated.

Even though a certain individual died, his or her living "stem cell" and DNA will not die and will be transmitted to the children. Such a cycle will be repeated. This phenomenon is the same as the business turnover, where the old business may decline or die but the new prospective business will be born and grow in the same company inheriting the DNA of the founder's philosophy and forward-looking attitude, so that the same company could sustain forever. The artificial products of automobile could also play a role of sustainable mobility with the eternal cycle of energy regeneration.

Appendix 1:

How the network organization can reach global optimal point

Suppose that the network organization consisting of the firms X_1 & X_2 is located at the initial peak P_1 (see Fig. 6). When the time elapsed from T_1 to T_2, this network has fallen into the valley P_2, which was under depression of the market. Thus, the top manager of this network tried to find some prospective chance in the new market and searched for a target firm that has some excellent technology for this new market.

Then the top manager found the firm Y who had the complementarity or synergy effect with the existing firm X_2. Thus, this network purchased the new firm Y and has moved to the point P_3 in the new market (i.e., new mountain).

Again the top manager found another firm Z who has the complementarity or synergy effect with the existing firm X_1. Thus, the network purchased the new firms Z as well as Y and has climbed up to the new peak P_4 of the new mountain (see Fig. 6).

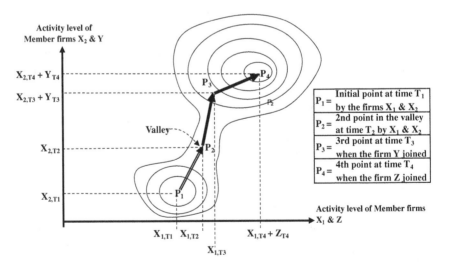

Fig. 6.   Sequential seeking approach to the new peak through M&A for the additional target firms Y and Z.

Sequential Seeking Approach to the New Mountain-Peak through M&A

There is no mathematical optimization algorism to reach the new peak P_4 of the new mountain (i.e., new market) from the current peak P_1 of the existing mountain (i.e., existing market) in Fig. 6 where there are two peaks of mountains and one valley between them, because the overall objective function is non-concave and the constraints are non-convex. The Kuhn–Tucker condition is merely the *necessary* condition for satisfying the global optimal solution, but not the *sufficient* condition.

The only way to reach the "global" optimal solution for the case of two peaks is the heuristic approach that the top manager of the network organization will sequentially seek for the additional target firms Z and Y one by one, each of which has the excellent technologies to create the synergy effect when it was merged. The author coins such method as the "Sequential Seeking Approach to the Global Optimum."

Further the target firms will be motivated to participate in the network by the allocation of joint profit (synergy effect) based on the method of cooperative game theory. (See the "cumulative opportunity cost method" of Monden (2012a; Appendix) originated by Monden (1989)).

Appendix 2:

Animism in the oldest cannon "Rig-Veda" of Hinduism

In this appendix the author introduces only five basic songs that glorify and preserve the gods of nature as samples, and also introduce the basic doctrine (teachings) of Veda (Shattack (1999) was also referred.).

The original poems of the songs in the quotation marks were cited by Sacred-Text Hinduism (2014). The author added some words in the parenthesis by using Tsuji (1970) and for better understanding of the readers.

(1) Song for Surya (God of sun)

Rig-Veda (1.115): "The brilliant presence of the Gods (sun) has risen, the eyes of Mitra, Varuna, and Agni (god of fire). The Sun (**Surya**) hath filled the air and earth and heaven. (As) soul of all that moveth not moveth (creatures and non-creatures)."

The air, earth, and heaven are three regions of the universe, and all of them are governed by various gods (called Savitar or Dyava) and are under the god of sun (Surya). Another region in the universe is the death world governed by Yama.

(2) Song for Savitar (God who represents activities of God of sun (Surya)). (Savitar is often called **Dyava**, and governs the creatures and non-creatures.)

Rig-Veda (2.38): "The wild beasts spread through desert places seeking their water share which thou hast set in waters. The woods are given to the birds. These statutes of the God **Savitar** none disobeyeth."

(3) Song for Parjanya (God of rain)
Parjanya showers mother earth with rain, wind, storm, and thunder.

Rig-Veda (7.101): "He is the Bull of all, and their impregner (who gives breeds and seeds): he holds the life of all things fixed and moving (creatures and non-creatures). May this **rita (order or rule of nature)** save me till my hundredth autumn (100 year old). Preserves us evermore, ye Gods, with blessings."

(4) Song for Varuna (God who preserves "rita" (order of universe)
Varuna will never permit any violation of rita; thereby keeps an order of the whole nature, religious services, and human moral. Although Varuna is fierce like Asura, he is also affectionate to those who reflect upon themselves and recover their freedom and health. Varuna accompanies God called **Mitra** who preserves social contract (promise). Thus, Varuna and Mitra together keeps the universe and human society in order.

4-1 Rig-Veda (2.28-5): "Loose me from sin as from a bond that binds me; may we swell, **Varuna**, thy Spring of Order (Rita)."

4-2 Rig-Veda (2.28-6): Far from me, **Varuna**, remove all danger accept me graciously, then Holy Sovran (Rita), cast off, like cords that hold a calf, my troubles: I am not even mine eyelid's lord without thee."

References

Abegglen, J. & Boston Consulting Group (1978). *Portfolio Strategy.* Tokyo: President (in Japanese).

Abernathy, W. J., Clark, K. B., & Kantrow, A. M. (1981). The New Industrial Competition, *Harvard Business Review*, September–October, pp. 68–81.

Abernathy, W. J., Clark, K. B., & Kantrow, A. M. (1983). *Industrial Renaissance: Producing a Competitive Future for America.* New York: Basic Books.

Arrow, K. (1951). *Social Choice and Individual Value.* New York: John Wiley & Sons.

Boston Consulting Group (1968). *Perspectives on Experience.* (Reproduced in J. C. Abegglen and The Boston Consulting Group (1978). *Portfolio Strategy.* Tokyo: President) (in Japanese).

Bukkyo Dendo Kyokai (Buddhist Promotion Foundation) (1966). *The Teaching of Buddha.* Tokyo: Bukkyo Dendo Kyokai (both in Japanese and English).

Doume, T. (2008). *Adam Smith:The world of "Moral Sentiment" and "Wealth of Nations".* Tokyo: Chuokoron Sinsha (in Japanese).

Furumori, S. (2009). *Management of Fighting Spirit.* Tokyo: Toyokeizaishinposha (in Japanese).

Hardin, G. (1968). The Tragedy of the Commons, *Science,* 162(3859), pp. 1243–1248.

Hirota, K. (2010). *Electric Vehicles.* Tokyo: Nikkan Kogyo Shinbun.

Hori, J. (1979). *What is entropy?* Tokyo: Kodansha (in Japanese).

Lavie, D. & Rosenkopf, L. (2006). Balancing Exploration and Exploitation in Alliance Formation, *Academy of Management Journal,* 49(4), pp. 797–818.

March, J. G. (1991). Exploration and Exploitation in Organization Learning, *Organization Science,* 2(1), pp. 71–87.

Monden, Y. (2005). Sociological idea for the application of JIT system under the Hinduism society (in Japanese: unpublished).

Monden, Y. (2006). Nature faith in the oldest cannon "Rig-Veda" of Hinduism (in Japanese: unpublished).

Monden, Y. (2012a). From Adam Smith's division of labor to network organization: From the market price mechanism to the incentive price mechanism, In Y. Monden (ed.), *Management of an Inter-Firm Network,* Singapore: World Scientific Publishing Co. Pte. Ltd., pp. 3–30.

Monden, Y. (2013). Interpretation of the product life-cycle based on the phase-transition theory (in Japanese: unpublished).

Nakanishi, T. (2013). *Toyota vs VW.* Tokyo: Nikkei Inc.

Nonaka, I. (1993). Self-evolution of the organization: Proposal of the self-organizing paradigm, in H. Itami, T. Kagono, & M. Ito (eds.), *Japanese Corporation Systems, Vol. 2 Organization and Strategy,* Tokyo: Yuhikaku (in Japanese), Chapter 12, pp. 411–440.

Nonaka, I. (2013). Toward the Management that Utilizes "Knowledge Driving Force", *The Nikkei,* August 15. "Economic Seminar" (in Japanese).

Sacred-Text Hinduism (2014). Retrieved from http://www.sacred-texts. com/hin/ (search date June 2, 2014).

Schumpeter, J. A. (1926). *Theorie der Wirtschaftlichen Entwicklungen,* 2.*Aufl.* (Japanese translated version by Y. Shionoya, I. Nakayama, & S. Tohata (1977) was published by Tokyo: Iwanami Shoten).

Shattack, C. (1999). *Hinduism.* London: Laurence King Publishing Ltd.

Shimokawa, K. (2009). *Is There a Prosperous Future in the Automobile Business?*" Tokyo: Takarajima (in Japanese).

Shibata, T. (2009). Electric Vehicle Viewed from the Management of Technology: Be Prepared to the Communized Design Rules, *The Nikkei,* November 18. "Economic Seminar", (in Japanese).

Smith, A. (1759). *The Theory of Moral Sentiment.* London: Printed for A. Miller, in *The Strand;* and A. Kincaid & J. Bell, in *Edinburgh* (Japanese translations was made by H. Mizuta (2003)).

Smith, A. (1776) (1st edn.), 1789 (5th edn.). *An Inquiry into the Nature and Causes of the Wealth of Nations.* London: Printed for A. Strahan & T. Cadell, in *The Strand,* MDCCLXXXIX (Japanese translations for Smith (1789) were made by H. Mizuta (2000), Tokyo: Iwanami Shoten; and K. Okochi (1978), Tokyo: Chuokoron Shinsha).

The *Nikkei* (2011). Toyota & BMW announced the alliance in environmental technology, December 2 (in Japanese).

The Nikkei (2012). Toyota & BMW announced their expansion of alliance to the FCV, June 30 (in Japanese).

The Nikkei (2013a). Toyota & BMW announced their alliance in core parts of FCV, January 25 (in Japanese).

The Nikkei (2013b). Nissan & Renault, Daimler and Ford jointly begin to develop the FCV, January 29 (in Japanese).

The Nikkei (2013c). Main supply relations of the lithium-ion battery for automakers, June 20 (in Japanese).

The Nikkei (2013d). Honda and GM announced the alliance for joint development of FCV, July 3 (in Japanese).

The Nikkei (2014a). Panasonic establishes the joint-venture battery plant in America with Tesla, February 26 (in Japanese).

The Nikkei (2014b). IPCC suggests that the warming gas must be reduced by 40–70% by 2050, April 14 (in Japanese).

The Nikkei (2014c). Toyota renewed fuel-efficiency, competing with HV and mini-cars, April 24.

The Nikkei (2014d). The planet will be warmed by 4 degree in 100 years, warned by the United Nations report, May 6 (in Japanese).

Toko, K., Ezaki, S., & Hayashi, K. (1999). *What is Self-Organizing? — Exploring the Rules of Emerging the Forms and Rhythm in the Biological World.* Tokyo: Kodansha (in Japanese).

Toyoda, S. (2014). Severe Requirement for the Exhaust Gas Became a Moment or Opportunity for the Innovation and Growth. *My Curriculum Vitae* 16, *The Nikkei*, April, 17 (in Japanese).

Tsuji, N. (1970). *Hymn of "Rig Veda"*. Tokyo: Iwanami Shoten (in Japanese).

Vernon, R. (1966). International Investment and International Trade in the Product Cycle, *Quarterly Journal of Economics*, 80(2), pp. 190–207.

6

Communization Strategy and Performance Management in the Japanese Automobile Industry

Noriyuki Imai
Meijo University

1. Introduction

Communization strategies for car platforms, units, and parts are becoming major linchpins within auto industry strategies that aim to increase profitability and strengthen price competitiveness by lowering automobile production costs in the face of global competition and the expansion of emerging markets. Within this competitive environment, there are generally two types of product design architectures, as indicated by Fujimoto (2004), i.e., integral architecture and modular architecture.

Monden & Larsson (2013) noted a recent change in product development in the global automobile industry, wherein the promotion of automobile modularization strategies is contributing to the transition of automobile product design architectures from mainly traditional integral architectures to a combination of modular architectures and integral architectures known as "hybrid architecture".

Here, communization strategies that aim to decrease the cost of automobile production, through economies of scale, have a high affinity for mass production and a "push" mentality that stems from the Ford system of the 20th century. This is a perspective wherein the Platform Chief Engineer system is utilized to affect a transition toward a performance management system that aspires to improve business performance by expanding the quantitative supply of the platform, based on a push mentality.

On the other hand, in the limited production and "pull" mentality of the Toyota Production System (TPS), utilized by Toyota, an April 2013 reorganization designated regional headquarters as profit centers with responsibility (specifically, Toyota One, which is in charge of both product and pricing strategy for markets in developed nations and Toyota Two, in charge of product and pricing strategy for markets in emerging nations) for taking orders from customers and delivering the finished product (in other words, from start to finish in the TPS supply-chain process).

By positioning unit centers, which fulfill a central role in the communization strategy (positioned as a midpoint within the TPS supply-chain process), as cost centers, a company is able to plan and formulate an organizational structure, as well as a performance management system, thereby enabling both lean supply chain management (limited production, pull mentality, Just-in-Time (JIT), *Jidoka*, and shortened lead times) based on the TPS and reduced cost, based on unit communization.

In this chapter, the new organizational structure and performance management system, which integrate the TPS and the communization strategy within Toyota, are defined as the "Organization Model of Lean Strategy". The significance of this model can be explained as an "Optimal Balance between Efficiency and Attractiveness", as indicated by Monden & Larsson (2013). In other words, the lowering of product costs, through communization strategies of lean supply chain management centers based on the TPS, results in a shift to the upper right of the efficient frontier curve of product efficiency and attractiveness in a tradeoff relationship. On the other hand, sales divisions (profit centers) can strategically select the optimal points of product efficiency and attractiveness in an efficient frontier curve, based on the product needs for target customers.

For instance, Toyota One, which is in charge of markets in developed nations, is able to strategically select a ratio with more attractiveness (i.e., an integrative architecture) as a high point, while Toyota Two is able to select a ratio with more efficiency (i.e., a modular architecture) as a high point, thus enabling the maximization of business profitability.

It should be noted that "Toyota" generally refers to the Toyota Group in this chapter and does not indicate the name of an individual corporation.

2. Product Design Architecture and Communization Strategy

First, let us consider the changes in product development trends within automobile product design architectures in the global automobile industry in recent years, as a background, wherein communization strategies are becoming major linchpins within automobile industry strategies. According to Fujimoto (2004), when people on the factory floor design some type of new product or process, the thought process employed in the design differs depending on the target product. This fundamental concept of product/process design is called "architecture". Moreover, the most important dichotomy for fundamental types of product design architecture is the distinction between integral architecture and modular architecture. Products of integral architecture are those wherein product functionality is not fully achieved, as a total system, if mutual adjustments are not subtly carried out among optimally designed multiple parts that have been designed specifically for that product.

For instance, an automobile's overall performance as a product, drastically changes simply by virtue of subtle changes in mutual relationships between units and parts, such as the balance between engine, body placement, and functionality (for instance, the engine center of gravity is relative to the entire car, and how the balance between engine functionality, body weight, and rigidity are maintained) in automobiles that have been traditionally targeted for developing nations. Included among these types of products are traditional automobiles and motorcycles produced for developed nations; electronic products that are advanced in miniaturization, complexity, and thickness; a wealth of precision machinery; individually produced general machinery; and core parts, such as the bearings, which comprise them.

On the other hand, based on the modularity concept of Baldwin & Clark (1997, 2000), modular architecture products are those from which various final products can be produced and the uniqueness of various combinations is demonstrated when existing parts that have already been designed are skillfully assembled. Characteristic of these types of products, the interface configuration, as well as communication procedures are standardized and the parts themselves are functionally complete. Included among these types of products are bicycles, personal computers (combinations of hardware and software), and products associated with the internet and digital electronics.

According to Monden & Larsson (2013), all products, whether automobiles or digital electronics, are "hybrid products" comprised both integral and modular architecture parts. Based on such a premise, and by virtue of the promotion of modularization strategies within the global automobile industry in recent years, automobile part design architectures are in the process of transitioning from mainly traditional integrative architectures toward "hybrid architectures", which combine both modular and integral architectures. This phenomenon forms the background wherein communization strategies have become a major linchpin of automobile industry strategies within the global automobile industry.

3. The Global Automobile Industry and Communization Strategies

At the dawn of the 21st century, amidst this ever-increasing economic globalization, global strategies are increasingly intensifying within the automobile industry. A particular catalyst to the intensification of this global competition is the rise and expansion of markets in developing countries. The overall global automobile market (number of vehicles sold) increased by 24.9 million vehicles between 2000 and 2012, moving from 57.4 million vehicles to 82.3 million vehicles. The breakdown includes a decrease of 4.9 million vehicles, from 46.7 million to 41.8 million vehicles in developed countries, and an increase of 29.8 million vehicles, from 10.7 million to 40.5 million vehicles in emerging countries. In other words, almost all of the increase in the automobile market (number of vehicles sold), in recent years, is due to the rise and expansion of markets in developing countries. This demonstrates that the main battlefields of global competition in the industry are the developing markets.

In the background of this business environment, communization strategies of automobile platforms, units, and parts, aimed at strengthening price competitiveness and improving profitability by lowering the cost of automobile production, are becoming a major linchpin of automobile industry strategy within the global automobile industry. In other words, because income levels are lower in the emerging countries, where automobile markets are expanding in comparison to developed countries, products (automobiles) are introduced with significantly lower prices compared to the products (automobiles) traditionally targeted for developed countries. Hence, the breakthrough cost reductions achieved by making extensive inroads into new areas of product development (design) and cost reductions through traditional continuous improvement are essential. The strategies that arise from this type of process are called communization strategies of automobile platforms, units, and parts.

While advanced products such as automobiles are comprised a large number of components, the main elements are classified into the three categories of platforms, units, and parts. A unit refers to a key element of the automobile, such as an engine or transmission, comprised multiple parts that have specific functions, such as the creation or transmission of power. The platform is the car chassis, which comprises multiple units and parts, and constitutes the base of the automobile to realize its basic functionality, such as driving, stopping, and turning. The manner in which the communization of these types of automobile platforms, units, and parts is implemented among the different automobile models, as well as how price competition is strengthened by reducing automobile production costs and enhancing profitability, are major strengths in today's global automobile industry.

4. Communization and Performance Management — The Case of Japanese Company A

The aim of these types of communization strategies for automobile platforms, units, and parts, among differing automobile models, is to realize lower costs in automobile production based on economies of scale.

Economies of scale means the decrease in the average cost of producing each unit by expanding the scale of production and increasing the number of units produced. There are two major drivers of economies of scale: the product (design) side driver and the process (production, sales) side driver. Product (design) side drivers are strategies that implement the centralization and consolidation of retail products and specifications through reviews of product portfolios, or that implement the communization of parts among different products by means of modular architectures through interface configuration and communication procedures. Process side (production, sales) drivers are strategies that increase the unit production of specific products through proactive marketing initiatives and use production processes in planned mass production.

The concept of economies of scale stems from the Ford system of the early 20th century and has a high affinity with mass production and the push mentality. It was characterized by centralized and stock-tolerant production management techniques that focused on a single product, i.e., Model T.

Coming from this background, the focus of Company A, a large Japanese automaker, was to utilize the Platform Chief Engineer system as an opportunity to formulate and execute a communization strategy as a new type of platform strategy.

In other words, in Japan, in recent years, automotive analysts in financial and capital markets have adopted the automobile industry's perspective on transitioning to performance management systems. These are systems used to increase performance by simultaneously pursuing economies of scale, based on product (design) side drivers, such as the communization of platforms among different car models, and by implementing the Platform Chief Engineer as profit centers, and also economies of scale based on process (production, sales) side drivers, such as mass production and mass sales of platforms, using a push mentality.

5. Communization Strategies and Performance Management — The Case of Toyota

This section presents the case of communization and performance management at Toyota, the largest automotive company (group) in Japan.

As indicated by Oono (1978) and Monden (2006), Toyota utilizes limited production and a pull mentality in its TPS. Originally, the TPS was based on the mindset that, in order to respond sensitively to a variety of customer needs, high-mix, low-volume production must be efficiently executed in the relatively small-scale Japanese automobile market. In other words, if several types of products (automobiles) are developed in response to a variety of customer needs, and if there are customer orders for automobiles, high quality automobiles must be produced without waste and delivered to customers within the shortest delivery time possible.

Hence, the TPS is based on the concepts of "Limited Production", which signifies producing only the products for which customer orders are received. The "JIT" system is based on a "pull" mentality and implies producing only the required amount of the required product, at the required time, by "pulling" the product through downstream processes. The "*Jidoka*" system signifies instilling quality into production processes, and the "Shortening of Total Lead Times" from customer order to delivery.

Toyota has a long history of using the communization strategy. In the early half of the 1990s, after the collapse of Japan's bubble economy, the Toyota Group introduced communization activities in its parts production. This is a system that strategically expanded the production of specific key automobile units and parts, with high-cost-component ratios in relation to the overall vehicle. Furthermore, in the latter half of the 1990s, the creation of mechanisms for the standardization and increased diversification of parts was implemented in product development (design) as part of a communization strategy that was spurred on by the soaring value of the yen. After the dawn of the 21st century, Toyota was influenced by the proactive platforms of both communization and modularization strategies at one of its major competitors, Volkswagen AG. Toyota also began to study communization strategies in earnest. The Toyota New Global Architecture (TNGA) strategy was subsequently established and announced (April 9, 2012 and March 27, 2013).

The gist of Toyota's TNGA strategies are as follows: (i) development of new platform types and their communization in each global region; (ii) the development of new types of power-train units; (iii) an increase in the communization ratio of units and parts among automobile models through the introduction of "Grouping Development"; and (iv) the implementation of "Bundled Orders", straddling multiple car models, regions, and time zones, at global bases, in order to facilitate "Grouping Development".

As previously mentioned, the aim of communization strategies is to reduce the cost of automobiles with regard to platforms, units, and parts, based on economies of scale and the implementation of communization among different car models. The drivers of economies of scale are product (design) side drivers and process (production, sales) drivers. Although communization strategies are one of the product (design) side drivers, if the point of view is extended to process (production, sales) side drivers, in processes requiring economies of scale, the affinity for mass production and push mentalities increases, thereby incurring the risk of nonconformance with the previously mentioned TPS.

Toyota utilizes the TPS with limited production and a pull-type mentality. With the promotion of the TNGA strategy, organizational structures, and performance management systems that avoid the aforementioned risks were studied and formulated. As a rule, a traditional organizational structure, differentiated by job function, had been implemented at automobile companies since their establishment. In other words, divisions were formulated by job function units, such as technology research, product development, procurement, production, production technology, logistics, sales and after-sale services, with an organizational composition of mutual horizontal cooperation revolving around the functional axes of quality, price, and human resources at each division (Hino, 2002). In these traditional organizational structures separated by job function, distinctions by region, and finished product, unit, or parts, do not exist on the organization chart. Hence, the following two major organizational changes were implemented in the April 2013 reorganization. First, divisions distinguished by region were established. These took the form of a matrix relationship with the traditional divisions. Specifically, Toyota One was in charge of markets in developed nations, and Toyota Two was responsible for markets in emerging nations. As such, a transformation took place that enabled sufficient response to the needs of customers in both developed and emerging nations. Another change occurred in the bisecting of the organization by division. Each division was distinguished according to the work functions of technology research, product development, production and production technology, as well as classified according to whether they were responsible for the final product, unit, or part. By integrating the organizations responsible for units and parts into a newly independent unit center, the transformation to an organizational structure that enabled strong promotion of unit communization, based also on the TNGA strategy, was achieved. The newly established divisions of Toyota One and Toyota Two were classified by region through this organizational transformation. Their designated missions were primarily to function as profit centers, and they facilitated the establishment and execution of price and product strategies, based on customer needs, in both developed and emerging nations. They also facilitated an order-delivery management mechanism based on the TPS. In other words, in order to span from the start to the end of the TPS supply chain process, divisions distinguished by region were responsible for communicating the order information received from customers to the production divisions and then to accept the final products (automobiles) that were manufactured, based on the limited production and pull mentality of the TPS, as well as deliver them to the customers. In addition, the unit centers that had been newly established by the same organizational transformation were positioned as cost centers that focused on the core TNGA strategy as the communization strategy and the realization of lower costs, based on the development of new unit types. Hence, the communization of units became a major mission.

Here, unit production came to be positioned in the midway points of the TPS supply chain process, based on the attributes of the automobile units themselves. However, since the unit centers were positioned as cost centers, economies of scale were sought, based only on the product (design) side driver of unit communization among different car models. The non-expansion of perception to process (production, sales) side drivers of mass production and push mentality results in avoiding the risk of non-conformance with the TPS.

6. The "Lean Strategy Organization Model" and Its Significance

As previously mentioned, due to the April 2013 reorganization, organizational structures and performance management systems that enabled the full adoption of both lean supply chain management based on the TPS and cost reduction based on unit communization were studied and formulated.

There are two key points of this new organizational structure and performance management system:

(1) By positioning organizations that focus on communization strategies as cost centers, a reduction in product costs through the promotion of the communization of platforms, units, and parts is achieved, while avoiding mass production and the push mentality (risk of non-conformance with the TPS) that occurs in economies of scale.

(2) The entire supply chain process (sales → production → procurement (and suppliers) → production → distribution → sales) is based on the key concepts of the TPS (limited production, pull mentality, JIT, Jidoka, and shortened lead times).

In this chapter, the generalization of the new organizational structures and the performance management systems that incorporates these two points and integrates both the TPS and communization strategies are referred to as the "Organization Model of Lean Strategy".

The significance of this model is that it explains the model of Optimal Balance between Efficiency and Attractiveness proposed by Monden & Larsson (2013). In other words, while product cost reductions through cost-center communization strategies and lean supply chain management, based on the TPS, cause an upward shift (toward efficiency) of an efficient frontier curve that shows the tradeoff between product efficiency and attractiveness, the resulting efficient frontier curve shifts to the upper right due to the strengthening of both the elemental and cutting-edge technologies as general corporate behavior.

On the other hand, retail divisions (profit centers) strategically select the most appropriate points of efficiency and attractiveness, on efficient frontier curves, for products based on the needs of target customers. In the case of the automobile industry, for instance, developed nations have a high net worth market, a middle-class market, and a low-income market. Emerging nations also have these three similar markets. In general, customers in high net worth markets have a stronger need for products of high quality and a high level of attractiveness (i.e., a high ratio of integral architecture) compared to customers in low-income markets. Moreover, customers in emerging markets have a stronger need for products with high efficiency (i.e., a high ratio of modular architecture) at a lower price, compared to customers in developed markets. In other words, automobile product design architectures are gradually undergoing transformations from high-income markets in developed nations, to low-income markets in emerging nations, with less focus on the integral architecture that increases attractiveness, based on the upper body of the automobile, and more focus on modular architecture gradation that increases efficiency, based on the underbody (see Fig. 1).

This can be interpreted as Toyota is intent on maximizing business profitability through the strategic selection of a higher ratio of attractiveness (i.e., a integrative architecture) on an efficient frontier curve showing the efficiency and attractiveness of automobiles by "Toyota One", which

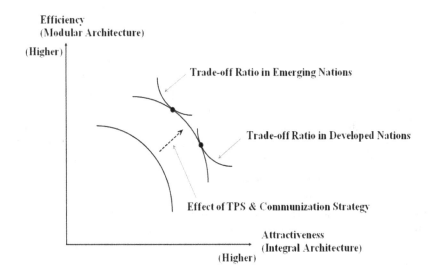

Fig. 1.   Optimal balance between efficiency and attractiveness.

Source: Based on Monden & Larsson, 2013.

is responsible for markets in developed nations, and the strategic selection of a higher ratio of efficiency (i.e., a modular architecture) by "Toyota Two", which is responsible for markets in emerging nations. The previously mentioned reorganization facilitated the execution of these types of product strategies through the placement of regional divisions, segmented by regions in developed nations and emerging nations, in order to respond to their respective customers' needs.

7. Conclusion

In this chapter, we considered how a communization strategy for automobile platforms, units, and parts, in the global automotive industry, is becoming a major linchpin in this sector's industrial strategy. We also highlighted that in the background, automobile product design architecture is transitioning from a traditional integrative architecture to a hybrid one that combines both modular and integral architectures. We discussed communization strategies in the Japanese automobile industry, and the organizational structure and performance management systems for the promotion of these strategies.

We also noted that Toyota, which utilizes the TPS, positioned unit centers that focused on communization strategies as cost centers, and implemented organizational structures and performance management systems that enabled the adoption of both supply chain management, based on the TPS, and cost reductions, based on communization of units, which was referred to in this chapter as the "Organization Model of Lean Strategy".

One of the unique characteristics of the considerations in this chapter is that the concept of economies of scale was more fully explored, and a definitive view was offered regarding the relationship between the TPS and communization strategies. Specifically, it was pointed out that, within economies of scale, there are two main drivers, the process (production, sales) side driver, wherein the affinity for mass production and a push mentality is high and the risk of non-conformance with the TPS is present, and the product (design) side driver that embraces communization and integration with the TPS. The importance of reflecting on the study and the formulation of actual corporate organizational structures and performance management systems within this perspective was also discussed.

With the expansion of markets in emerging nations, global competition in many industries is sure to intensify. In such an environment, communization strategies will spread even further to cross industry boundaries, and performance management systems that support communization strategies will become even more critical.

References

Baldwin, C. Y. & Clark, B. (1997). Managing in an Age of Modularity, *Harvard Business Review*, 75(5), pp. 84–93.

Baldwin, C. Y. & Clark, B. (2000). *Design Rules: The Power of Modularity.* Cambridge: MIT Press.

Fujimoto, T. (2004). *The Philosophy of Monozukuri in Japan.* Tokyo: Nihon Keizai Shinbun (in Japanese).

Hino, S. (2002). *A Study of Management Systems at Toyota.* Tokyo: Diamond Inc. (in Japanese).

Monden, Y. (2006). *The Theory and Structure of the Toyota Production System.* Tokyo: Diamond Inc. (in Japanese).

Monden, Y. & Larsson, R. G. (2013). Robust supply-chain management for the disasters: Based on the product design architectures, in Y. Monden (ed.). *Management of Enterprise Crises in Japan*, Singapore: World Scientific Publishing Co. Pte. Ltd., pp. 125–148.

Oono, T. (1978). *The Toyota Production System — The Management of Downscaling.* Tokyo: Diamond Inc. (in Japanese).

Toyota Motor Corporation: News Release (2012). Announcement of initiatives for the realization of "Better Car Manufacturing" (in Japanese). Retrieved from http://www2.toyota.co.jp/jp/news/12/04/nt12_0410.html (search date March 27, 2014).

Toyota Motor Corporation: News Release (2013). Announcement of the status of TGNA initiatives for "Better Car Manufacturing" (in Japanese). Retrieved from http://www2.toyota.co.jp/jp/news/13/03/nt13_018.html (search date March 27, 2014).

Part II

Lean Management and Performance Evaluation in the Business Operations

7

Financial Performance Measures for the Lean Production System

Zhi Wang
Nagoya University of Commerce and Business

Yasuhiro Monden
University of Tsukuba

1. Introduction

The lean production system as applied to manufacturing floors uses various performance metrics including the operation's lead-time, inventory size, quality (defect rate), actual number of employees, and machine breakdowns as physical indicators. There have been many proposals recently for integrating such physical measures into *financial* or *accounting* measures to understand the overall effects of the lean production system on company-wide performance. In this chapter, the authors examine and compare the existing proposals and develop some new, useful financial measures.

For managers, the controllable domain is dependent on the given authorities and managers' capabilities, and different management levels exist in a business organization. This research divides management levels into (i) local management, such as operators on the manufacturing floor, (ii) middle management, such as team leaders and plant managers, and (iii) top management which includes (a) the top management of an individual company and (b) the top management of a consolidated business group or a supply chain group. This chapter proposes suitable performance measures for each management level.

2. Performance Measures by Management Level

2.1. *Physical and financial performance measures*

Performance indicators could be classified into physical (non-financial) and financial measures and assigned to managers according to their authority and responsibility. While both types of measures use numerical scales to express production activities, they differ in essence. Physical measures consist of items such as weight, capacity, number of units, length, time (lead-time), and quality. These express the reality of production activities and are a low-level integration, that is, they are integrated at the point of manufacturing. Therefore, physical measures are a concrete concept. On the other hand, financial measures can also be called accounting indicators and include items such as operating profit and operating cash flow. These express the reality of production activities in monetary terms by aggregating various individual characteristics. Thus, financial measures are an abstract concept (Wang, 2010).

While management by physical measures focuses on efficiency from a material viewpoint, it directly and significantly influences production activities. In terms of timeliness, cost is managed at exactly the time it is incurred. This type of management provides both a faster way to manage production activities and a means to explore company performance that cannot be investigated by financial measures. Since local management has the opportunity to observe production activities in real-time, they are expected to improve production efficiency using physical measures.[1]

Physical measures are concrete concepts, and financial measures are abstract concepts. They exist in different dimensions. Financial measures convert physical indicators into financial or accounting indicators by abstracting the individual concrete characteristics to create an aggregated measurement. Thus, higher management levels use financial measures to manage production activities as a whole (Wang, 2010).

2.2. *The problem of traditional financial measures*

The lean production system affects not only costs, but also sales and cash flows through reduced lead-times (Wang, 2011). Improvements in profits (i.e., sales less costs) and cash flows strengthen the business structure, and their effects are hard to measure in the short term. In particular, since cash flow improvements do not appear immediately and completely

---

[1]However, when the team adopts *value-added per hour* (a financial indicator), like Kyocera's amoeba system, they could aim to improve this financial indicator.

in the earnings reported in the income statement, it is insufficient to simply calculate the effects of lean production based on reported earnings.

Local managers using physical measures can grasp the effects of the lean production system. However, accounting sections, plant managers, and top management use traditional financial measures based on the reported earnings in the income statement and these measures cannot evaluate the effects of lean production on cash flows. As the lean production system contributes to improvements to a company's business structure, if it is not properly evaluated, it may impair operators' motivation on the manufacturing floor.

3. Physical Measures for Local Management

On the manufacturing floor, the target cost reduction amounts assigned by *Kaizen Costing*[2] are converted into physical indicators, such as the amount consumed, time (lead-time), and quality, with the lean production system applied to achieve these targets. Therefore, the operation standards on the manufacturing floor are based on physical indicators and the results of improvement activities are usually measured using physical indicators — rarely are the results measured using financial indicators.

It is not difficult to understand physical measures such as reduced consumption and improved quality. However, managing and measuring lead-time likely needs an explanation.

At Toyota, lead-time is managed through takt-time. Takt-time is the time, measured in minutes and seconds, required to build one product according to the customer demand, and it is calculated by dividing the available production time per day by the customer demand per day (Ohno, 1988). The daily available production time is the time that the machine can work per day. The customer demand per day is calculated by dividing the monthly customer demand by the days of operation per month. Precisely matching the production to customer demand eliminates useless stock (stagnation) and creates a rhythm for the whole factory. For example, at an assembly line the lead-time is ideally calculated by multiplying takt-time with the number of processes. This is the net standard working time or processing time in the narrow sense. However, the lead-time also includes

---

[2]The assignment of target cost reduction amounts in *Kaizen Costing* is based on the target profit amounts. For more information about *Kaizen Costing*, please refer to Monden (1995). *Kaizen Costing* can measure the effects of a lean production system financially.

non-processing time, such as materials handling time, material waiting time, and setup time. To reduce this production lead-time, manufacturing floor operators try to reduce the setup time and the lot size, for example.

4. Financial Measures for the Team Leader and Plant Manager

At this management level, it is better to use financial rather than physical measures, since this level typically supervises some operators and some sections. In order to manage from an overall viewpoint, they use a monetary financial indicator to unify physical data. Two such financial measures are now proposed.

4.1. JIT Cash Flows based on a direct method of creating a cash flow statement

When evaluating the effects of the lean production system, the influence of cost reduction and sales increase on reported earnings and the influence of lead-time reduction on cash flows should be taken into account. Therefore, the new financial measures proposed in this research include reported earnings and cash flows.

In this research, we assume that the operating profit from a firm's regular business expresses and is the effect of reducing cost and increasing sales, and the change in cash flows that is not included in the operating profit reflects the effect of lead-time reduction. We collect the operating profit and cash flows from the operating cash flows in the cash flow statement. The operating cash flows are one base of free cash flows, and the present value of the future free cash flows represents corporate value. Therefore, performing an activity that increases the operating cash flow contributes to the corporate's value.

In this section, we propose a financial measure for team leaders and plant managers. At this management level, there is no information about the operating cash flow based on the indirect method of creating the cash flow statement, and hence, we use the direct method. *JIT Cash Flows*, Eq. (1), is based on the direct method, and it represents the sales amount less the amount of purchased direct materials and all cash-paid processing costs of obtaining such sales (Monden, 2012).[3] Sales are not the amount as

---

[3]Similar to the *JIT Cash Flows* theory, there is the *Theory of Constraints* (Goldratt and Cox, 2000) that aims at maximizing the throughput (throughput = sales revenue − cost of purchased direct materials). Additionally,

reported in the income statement created by the accrual basis of accounting but the cash income by sales. The amount of purchased direct materials is the total spending on direct materials, including not only the direct materials constituting the cost of goods sold, but also the direct materials included in the closing inventory. Cash-paid processing costs are the costs that involve cash outlays for meeting direct labor costs and manufacturing overheads. Non-cash costs, such as depreciation expense, are not included in the cash-paid processing costs.

JIT Cash Flows = sales amount − amount of purchased direct materials

$$- \text{all cash-paid processing costs.} \qquad (1)$$

JIT Cash Flows, Eq. (1) can be measured daily or monthly at each process or line and each plant. However, when the finished goods are not sold to the external market, the goods sent to the following process (i.e., an intra-company transfer price will be applied) are equal to the sales amount. About *JIT Cash Flows* of a team and a factory, the amount of latter becomes larger than the former, but the calculation method is the same (Monden, 2012).

Equation (1) is essentially similar to the added-value equation of the mini-profit center that is applied in Kyocera's amoeba system.[4] Dividing

---

net profit = through put − operating expense; operating expense = direct labor cost + manufacturing overhead + selling, general and administrative expenses. Operating expenses may have some variable cost characteristics but are generally fixed costs.

[4]Kyocera Corp. developed the amoeba management system, a simple system of management accounting easily understood by the operators of the manufacturing floor. Generally about 10 operators are organized together as a profit center called an amoeba (Inamori, 1998 and 2006; Miya, 1997). This system uses the financial measure called *value-added per hour* or *profit per hour*. To calculate *value-added per hour*, first the added-value is obtained by subtracting the total cash paid (purchases from the internal market and total expenses other than amoeba labor costs) from the total cash received (sales to the external and internal markets) and then dividing the added-value by the total labor hours. This financial indicator makes each amoeba aware of exactly how much added-value it creates per hour for the company. Furthermore, this financial indicator also makes it possible to compare oneself with others, promoting competition among amoebas (Inamori, 1998 and 2006; Miya, 1997; Hamada and Monden, 1989).

To raise this *value-added per hour*, each amoeba may increase sales, decrease costs, or reduce labor hours. This financial indicator serves as a total profit measurement, including not only cost reduction but also sales increases, and it is more than a measurement of the reported earnings recorded in the income statement.

Eq. (1) by the labor hours as in the mini-profit center at Kyocera yields a result similar to the *value-added per hour*.

Within the amoeba system, if a material is purchased, it will be counted as a cost at the time, and the account inventory as a current asset will not be created. Therefore, to reduce the purchase expenditure recorded in this way, the amoeba system reduces the inventory of purchased materials and shortens the lead-time. These help to reduce expenses. The amoeba system affects the profit and cash flows of a company, and it serves as a method of cash-based accounting.

The equation of *value-added per hour* in the amoeba system motivates people to be profit conscious and to use various JIT techniques to make continuous improvements. It can also be used to measure the effects of the lean production system (Monden, 2002). In many Japanese manufacturing companies, such as Kyocera and NEC, in many cases, the JIT production system is used concurrently with the mini-profit center.

4.2. *JIT Residual Income*

The lean production system reduces lead-time and affects inventory size, saving the cost of carrying inventories. Using residual income, we define *JIT Residual Income* as follows (Monden, 2013b):

$$JIT\ Residual\ Income = \text{contribution margin} - \text{plant workforce expenses}$$
$$- \text{cost of capital} \times \text{closing inventory.} \qquad (2)$$

The contribution margin is the selling price per unit minus the variable cost per unit. Since it is computed using the processing cost under variable costing, it eliminates the problem of traditional absorption costing. That is, when using absorption costing, an entity could generate extra profits simply by manufacturing more products that it does not sell. Fixed costs, such as depreciation expense, are treated as the period expenses. The plant workforce expenses are calculated by multiplying the personal expenses per employee by the total number of employees. "Cost of capital × closing inventory" measures the costs of working capital captured in the closing inventory that includes work-in-process inventory at each line and finished goods inventory. Typically, the cost of capital is computed using *capital asset pricing model* (CAPM), but in practice, it could use the minimum acceptable profit ratio.[5]

JIT Residual Income is a profit indicator that becomes the basis to evaluate the corporate value and shareholders' value, as discussed in Sec. 5.3. When the team leader and plant manager act to raise *JIT Residual Income*, they contribute to improvements in both these values.

	Accounts	Given data	Actual data	Equation	Calculation
	A	B	C	D	E
1	Selling price per unit	10,000			
2	Variable cost per unit	7,000			
3	Number sold		80		
4	Personal expense per employee	10,000			
5	Number of employees		5		
6	Cost of capital	0.1			
7	Closing inventory size of finished goods		20		
8	Cost per unit of pressed parts	4,000			
9	Closing inventory of pressed parts (at the store of pressing line)		6		
10	Closing inventory of pressed parts (beside the assembly line)		6		
11	Contribution margin			= (B1-B2)*C3	240,000
12	Plant workforce expenses			= B4*C5	50,000
13	Closing inventory of finished goods			= B2*C7	140,000
14	Closing inventory size of pressed parts			= C9+C10	12
15	Closing inventory of pressed parts			= B8*D14	48,000
16	Total closing inventory			= D13+D15	188,000
17	Total capital costs			= B6*D16	18,800
	JIT Residual Income			= D11–D12–D17	171,200

Fig. 1. The simplified *JIT Residual Income* equation using an Excel sheet.

---

[5]Figure 1 is a simplified *JIT Residual Income* equation using an Excel worksheet, based on the JIT game created by Monden (2013a, 2013b, 2013c, and 2013d) for educational purposes. Adding the "actual data" into the Excel worksheet will automatically generate the result. To simplify the idea, it is assumed that the manufacturing process includes only pressing lines and assembly lines, with no closing work-in-process inventory at each. Moreover, since the lean production system is adopted between the pressing line and assembly line, there are pressed parts inventories stored at the pressing and assembly lines (therefore, the pressed parts inventory account is prepared in cost accounting).

5. Financial Measures for the Top Management of an Individual Company

5.1. *Traditional financial measures, ROA, and ROI*

The ultimate goal of the lean production system is to improve the company's efficiency or productivity from the shareholders' viewpoint. Return on investment (*ROI*) and return on assets (*ROA*) can be used to measure this efficiency or productivity.[6] These two financial measures are intended for the top management of an individual company, consolidated business group, or supply chain group.

Let us have a look at *ROA*. *ROA* is a performance indicator that indicates how efficient management is at using its assets to generate profits. *ROA* is calculated as (profit margin × asset turnover = (profit/sales) × (sales/assets)). To improve the profit margin ratio, when sales are constant, costs must be reduced, since profit = sales − costs. To improve the asset turnover ratio, the amount of assets must be reduced in relation to sales. If lead-time is reduced, then inventory decreases, thereby reducing total assets. *ROA* can measure the effect of the lean production system.

5.2. *Operating Cash Flows based on an indirect measurement method*

*JIT Cash Flow*s, Eq. (1), proposed measuring the effect of the lean production system by three elements, sales amount, amount of purchased direct materials, and all cash-paid processing costs, at the team leader and plant manager level. At the top management level, there is information about the earnings before interest and tax. Moreover, cash flows change according to increases and decreases in inventory. That is, inventory increases mean cash outflow, and inventory decreases mean cash inflow. Inventory increase or decrease shows the inventory carrying time that makes up the lead-time and reducing useless inventory will reduce lead-time. Thus, the effect of lead-time reduction could show through the changes in inventory.

---

[6]As a concept similar to *ROA*, Kawada (2009) proposed *profit potential,* which measures profitability by replacing *ROA*'s ordinary profit with operating profit, and replacing total assets with inventory assets.

Therefore, the top management of an individual company can use Eq. (3) as a performance measure of the lean production system. It is an indirect method of measuring operating cash flows.

Operating Cash Flows

= earnings before interest and tax + non-cash expense (depreciation)

$-(+)$ increase (decrease) in accounts receivable

$-(+)$ decrease (increase) in accounts payable

$-(+)$ increase (decrease) in inventory + receipts of interest

$\times$ and dividend $-$ payment of interest $-$ income taxes.   (3)

5.3. *Primary Residual Income*

The primary *Residual Income* used to evaluate corporate value is determined using the following:

Residual Income = operating profit before interest and tax

$-$ cost of capital $\times$ (liabilities with interest

$+$ shareholders' equity).   (4)

Here, the "operating profit before interest and tax" is the operating profit before deducting interests and taxes, and the cost of capital is the weighted average cost of capital (*WACC*).

Since the present value of future residual income plus the opening book value of equity equals shareholders' value (or market capitalization), both the *Residual Income* and *JIT Residual Income* are basic measures of shareholders' value. In addition, as the present value of future residual income plus the opening book value of total assets equals corporate value, both the *Residual Income* and *JIT Residual Income* are basic measures of the corporate value.

Primarily, residual income as a financial indicator aims to maximize shareholders' value or corporate value, both shareholder goals. However, for example, if a company sacrifices employees' needs to satisfy the goals of shareholders, such as cutting wages to pay dividends, it cannot obtain employees' cooperation in the long term. To improve the corporate value or shareholder's value, the constraint condition is that the needs of stakeholders other than shareholders must first be met.

6. Financial Measures for the Top Management of a Consolidated Business or Supply Chain Group

At this level, the top management of a consolidated business or supply chain group should ensure not only lead-time reductions and inventory decreases in the manufacturing department of an individual company, but also monitor the sales and purchase activities of the whole group. In accordance with the principles of the lean production system, the top management should improve the efficiency of capital collection throughout the supply chain.

To improve the efficiency of the wider operating activities, the *Consolidated Operating Cash Flows* is used instead of *JIT Cash Flows* as the performance measure of the lean production system. The *Consolidated Operating Cash Flows* is based on the indirect method of creating the cash flow statement.

In addition, the two methods of creating the consolidated statement of cash flows are as follows:

(1) Basic method: combining the cash flow statements of all individual companies, and adjusting this by eliminating the debits and credits between the companies.
(2) Simplified method: creating the consolidated statement of cash flow directly from the consolidated balance sheet and income statement.

By either method, if the sales company is consolidated with the manufacturer, the sales of the manufacturer to the sales company and the purchases by the sales company from the manufacturer are offset. The manufacturer's related share of unrealized profit will also disappear when a portion of goods sold is held by the sales company at the end of the period. This amount decreases the gross profit of the manufacturer and decreases the same amount of inventory at the sales company. In addition, the manufacturer's accounts receivable from the sales company and the accounts payable from the sales company to the manufacturer are offset. However, the year-end stock (the amount after eliminating unrealized profit) at the sales company remains on the consolidated balance sheet. Moreover, the increased portion of this year-end stock will also be recorded in the consolidated statement of cash flow as a cash outflow. Therefore, the top management of the parent company is motivated to decrease this stock.

6.1. *When the sales company is not consolidated to the business group, the manufacturer still has an incentive to reduce the inventory of the sales company*

If the sales company is not consolidated with the manufacturer, the manufacturer's accounts receivable related to the sales company still appear on the manufacturer's consolidated balance sheet or cash flow statement. Therefore, the top management at the manufacturer has an incentive to decrease the excess accounts receivable and also the excess stock that the sales company owns.

As mentioned earlier, activities that increase the *Operating Cash Flows* (or *JIT Cash Flows*) and *Residual Income* (or *JIT Residual Income*) will improve the performance of a consolidated business group. Therefore, if the top management of the manufacturing entity uses *Operating Cash Flows* and *Residual Income* as performance measures, it will help to raise the overall enterprise value.

7. Conclusion

This chapter discussed the types of performance measures that could be used to evaluate the effects of the lean production system, arguing that manufacturing floor operators use physical measures, and upper management levels use financial measures. When using a financial indicator for measurement, it should consider not only the effect of reduced costs and increased sales, but also the effect of lead-time reduction.

The authors therefore propose the following:

(1) Manufacturing floor operators use physical measures such as lead-time (machine breakdown time, material waiting time, inventory carrying time, setup time, and processing time, among others), inventory size (direct materials inventory, work-in-process inventory at each process, finished parts inventory at each process, and finished goods inventory, among others), production volume, quality, and the number of employees.

(2) Team leaders and plant managers use financial measures such as *JIT Cash Flows,* based on the direct method of creating a cash flow statement, and *JIT Residual Income.* However, to improve these financial

indicators, team members modify manufacturing activities based on the physical indicators.

(3) The top management of an individual company use financial measures such as the *Operating Cash Flows*, based on the indirect method of creating a cash flow statement, and the primary *Residual Income*.

(4) The top management of a consolidated business group or a supply chain group use the *consolidated Operating Cash Flows* based on the indirect method.

References

Goldratt, E. M. & Cox, J. (2000). *The Goal, Second Revised Edition*. Great Barrington: The North River Press.

Hamada, K. & Monden, Y. (1989). Profit management at Kyocera corporation: The amoeba system. In *Japanese Management Accounting*, Y. Monden and M. Sakurai (ed.), pp. 197–210. Cambridge: Productivity Press.

Inamori, K. (1998). *Practical Learning of Kazuo Inamori*. Tokyo: Nikkei, Inc. (in Japanese).

Inamori, K. (2006). *Ameoba Management*. Tokyo: Nikkei, Inc (in Japanese).

Kawada, M. (2009). *Toyota Way — Reindustrializing Management Accounting for New Age*. Tokyo: Chuokeizai-Sha (in Japanese).

Miya, H. (1997). Management Control for Empowerment: The Kyocera Amoeba System. *The Journal of the Department of Economics of Gakushuin University*, 34(3/4), 135–148 (in Japanese).

Monden, Y. (1995). *Cost Reduction System: Target Costing and Kaizen Costing*. Cambridge: Productivity Press.

Monden, Y. (2002). The Relationship Between Mini Profit-center and JIT System, *International Journal of Production Economics*, 80(2), 145–154.

Monden, Y. (2012). *Toyota Production System* (4th edition). Boca Raton: Taylor & Francis Group.

Monden, Y. (2013a). Play "JIT Game" for Learning the Lean Production System. *Factory Management (Kojo Kanri)*, 59(5), 72–78 (in Japanese).

Monden, Y. (2013b). Play "JIT Game" for Learning the Lean Production System. *Factory Management (Kojo Kanri)*, 59(7), 73–80 (in Japanese).

Monden, Y. (2013c). Play "JIT Game" for Learning the Lean Production System. *Factory Management (Kojo Kanri)*, 59(8), 113–115 (in Japanese).

Monden, Y. (2013d). Play "JIT Game" for Learning the Lean Production System. *Factory Management (Kojo Kanri)*, 59(9), 76–80 (in Japanese).

Ohno, T. (1988). *Toyota Production System: Beyond Large-Scale Production.* New York: Productivity Press.

Wang, Z. (2010). A Study on how to Relate the Physical Measures to Accounting Measures. *Financial and Cost Accounting (Sangyo Keiri)*, 70(1), 143–153 (in Japanese).

Wang, Z. (2011). The New Integrated Indicator for the Performance Evaluation of Shop Floor Management. *Accounting (Kigyoukaikei)*, 63(8), 133–138 (in Japanese).

8

Management Control Systems for Lean Management in Medical Services — A Case Study at Lund and Kameda

Rolf G. Larsson
Lund University

Yoshinobu Shima
Kinki University

Chiyuki Kurisu
Kameda College of Health Sciences

1. Introduction

The cost crisis in health care and medical insurance systems is evident in Japan, in Sweden, in the US, and in many other nations. To try to solve this crisis seems to be a global top priority question. In Japan, the Ministry of Health, Labor and Welfare has promoted medical reforms, to reconstruct the financial balance of the medical insurance system. As one of these efforts, a fixed payment system for medical services based on (Diagnosis Procedure Combination) "DPC" was introduced to a number of hospitals in Japan. Also in Sweden a series of health care reforms have been discussed, including a European version of DPC. The question for this study is how can Japanese and Swedish hospitals develop Management control systems (MCS) that may help to provide high quality medical services at lower cost, in order to balance their books?

As a response to the critique, some hospitals have tried to introduce ideas of lean production systems (LPS) to their medical treatment processes. The essence of the lean concept is to provide good quality products or services with lower cost through continuous process improvement. When such lean concepts are applied to medical services, the MCS also has to be redesigned to support the lean medical processes. However, little has been known about how the MCS of medical institutions could be redesigned for the Lean concepts in medical services. One idea comes from Kaplan & Porter (2011) who suggest Time-Driven Activity-Based Costing (TD-ABC) as a means to measure cost per minute in the value chain. But they do not combine the TD-ABC with the Lean process maps, or to Lean accounting.

In this chapter, the authors discuss the principal features of MCS packages in Lean medical services by examining two advanced cases: One is the case of Kameda Medical Centre (KMC) in Japan, and the other is of Lund University Hospital (LUH) in Sweden. By comparing the Lean processes and accounting models in Japan and Sweden, the authors hope to be able to analyze both philosophical and technical differences between the two hospitals.

1.1. *Purpose*

The aim of the study program is to explore MCS package for process innovation in medical services. More specifically, this chapter sets out to study, create, and test models of management accounting and control following the Lean processes. The models will be based on a combination of ideas from Lean Health care and TD-ABC, and similar models for Lean Accounting.

1.2. *Methodology*

This chapter is based on two case studies (Yin, 2003), one Japanese hospital and the other Swedish. Within the case studies we have used action research (Argyris *et al.* 1985; Kaplan, 1998) to build and test Lean-TD-ABC prototypes and similar cost allocation models. However, as the study covers a period of more than a year, its focus has shifted over the period and this has affected the way in which specific research methods have been used. In the quest to implement a TD-ABC prototype or similar model in the case organizations, different methods were used in different phases of the research. During spring 2013, the researchers took an active role in experimenting with prototypes for TD-ABC in the Lean process of Endobronchial Ultrasound (EBUS) in the Swedish case organization. From autumn 2013, the study changed as the interest became more focused on the use of the TD-ABC model for improved MCS. In this phase, the researchers tried to understand and explain the possibility of improved cost efficiency and resource allocation within the Lean patient flow. The Japanese case study started in the autumn 2013, with interviews. In the spring 2014, the researchers started the experimenting process with prototypes for Lean Accounting, personal responsibility centers and quality systems in the Japanese case organization. Follow up interviews were performed for both cases in autumn 2014.

1.3. *Theoretical perspectives*

In the *New England Journal of Medicine*, and in *Harvard Business Review*, we have been able to follow three distinguished researchers, Porter (2009, 2010), Mintzberg (2011, 2012) and Kaplan (2011) and their debate on how to solve the cost crisis in health care. They seem to agree on a suggestion that all costs should be based on patient care cycles and processes, and that a reimbursement system based on value for patients should be used. Proposed techniques are cooperative managing styles, process value streams and TD-ABC. Unfortunately, they find that almost all MCS ideas used today, stand as barriers against their proposals; including — organizational strategies and structures, reimbursement systems, information systems, accounting, budgeting, and costing models.

But before we go into the details of MCS we will give a brief background of Lean processes in hospitals. During the last two decades the Lean principles from Toyota (Monden, 1992) has been translated into health care organizations. Kollberg *et al.* (2007) noted that the quest of eliminating wastes in the value chain is rather similar in the health care activities and processes. They saw that the goal in health care, to build value adding patient flows, is equivalent to creating value adding flows at Toyota. This is in line with Spear's (2005) comment that the first priority in Lean health care, is to shorten lead times and eliminate wastes. Another important part of the Lean principles is to even out variations in the flow. Spear (2005) further claimed that Lean is not about drastic change rather it is about giving employees a mandate to solve problems and to improve the way that work is carried out. Continued improvement is a corner stone in Lean, which the author believed will also improve the motivation among employees. Another important part of Lean is quality, which coincide with the quality demands in health care. In Lean health care, these two demands for quality are combined (Kollberg *et al.* 2007). A problem with Lean health care implementation is that it also affects the MCS of the organization.

In this study, we use the definition of MCS that Anthony & Govindarajan (2007, p. 6) framed as; *"Management control is the process by which managers influence other members of the organization to implement the organization's strategies"*. For a more practical description of the tools and techniques that organizations use for MCS, we follow the notion of a MCS package presented by Malmi & Brown (2008). Their MCS package — Management Control Package (MCP) included a core of; strategic planning, cybernetic controls with budgets, financial and non-financial measuring systems, and rewards. The inner core was complemented by; cultural controls, government structure, organization structure, and policies and procedures.

It seems imperative to go from a situation where the MCS is believed to have had barriers against the proposals from Porter, Mintzberg, and Kaplan — to a situation where the MCP becomes enablers of the suggested solutions to the cost crisis in health care. But change is hard to get, as already Machiavelli (1513) noted. Rowe *et al.* (2008) studied the effects of organizational process changes on MCS and found that slow and continuous changes in the organization were possible to implement in the MCS, but that discontinuous organizational changes at a higher speed were much harder to implement. In a later study, Rowe *et al.* (2012) found that soft parts of the MCS, like Activity-Based Costing (ABC), was impossible to implement until it was "hardened" and more persuasive, which could take several years. This relative stability of MCS was also studied by Burns & Scapens (2000), who explained this resistance to change with institutional theory: The same explanation for stability and resistance to change in MCS was also used by Granlund (2001).

However, despite the evidence that it seems hard to change the MCP with its organizational strategies and structures, reimbursement systems, information systems, accounting, budgeting and costing models, performance measurement, reward, and cultural controls, several authors have tried to introduce new ideas for MCS. In this study, we will focus on Lean Accounting, individual responsibility centers and TD-ABC. Lean Accounting is suggested as a form of accounting that is tailored for organizations that work with Lean strategy. Lean Accounting focuses on revenues and costs in the value creation processes, sometimes known as the value stream, from an order to a finished product or service. This implies a cost and revenue analysis of the entire organization's activities and processes, rather than focusing on individual products (or services) and product groups as in traditional costing (McNair in Stenzel, 2007). However, Lean Accounting is a relatively new method and there are still few studies that show examples of how MCS, accounting, budgeting, and costing can be incorporated into the Lean strategy. Anthony & Govindarajan (2007) discuss variations in responsibility centers where profit centers are of a special interest. When a manager takes on full responsibility for revenues, cost, and profit, he gets committed to the value creation and quality of the center. In the Japanese case, this kind of commitment in a Lean organization will be studied.

A similar idea to McNair's was presented by Kaplan & Porter (2011) with their advice that an effective way to measure the cost in health care is to use time as the primary cost driver in a TD-ABC model. For a more detailed description of TD-ABC we refer to Kaplan & Anderson (2007). In the Swedish case we will use Kaplan & Porter's (2011) TD-ABC model and its claim that costs for various operators such as personnel, equipment, facilities and materials should be allocated on the basis of the time it takes to process the various activities. In the Japanese case, we will use a similar model of Lean Accounting. In the projects, we seek to follow the patient flow in the Lean process map, and try to use that as a basis for measuring the time each activity takes and use that as a basis for cost allocation. Implementing the TD-ABC model would thus be a first step in expanding the Lean Health care approach from the Lean process map by adding time estimates and costs for all value creating activities. The Kaplan & Porter article was recently published, so there are a few other studies in the field of TD-ABC in health care (Demeere *et al.* 2009; Tanis & Öxyapici, 2012; Vogl, 2013) that we may use for comparison. The TD-ABC model that Kaplan & Porter suggest consists of seven steps;

(1) *Select the medical condition and/or patient population to be examined;*
(2) *Define the care delivery value chain;*
(3) *Develop process maps of each activity in patient care delivery; identify the resources involved;*
(4) *Obtain time estimates for each process step;*
(5) *Estimate the cost of supplying each patient care resource;*
(6) *Estimate the practical capacity of each resource provider, and calculate the capacity cost rate;*
(7) *Compute the total costs over each patient's cycle of care.*

Based on data from the TD-ABC model, Kaplan & Porter implies some promising management opportunities for cost reduction and improved efficiency without quality losses, what we will call Time-Driven Activity-Based Management (TDABM). Moreover, the authors claim that TDABM can actively engage physicians, clinical teams, administrative staff, and management accountants in joint work on improvements and innovation, compared to the traditional costing and accounting models that tended to lead to tensions and everlasting discussions. Kaplan & Porter suggested a nine step model for implementing TDABM;

(1) *Eliminate non-value activities*;
(2) *Improve resource capacity utilization by increasing bottle neck resources and decreasing wasted resources*;
(3) *Deliver the right processes at the right locations*;
(4) *Match clinical skills to the process*;
(5) *Speed up cycle time*;
(6) *Optimize over the full cycle of care*;
(7) *Capture the payoffs of unused capacity*;
(8) *Use the TD-ABC model for budgeting (TDABB)*;
(9) *Reinvent reimbursement to Value-based reimbursement.*

However, the authors do not provide any guidelines for how the actual change from traditional MCS to the new ideas of TD-ABC should be managed. This is problematic, as they claim that almost all MCS ideas used today stand as barriers against their proposal, and thereby needs to be changed. At the same time Rowe *et al.* (2008, 2012) has proved that change in MCS is hard to get. There is an institutional resistance to change in MCS, according to Burns & Scapens (2000) and Granlund (2001), or as Niccolo Machiavelli,[1] 400 years ago claimed; *"It must be considered that there is nothing more difficult to carry out, nor more doubtful of success, nor more dangerous to handle, than to initiate a new order of things."*

2. Case Studies

2.1. *Case of Lund University Hospital (LUH)*

LUH has worked with Lean Health care since 2007. Today, Lean is considered a fundamental philosophy for all improvement work within the hospital.

One of the units that has been working with the implementation of Lean Health care the longest, is Division 3, which will be the focus of this case. In this work with process improvement, they have given priority to really understand the work processes in cooperation between nurses, medical doctors, and other hospital staff. This work is known as "Go to Gemba",

---

[1]Machiavelli (1513). II Principle.

inspired from Toyota (Ohno & Bodek, 1988). However, the hospital's work with Lean Health care has so far been directed towards quality of care, reduction of queues, time efficiency, and productivity standpoint. The Lean process maps and, process improvements had prior to 2013 not been linked to accounting or MCS. Within the Division this case is primarily focused on the ward that deals with diagnosis and staging (how far the cancer has spread) in the treatment of lung cancer. In this process, an ultrasound guided bronchoscopy called the EBUS is used. The EBUS patient's flow chart is illustrated in Fig. 1, including the activities performed by nurses, medical doctors and support staff.

The EBUS patient's flow is also an example of a Lean process map, which is a vital part of Lean health care at LUH. Such Lean process maps are the basis for process improvement like; shorter queues, reduced lead times and more efficient patient processes. The idea is that with continuous improvement of work routines the hospital care processes will be more effective which will benefit both patients and staff. One of the cornerstones in Lean health care at LUH is to level out variations in work load and the patient flow. More effective production planning will lead to better care and less stress among employees. Another corner stone is to create common work practices for an easier identification of quality deviations and nonconformity errors. This will put a focus on processes and quality. As soon as an error is detected, a task force will start looking for the cause, identify the root cause of the problem. In this process, new knowledge is gained and quality will be improved. All such work should be carried out with respect for both patients and personnel.

So far the Lean health care project in the EBUS flow has focused on eliminating wastes of resources and materials, which has created a sense of urgency among the staff. They have started to question why a more expensive material has to be used if there is a cheaper equivalent. When a new patient examination process is started, nurses do not open the more expensive material packages until the last minute, in case the examination is not carried out for different reasons. Another result was that the operating theater and connecting rooms used in the EBUS process were redesigned for a better flow of the care activities, which saved time and effort and reduced wastes in the long run. However, "It may be easy to reduce wastes in materials and buildings, but much harder when it comes to humans and the way they work" as one of the controllers at the division commented.

The practical work with the Lean strategy at LUH is built on meetings where deviations from quality and time levels are discussed. Every such

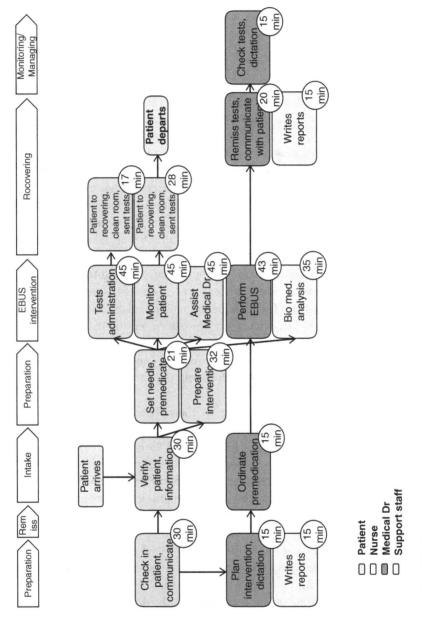

Fig. 1. The EBUS patient flow.

deviation is the starting point of a new project with the responsibility to investigate the cause of the deviation or non-confirmity and to come up with a suggestion for improvement. For each such project, new learning is gathered. However, despite the previous work with Lean at EBUS, the target of maximum 12 days from remiss to diagnosis, has not been reached yet. When the Lean-TD-ABC project started at LUH the researchers could follow the seven step model that Kaplan & Porter (2011) had suggested. The selected medical condition to be examined was found in LUH Division 3, a lung cancer ward that already had a well defined value chain and a process map. To combine the physical process map with resources involved, we measured the time that was used for the patient at each process step. These time measures were relatively simple to obtain from interviews and from actual time studies of the different processes. A trickier part was to estimate the cost of supplying each patient care process step to resource consumption. The process map is illustrated in Fig. 1.

We started to look for information on cost for personnel, facilities, medical equipment, and materials. The calculation of cost for staff was based on the budget for 2013. Staff costs were divided into three categories: doctors, nurses, and medical secretaries. In accordance with the TD-ABC idea there should be a distinction between theoretical and practical capacity. As LUH is a University hospital both doctors and nurses are involved with research for about 25% of the time. As research this time cannot be traced to specific patients we reduced the capacity to 80%. The annual cost of staff is also a basis for management overhead costs (16%) which was added to the total cost of labor. The price per minute for the different staff categories is illustrated in Table 1.

Costs for personnel account for about 50% of the total cost. When studying medical personnel at work it is easy to see the logic of using minutes to account for their activities. It is perhaps not obvious that costs for resources

Table 1.   Price per minute by employee (SEK) Staff category.

	Medical Dr	Nurses	Secretary
Annual costs	1,238,413	2,613,871	425,803
Minutes per year (80% capacity)	88,320	521,088	88,320
Cost per minute	14.02	5.02	4.82
Cost incl. overhead	16,29	5,83	5,60

like facilities, medical equipment, and materials behave in the same way. However, when we started to look at facilities used in the patient care process, we could see that it was budgeted to cost SEK 238.268 for 2013, which could be divided into 365 days, or 8,760 hours, or 525,600 minutes. But again, the problem with capacity usage must be applied and we decided that facilities without personnel did not create value, which led back to the same amount of minutes as for personnel. The annual cost of SEK 484.612, divided by annual used minutes gave a price per minute of SEK 4.85. The same logic was used for medical equipment compiled from the inventory list that clinicians used last year, giving a price per minute calculated to Kronor 15.23. Cost for material used for an EBUS-examination we found already listed, as this price list had been used earlier as a basis for charges from one hospital to another. However, as a research group member estimated that it contained several inaccuracies, the staff of the department conducted a review of consumption and prices for these materials. The list includes all materials, from paper cloth lying on the examination table, which costs just SEK 1, to the high tech needle used in biopsy priced at SEK 1,800. After the review, the current cost estimate for each material used in the process could be directly copied into the prototype we constructed.

In the last step of the TD-ABC model, we calculated the total cost of patient care in the EBUS process. The per minutes rates that have been calculated was added to the flow as it was multiplied by the actual time, as shown in Fig. 1. Staff costs amounted to a total of SEK 3,715 per EBUS-examination, where doctors and nurses accounted for nearly 50% each, as illustrated in the Fig. 2. The cost of facilities totaled SEK 585 based on the price per minute 4.85. To assess whether this could be reasonable or not, the facility rate was compared with the total cost of the premises at the Division 3, which turned out to be SEK 501 per procedure. As EBUS is one of the more complex interventions carried out by the intervention team, we believed that it was reasonable that the EBUS process cost could be slightly higher than the average price per minute.

The model was discussed at a meeting in the project group, where we found that when both revenues and costs are measured in the actual lean process maps, it empowered employees to start to discuss the reduction of non-value adding activities and to improve the efficiency of the value creating activities in the patient care processes. However, the lean accounting TD-ABC model showed that the studied lean process (EBUS) was "unprofitable" as the DPC-based price did not cover all costs. This problem put a

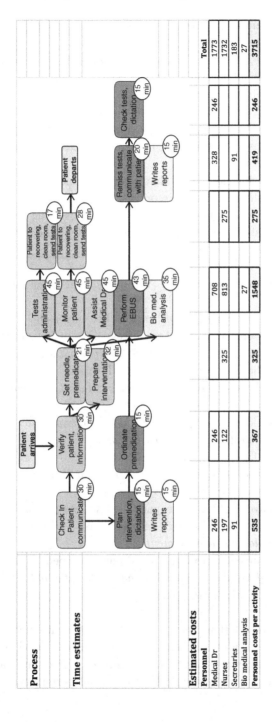

Fig. 2. The Lean EBUS process in TD-ABC.

pressure on the group to start to discuss this problem. Is it the DPC price or the cost that is wrong, or both?

In the next phase of the project, a follow up meeting was held between the researchers and all personnel at the EBUS group. The researchers wanted to discuss the model and its virtues, but the outcome of the meeting was not as intended. The researchers tried to discuss how to eliminate non-value activities, how to improve resource capacity utilization by increasing bottle neck resources and decreasing wasted resources, and how speed up cycle time.

The answer was that no one felt that he or she wanted to be eliminated, no one wanted to discuss wasted resources, but many had things to say about scarce resources, and no one was interested in speeding up cycle time. The argument can also be summed up in the nine step model suggested by Kaplan & Porter (2011):

(1) Eliminate non-value activities — *No one felt that he or she wanted to be eliminated.*

(2) Improve resource capacity utilization by increasing bottle neck resources and decreasing wasted resources — *No one wanted to discuss wasted resources, but many had things to say about scarce resources.*

(3) Deliver the right processes at the right locations — *To people from Malmö, the right locations where placed in Malmö, and vice versa for people from Lund.*

(4) Match clinical skills to the process — *Most personnel thought that this was what they had done for the last 8 years.*

(5) Speed up cycle time — *No thank you!*

(6) Optimize over the full cycle of care — *Yes, but they thought that this was already included in the EBUS flow.*

(7) Capture the payoffs of unused capacity — *No one felt "unused".*

(8) Use the TD-ABC model for budgeting (TDABB) — *Not this year, this will take much longer to implement.*

(9) Reinvent reimbursement to value-based reimbursement — *Yes, this was the only part of the list where people agreed that the old DPC was not a good model for reimbursement.*

This part of the LUH project is now at a hold until further notice. However, the project will continue on a more general level, the whole Lean process of cancer treatment. In this project, one of the participant medical doctors will be responsible for the overall performance of; time,

Just-in-Time (JIT), queues, budget, DPCs, other types of revenues, and of course cost and quality of the medical services.

2.2. *Case of Kameda Medical Center (KMC)*

KMC is one of the largest private hospitals in Japan. KMC is the corporate designation of their medical service facilities located in the south part of Chiba prefecture, which consists of the Kameda General Hospital, Kameda Clinic and Kameda Rehabilitation Hospital. KMC has 33 medical departments and 925 beds, and receives 3,000 outpatient visits every day on average. It employs about 2,400 staff, including 420 general physicians and specialists, and 800 nurses. KMC is known as the first hospital to make use of the Electronic Medical Record and to acquire Joint Commission International (JCI) certification in Japan. The mission of KMC is "In order to contribute to the happiness and well-being of everyone involved with the Kameda Medical Center, we endeavor to provide the highest level of medical service." And one of their values is "We will hold our patients in the highest esteem, with their needs being the highest priority of all." In accordance with its mission and values, KMC provides advanced medical care to every patient with high quality and it is known as one of the best hospitals in Japan.

Although KMC has not explicitly introduced Lean philosophy or the Toyota Production System (TPS) into their management systems, it does have a set of control mechanism to implement continuous improvement (Kaizen). Medical staff always ask "Is there any problem or obstacles to provide the most appropriate and efficient medical care to patients?" Whenever they face a problem, they hold a meeting and discuss how the problem can be solved. Finally, they revise their treatment manual or re-organize cross functional work processes. These practices of continuous improvement have been introduced and facilitated through the re-engineering of the management control system.

Around 1998, the financial condition of KMC was deteriorating because of the heavy investments in the Electric Medical Record system and other facilities. To cope with the difficulties they were facing, the director of KMC re-engineered the management control system. One change was to delegate spending authority to the director of each clinical department so that each department could be managed as a profit center. The other was to acquire ISO 9001 certification. The director of KMC aimed to utilize ISO 9001 for making the medical staff manage their processes.

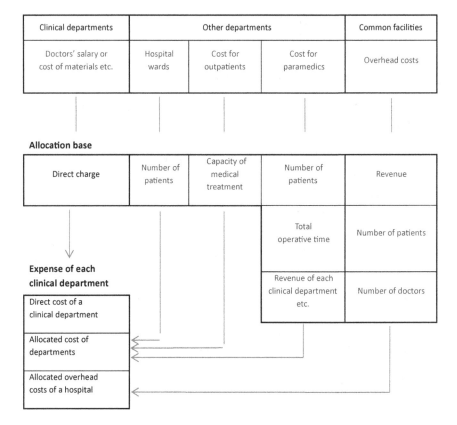

Fig. 3. The cost allocation process in KMC.

2.2.1. *Introducing a divisional profit and loss statement (P/L)*

The purpose of introducing a divisional P/L is to make the managers of the clinical departments to be conscious of the profitability of their departments so that they can independently make an effort to improve their business process. Figure 3 shows how the cost allocation process is carried out in KMC.

First, all medical expenses are traced to the direct cost pool of the clinical departments, the direct cost pool of the other departments, and the common facilities overhead cost pool. The direct cost traced to clinical departments consists of doctors' salary, the cost of materials, and other traceable expenses. The direct costs of other departments consist of the cost for hospital wards, outpatients, and paramedics. The cost for hospital

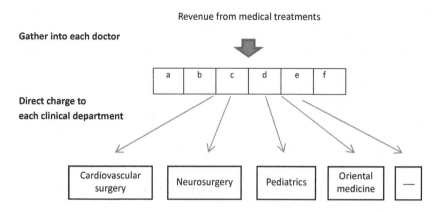

Fig. 4. The distribution process of revenue in KMC.

wards are allocated to the clinical departments using the number of patients as the cost driver. The costs associated with outpatients are allocated using the capacity of medical treatment in each clinical department. The costs of paramedics are allocated using the number of patients, the total operative time, the revenue of each clinical department as well as other measures. The overhead costs are then allocated using the revenue, the number of patients and the number of doctors.

Figure 4 shows how KMC measures the revenue of each clinical department. At the beginning, they calculate how much revenue each doctor yields from medical treatments. Then, the revenue yielded by each doctor is added together within each clinical department to give the total revenue for the department. This can also be achieved by just calculating the revenue of the clinical department, but they think that it enhances doctors' motivation to know the revenue they yielded, so when some doctors often ask a question at the meeting, "How much money have I made this month?" they can tell them.

Since the profitability of a department is used as one of the performance indicators that managers are responsible for, KMC thinks it is important to make the calculation process fair for all the managers. Therefore, when they allocate indirect cost to the departments, they often adjust the allocation bases for the consumption of actual resource using an adjustment factor. For example, the cost of using an operating room is allocated using the sum of operating hours among the departments. But it is allocated at one and a half times to some departments, such as the cardiovascular surgery department and the neurosurgery department because they usually need more support from the paramedics, which is an additional expense.

On the other hand, the medical treatment fee, which is a major part of the revenue of hospitals in Japan, is paid based on the National Health Insurance (NHI) point system that the Ministry of Health, Labor, and Welfare implemented. It seems that when the NHI point system was put in place, every clinical department was shown to make a profit. But since the NHI point system has not been updated using the rigorous cost calculation, it has caused some clinical departments to make a profit but some are always shown to make a loss.

In general, the pediatrics department that provides advanced medical care or operations are barely profitable. That is because most children who come to the pediatrics department have minor illnesses and do not need very much treatment so the department does not gain enough from the NHI point system to be profitable. In addition, as the KMC provides 24 hours emergency medical services as well as pediatrics, a few doctors and paramedics always have to stand by all day long whether a patient comes in or not, which increases medical expenses as they are a fixed cost. In another case, some departments, such as the oriental medicine department, the dermatology department and the psychosomatic medicine department, provide not only medical treatments to their own patients, but often also supports or advises patients in other clinical departments. As these support activities do not bring any additional benefits through the NHI point system, these departments also tend to be unprofitable.

As mentioned earlier, the purpose of introducing a divisional P/L was to make the clinical departments more conscious of their profitability and to improve their business process. The financial results of each department are reported at the management meeting to which managers of all clinical departments attend. Since a part of the financial result is used as an indicator of the doctors' performance, the doctors whose departments make a loss are motivated to explore how to decrease the cost or increase the revenue of their departments. However, the doctors whose department are always unprofitable because of factors outside their control may lose the motivation to improve their departments. It seems that in this setting the process to provide good medical service may never improve the financial results, thus doctors ignore the financial results and the divisional P/L. Accordingly, they reduce the allocation of the indirect costs to the clinical departments, which make a loss under the current NHI point system, in order to make the financial results of all clinical departments apparent to be profitable.

In other words, they evaluate the contribution which does not bring any additional revenue, but makes good medical services to the whole hospital. The extent of the allocation cost reduced is decided subjectively by the board chairman of KMC after interviewing doctors.

The results of the financial measures are reported to the board of directors, the hospital's management conference and the management meeting in order to monitor the financial performance of each clinical department. In addition, the financial measures are used when the board chairman conducts interviews with the department managers to prepare the annual budget for the following year. Basically, almost of all the doctors, including the managers of the medical departments, think that their mission is to provide a good medical treatment to their patients, and they do not have much interest in financial performance. Therefore, in order to make the doctors to be concerned about the financial performance, the board chairman thinks it is good to show them how much profit they have to earn to provide a good medical treatment that they desire to realize.

When interviewing doctors, the project manager explains the previous results and suggests future targets to the department managers. The management and the doctors exchange ideas so that it is clear how they will attain the targets. For example, at first, the board chairman and the project manager decide the financial targets each year and give it to the department manager. Then the project manager illustrates the effect of the number of patients and operations on the monthly profit performance of the department and its effect on KMC's profit, using the data from department P/L. In order to attain the financial target, the department manager and the project manager examine how much cost they need to decrease in each department, how many doctors they need for the number of patients or operations they have, and how much they need to invest in the medical equipment.

The interview that the board chairman conducts to involve the department managers in the budgeting process, has brought desirable changes to the management of the clinical departments. The project management manager draws up a draft budget for the following year, because he can get useful information from the interview to forecast future business accurately. The department manager develops a sense of responsibility to attain the financial target so that the doctors in the department should take the contribution to the financial performance into consideration when they conduct their medical treatments. When they have alternative medical treatments, for example, the choice between outpatient day treatment or hospital treatment, the doctor can check with the project manager which alternative would increase the profit of the department and the hospital.

2.2.2. *Acquiring ISO 9001 certification*

ISO 9001 is one of the quality management system standards that provide guidance and tools for organizations to ensure that their products and services satisfy customer's requirements. This standard is based on a number of quality management principles, including a strong customer focus, involvement of top management, a process approach, and continuous improvement. The ISO 9001 certification project started in the summer of 1998. First, KMC established a preparation committee, including managers, doctors, nurses, other specialists, and the board chairman. Then, it held a study meeting for the preparation committee members with an outside consultant. Even with the help of a consultant, the members could not understand the merit of applying the standards of ISO 9001 in their medical processes. That might be partly because the requirements of ISO 9001 were translated into Japanese on the assumption that it should be applied to manufacturing, not to service entities. The committee chairperson said "I had no idea what an outside consultant was talking about, nor was I sure whether introducing ISO 9001 would increase the quality of medical care, the number of patients, sales, or decrease costs."

Even if they did not grasp what ISO 9001 really meant, they did their best to introduce the process. The committee chairperson said "OK, we'll try, without thinking about what the merit of ISO 9001 is. We should do it first, after that we'll discuss how to utilize the standards for our business management." This is the type of cooperative attitude that has been fostered by the catchphrase "Do & Think" which the board chairman would always say to the staff members. That means, we should think the value of something after challenging it. Next, the preparation committee held workshops to train internal examiners selected from each department. The internal examiner, who had taken lessons on how to examine the work process, checked operational processes in the department, and they found that the medical processes were not standardized at all in the hospital. For example, the safety standards for medical treatment procedures were not unified and that there were different forms of incident reports used in different departments. Therefore, each department staff needed to make an improvement plan for standardization of medical process and executed it before the next examination. An internal examiner was also expected to be a mediator who presented improvement methods to one department, which were applied in the other department. Under these processes, standardization of medical process, safety standards, and forms of reports progressed through the whole hospital.

On the other hand, Standardized medical processes and rules were documented using a common form. Proceedings in the preparation committee were also documented. These documents were shown to all staff at meetings in each department so that every staff in the hospital could share the standards and information. Moreover, these documents were uploaded to the Electronic Medical Record system. This made it easy to share the standards and information among the medical staff. In addition, it made the medical process more safe and effective, because all staff could get information of medical treatments from the system anytime they needed them. For example, when a nurse gave medical treatment to an inpatient that was in another department, he or she could refer to the standard procedure which had been uploaded to the system.

Top management were also involved in this project and kept informed of the progress of the project at management reviews, where each department reported their outcomes in the previous term and showed their goals and road maps for the following term. There, top management checked the progress of the project and commented on each presentation. Management reviews were an important opportunity for top management to show the firm intention to acquire ISO 9001 certification. This increased awareness of the value and significance of ISO 9001 for all staff. The records from management reviews were also documented and uploaded to the information system. KMC acquired ISO 9001 certification in 2000 after an external examination and they have renewed it until the present. They make good use of ISO 9001 to encourage continuous process improvements so that every staff became accustomed to fulfilling it. It seems that the Plan-Do-Check-Action (PDCA) cycle for improvement activities have really taken root in their daily work and has achieved the desired outcomes, such as decreasing the average number of hospitalization days, raising the turnover rate of beds, and shortening the waiting time of patients.

One of the most remarkable outcomes is the improvement of the cancer treatment processes. Formerly, a variety of medicines were used for patients in cancer treatment because each medical oncologist tended to use a different anticancer medicine. A number of nurses pointed out that there was a high risk of medication error. Therefore, they formed an ad hoc committee composed of medical oncologists, medical hematologists, nurses, and pharmacists in order to discuss how to decrease medication error rate. After discussing the issues, the committee decided to set a few usage patterns for anticancer medicines according to the condition of a patient so that it would not lead to a deterioration of medical quality. This practice has brought about good results in all aspects. It has decreased not only the risk of medication error in medical processes, but also the amount of work for pharmacists and purchases, because the kind of medicines which they need to prepare for the medical treatment has been limited.

3. Comparisons of Cases and Analysis

The comparisons of the Kameda and Lund cases will be based on the MCP (Malmi & Brown, 2008). The MCP originally consists of five parts, of which we will use three: cultural controls, cybernetics controls, and administrative controls. The other two parts, planning and rewards, has not been investigated in the two case studies. The three parts that we will concentrate on will be further explained in the theoretical part of the chapter. Here follows a short summary of the main contents as a basis for the comparisons of the two cases. Cultural controls are the set of values, beliefs, and norms which are shared by the members of an organization and thereby influence their thoughts and actions. Malmi & Brown (2008) presents three aspects of cultural controls; clans, values and symbols. The clan control consists of distinct subcultures within an organization, often based on professions with specific education, ceremonies, and rituals. Both nurses and medical doctors are typical examples of clans. The values control consists of mission or vision statement, credos and statements of purpose which convey values that senior manager expect subordinates to adopt.

Cybernetic controls are defined by Malmi & Brown (2008) as a process including a feedback loop where actual performance measures are compared with standards. In the MCP four basic cybernetic systems are: budgets, financial measures, non-financial measures, and hybrids (e.g., The balanced scorecard). In this study, we focus on financial measures and non-financial measures in the form of Key Performance Indicators (KPIs). Administrative controls aims at directing behavior through the organization of groups and individuals, and by specifying how tasks should be performed. Governance structure, organization structure, policies and procedures are examples of administrative controls. According to Malmi & Brown "governance" is the formal lines of accountability both vertically and horizontally, meetings and meeting agendas are typical governance examples. Organization structures specify contacts, and relationships between groups, typical examples are functional specializations, or process oriented structures. Policies and procedures may be bureaucratic and formal documents, but also more informal practices and codes of behavior.

If we compare the two cases, it is obvious that they share the same cultural control, they are both affected by the clans of nurses and medical doctors. However, we found that hospital managers could be described as a category of clans as they represent a third distinct sub-culture based on their professions and education, but also on their "ceremonies and rituals" of improvement programs, like Lean or Kaizen. In addition, Kameda used the values controls, the catchphrase of the board chairman "Do & Think", to change the mind of the medical staff at the stage of the introducing ISO 9001. This values control also facilitated the introduction of the continuous process improvement. Moreover, it seems that Kameda used this values control to weaken the effect of the clan controls on the thoughts and behavior of the professions, so that they obtained the cooperation in the process improvement among them. Also Lund worked with cooperation in their process improvement, called "Go to Gemba", inspired from Toyota (Ohno & Bodek, 1988).

In the first part of Cybernetic control, Kameda used the individual revenue of each medical doctor and P/L statement for each department to evaluate the outcomes from process improvements for the PDCA cycle. The Lund case illustrated the financial measurement system as Cybernetic control, that TD-ABC used as a Lean accounting system could reveal profitability, or as in the case unprofitability, of the EBUS lean process. However, to solve this unprofitability remains to be unsolved in both cases. If we move to the non-financial measurement system part, we could see that the same two KPIs were used. Shorter waiting time for patients is an important KPI in most Lean and continuous improvement projects, as waiting time is an obvious waste that needs to be reduced in all businesses, but especially in medical services. More efficient treatment of cancer is a global challenge for hospitals and researchers, but as leading University hospitals both Kameda and Lund take an extra interest. The efficiency of cancer treatment is dependent on the time from diagnosis to treatment which links this KPI to the KPI for shorter queues and waiting time, they should be regarded as a duality.

For the Administrative controls, we noted that both Kameda and Lund had introduced new improved medical processes as an important part of their Governance structure. Process maps and patient flows seem to be the keys to the hospitals improvement programs. Another key to improvements are a decentralized Organization structure in combination with profit centers. Both cases show that a decentralized structure, whereby every employed nurse and doctor is empowered to take on the responsibility of improving the daily situations in the different wards, is essential for the success of the Lean ideas. This brings us to the last part of the Administrative controls; Policies and Procedures. In the Malmi & Brown MCP Policies and procedures is presented in the down, right corner as the last part of the package. However, in the Kameda and Lund cases, we can just as easy put policies and procedures as a starting point. In Kameda, standardized medical process, rules, and proceedings in the committee were all documented and uploaded to the Electronic Medical Record (EMR) system so that every staff in the hospital could share the information. This documentation made it clear how to treat a patient in any situation and it decrease the medical incidents. It is clear from both cases that the Lean ideas, although expressed differently, is the cornerstone to provide continuous improved quality of their medical services without using more resources. In the Kameda case, we could follow the Kaizen and ISO 9001 certification process and how that gave the hospital continuous process improvement and standardized patient flows at the same time. In the Lund case we could see the same continuous process improvement and standardized patient flows, but based on the Lean and Lean accounting ideas. Lean projects seem to have many faces, and they have different names, but they share the power of Policies and procedures and they give the same results.

4. Concluding Discussions

When we studied the MCP for process innovation in the two hospital cases, it was clear that they have adopted many of the Lean principles from Toyota (Monden, 1992) and that one of their priorities was to eliminate wastes in their value chain (Kollberg *et al.* 2007). Both Kameda and Lund worked hard with new and improved medical processes to shorten lead times and to even out variations in the flow (Spear, 2005), and they had done this for many years together with their employees in continued improvement, or kaizen, projects. In both hospitals motivation among employees was important as motivated and satisfied employees were seen as cornerstones in providing a better quality and more efficient treatment of cancer. In Lean health care the demands for quality in personnel and patient processes are combined (Kollberg *et al.* 2007).

Table 2.   Case comparison.

		Kameda	Lund
Cultural Controls	Clans	Nurses, medical doctors, hospital managers	Nurses, medical doctors, hospital managers
	Values	"Do & Think"	"Go to Gemba"
Cybernetic Controls	Financial measurement systems	Individual Profit & Loss statements	TD-ABC as Lean accounting
	Non-financial measurement systems	2 KPIs; — Shorter waiting time for patients — More efficient treatment of cancer EMR	2 KPIs; — Shorter waiting time for patients — More efficient treatment of cancer
Administrative Controls	Governance structure	New, improved medical processes	New, improved medical processes
	Organization structure	Decentralized, Profit Centers	Decentralized, Profit Centers
	Policies and procedures	Kaizen (Lean) Documentation (ISO 9001)	Lean Lean accounting (TD-ABC)

In both cases we could see that MCS was prioritized as *"Managers influenced other members of the organization to implement the organization's strategies"* (Anthony & Govindarajan, 2007, p. 6) and that the idea of MCS as a package (Malmi & Brown, 2008) could be a basis for comparisons and understanding of the cases. In the study, we only used three parts of the MCP; cultural controls, cybernetics controls, and administrative controls, but it is evident from Table 2 that these three parts were suitable for the comparison. Of the seven items in Table 2 we found that four were identical between the two cases; they both had three types of Clans (nurses, medical doctors, and hospital managers), the Non-financial measurement systems showed the same two KPIs (shorter waiting time for patients and more efficient treatment of cancer), the Governance structure were the same (improved medical processes), and the organization structures corresponded (decentralized profit centers). The remaining three items were also similar. The Values were both versions of Lean mottos; "Do & Think" at Kameda and "Go to Gemba" at Lund. The Financial measurement system at Kameda was built on the individual revenue of each medical doctor, and divisional profit & loss statements, and at Lund it was TD-ABC as Lean accounting. Of course, the techniques are different, as we could see in the cases, but we also noted a similarity in the form of outcome as "profit or loss" after the costs for all activities in the department were deducted from the DPC-based revenues. In the last item in the MCP, Policies, and procedures, it is clear that different versions of Lean is at the base, but that Kameda favored Kaizen and ISO 9001 where Lund used TD-ABC and Lean accounting. In addition, it seems that there may be some complementary relationships among MCS, which means that the use of one management control factor increases the benefits of another one as a system (Grabner & Moers, 2013).

However, even though the MCP could explain how the two cases worked with Lean and process innovation, many problems remain to be solved when a hospital wants to break through the barriers that Porter, Mintzberg, and Kaplan discussed. In both cases we could see that change is hard to get (Machiavelli, 1513) and that the pace of organizational process changes and MCS changes is a delicate matter (Rowe *et al.* 2008). In the Lund case we could see that the lean patient process and the TD-ABC prototype could not be implemented on a larger scale because of problems with change management. To change well established MCS models will take a long time. It will require slow and continuous changes, as Rowe *et al.* (2008) claimed, which is also in line with Lean principles. In the slow process people at LUH will have the opportunity to get used to the "hardened" TD-ABC model, which Rowe *et al.* (2012) found essential. In the Kameda case we could see similar problems with the divisional profit centers and their cost allocation. In both Kameda and Lund the problems with "unprofitable" medical care was evident.

As a summary from the two case studies, we could see that some parts of the ideas to solve the cost crisis in health care from Porter (2009, 2010), Mintzberg (2011, 2012) and Kaplan & Porter (2011) could be implemented. In both Kameda and Lund we could see cooperative managing styles where nurses and medical doctors were taking great interest in projects for continued improvement, Kaizen and Lean. Both hospitals had worked for many years with new improved medical processes in value streams. We could also see that all costs in the lean hospital flows could be based on the patient care process, and that a DPC reimbursement model was used. However, we also noted that the processes were unprofitable as the total costs exceeded the DPC based reimbursement. The suggested solution to this problem, from Mintzberg, Porter, and Kaplan, was to use value based reimbursements which could not be tested as such systems did not exist in Japan or Sweden. We may conclude that more research is needed to help Japanese and Swedish hospitals to provide high quality medical services at lower cost in order to balance their books.

References

Anthony, R. N. & Govindarajan, V. (2007). *Management Control Systems*. Boston: McGraw-Hill.

Argyris, C., Putnam, R., & McLain-Smith, D. (1985). *Action Science: Concepts, Methods, and Skills For Research and Intervention*. San Francisco: Jossey-Bass Inc.

Burns, J. & Scapens, R.W. (2000). Conceptualizing Management Accounting Change: An Institutional Framework, *Management Accounting Research*, 11, pp. 3–25.

Demeere, N., Stouthuysen, K., & Roodhooft, F. (2009). Time-Driven Activity-based Costing in an Outpatient Clinic Environment: Development, Relevance and Managerial Impact, *Health Policy*, 92(2/3), pp. 296–304.

Grabner, I. & Moers, F. (2013). Management Control as a System Or a Package? Conceptual and Empirical Issues. *Accounting, Organizations and Society*, 38(6–7), pp. 407–419.

Granlund, M. (2001). Towards Explaining Stability in and Around Management Accounting Systems, *Management Accounting Research*, 12, pp. 141–166.

Internal material from Kameda and Lund University Hospitals.

Kaplan, R. S. (1993). Research Opportunities in Management Accounting, *JMAR*, 5(Fall), pp. 1–14.

Kaplan, R. S. (1998). Innovation Action Research: Creating New Management Theory and Practice, *JMAR*, 10, pp. 89–118.

Kaplan, R. S. & Anderson, S. R. (2007). *Time-Driven Activity Based Costing*. Boston: Harvard Business School Press.

Kaplan, R. S. & Porter, M. E. (2011). How to Solve the Cost Crisis in Health Care, *Harvard Business Review*, September, 89(9), pp. 47–64.

Kock, N. (2004). The Three Threats of Action Research: A Discussion of Methodological Antidotes in the Context of Information Systems Study, *Decision Support Systems*, 37, pp. 265–286.

Kollberg, B., Dahlgaard, J., & Brehmer, P. O. (2007). Measuring Lean Initiatives in Health Care Services: Issues and Findings, *International Journal of Productivity and Performance Management*, 56, pp. 7–24.

Lukka, K. (2006). Management Accounting Change and Stability: Loosely Coupled Rules and Routines in Action, *Management Accounting Research*, 18(1), pp. 76–101.

Machiavelli, N. (1513). *The Prince* (II Principe). Florence Antonio Blado d'Asola.

Maskell, B., Baggaley, B., & Grasso, L. (2011). *Practical Lean Accounting: A Proven System for Measuring and Managing the Lean Enterprise*, Portland: Productivity Press.

McNair in Stenzel, J., (eds.), (2007). *Lean Accounting — Best Practices for Sustainable Integration*. Hoboken: Wiley.

McNiff, J. (2013). *Action Research: Theory and Practice* (3rd edn.). London: Routledge.

Mintzberg, H. (2011). Managing the Myths of Health Care (extract). To appear in *Harvard Business Review*.

Mintzberg, H. (2012). Managing the Myths of Health Care, *World Hospitals and Health Services*, 48(3), pp. 4–7.

Modig, N. & Åström, P. (2011). *Detta är Lean: Lösningen på Effektivitesparadoxen*. Stockholm: Stockholm School of Economics.

Monden, Y. (1992). *Cost Management in the New Manufacturing Age: Innovations in the Japanese Automotive Industry*. Portland: Productivity Press.

Ohno, T. (1988). *The Toyota Production System: Beyond Large Scale Production*. Portland: Productivity Press.

Porter, M. E. (2009). A Strategy for Health Care Reform — Toward a Value-based System, *The New England Journal of Medicine*, 361(2), pp. 109–112.

Porter, M. E. (2010). What is Value in Health Care? *The New England Journal of Medicine*, December, 363, pp. 2477–2481.

Romney, M. B. & Steinbart, P. J. (2014). *Accounting Information Systems*. Boston: Pearson.

Rowe, C., Birnberg, J. G., & Shields, M. D. (2008). Effects of Organizational Process Change on Responsibility Accounting and Manager's Revelations of Private Knowledge, *Accounting, Organizations and Society*, 33, pp. 164–198.

Rowe, C., Shields, M. D., & Birnberg, J. G. (2012). Hardening Soft Accounting Information: Games for Planning, Organizational Change, *Accounting, Organizations and Society*, 37, pp. 260–279.

Spear, S. J. (2005). Fixing Health Care From the Inside, Today, *Harvard Business Review*, 83(8), pp. 78–91.

Stenzel, J. (eds.), (2007). *Lean Accounting — Best Practices for Sustainable Integration*. Hoboken: Wiley.

Tanis, V. & Özyapici, H. (2012). The Measurement and Management of Unused Capacity in a Time Driven Activity Based Costing System, *Journal of Applied Management Accounting Research*, 10, pp. 43–45.

Vogl, M. (2013). Improving Patient-level Costing in the English and the German "DRG" System, *Health Policy*, 109(3), pp. 280–300.

Yin, R. K. (2003). *Case Study Research: Design and Methods* (3rd edn.). London: Sage Publications.

9

Management Control for Horizontal Network Organizations of SMEs — In the View Point of Profit Allocation Mechanism of Joint Manufacturing on Order

Yoko Ogushi

Niigata University

1. Introduction

In the industrial integrated region, small and medium-sized companies (SMEs) are collaborating closely due to geographical proximity, which reduces the cost of reliability, information cost, and coordination cost because most transaction costs are absorbed in the communication cost in the region. A lowness of division-of-labor coordination cost facilitates acquiring information on other enterprises, arranging the division of labor, and the collaboration among the companies. Moreover, there are many expertise companies surviving in their specialized field in the region, though the expertise companies cover only a few business processes. It means there is a climate that encourages newcomers. Of course, newcomers have to seek ways to differentiate themselves. As a result, it has been possible to combine business processes in response to a request for product with competitiveness of quality, delivery, and price (see Fig. 1) (Ogushi, 2005, p. 27).

In other words, industrial agglomerations have kept the advantage for long periods. However, in recent years, the regions lost their advantage of cost and/or speed of making product because many SMEs discontinue or move to the overseas with big companies. In other words, the geographical accumulations of SMEs have begun to collapse. At the same time their advantage of transaction cost based on the geographical proximity has disappeared. Accordingly, efficient and prompt management which is achieved as the virtual business group by sharing the information among

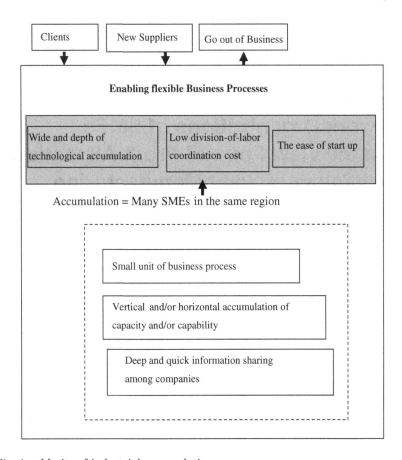

Fig. 1.   Merits of industrial accumulation.

the respective different business entities have almost disappeared. In the same way, the concept of management control needs to extend for a sub-contractors and/or inter organizational control (Otlay, 1994; Mouristsen, 1999; Mouristsen, Hansen & Hansen, 2001).

Utilization of IT can be the countermeasure against this situation. IT breaks geographical limitation of "integration", if it is possible to build a new network out of their place. To obtain the efficiency of cooperation among enterprises is the most important issue for SMEs because they cannot survive without cooperative business processes with cheap cost. As Davenport mentions that the cooperation with many companies, as such has been achieved in the industrial agglomeration area to enable low-cost, and support their business (Davenport, 2000, p. 268).

In this chapter, first, I will describe the definition of the network organization and its features. Then, I will overview the previous researches of the management and the operations of it from the point of view of inter-organizational management control (MC). Then, by using the case analysis with interviews, I will make a classification in three types of purposes in each joint orders network organization. It helps us to understand which kind of information is shared among organizations and how MC is done, and the role of IT.

2. The Definition of the Network Organization and its Features

2.1. *Definition of network organization*

This chapter adopts the following two elements as a definition of network organization.

- It means a particular group of corporations, where each member has a purpose but gather and share resources in order to achieve a same objective (Castells, 2000, p. 187).
- It is the networks of plural companies joined together, and it acts like a single company with the constitution companies' cooperation (Monden, 2009, p. 21).

2.2. *Five features of the network organization*

Network organization as earlier defined has the following five features:

- The network possesses the property of the horizontal organization because it is relatively flexible.
- Management among organizations is necessary in the network because plural organizations with an individual purpose participate.
- An incentive to raise the commitment of participant companies is necessary to bring about synergy effect.
- Mechanism to distribute synergy effect fairly is necessary.
- Because a coordinator plays an important role, his/her position and the authority in the organization influence the administration of the network.

As a flexible network organization of SMEs have the nature of horizontal organization, we overview MC of the horizontal organization in the next section.

3. The Previous Studies on Management Control of the Horizontal Organization

Mouritsen *et al.* (2006) focus on MC of the horizontal organizations network analyzed for three cases. At first, they insist that it is important to raise each other's reliability for the maintenance of the network and the effectiveness. In addition, when the company in the network uses the assets of the other member company, it is important to set a transfer price, or carry out a "fee" explicitly. They insist that it leads self-regulation for stability and maintenance of the networks. In other words, in addition to the relationship and trust among members, those networks require a fair mechanism for the distribution of income.

There are also same kinds of mechanisms in joint orders organizations which we will discuss in this chapter. On the other hand, the order coordination among participants may run into difficulties because an interest is opposed with following four points:

- Distribution of the quantity of order;
- Coordination among plural processes;
- How and who guarantees quality, delivery, and cost (QDC);
- Quality and the equitableness of the coordinator.

The distribution of the quantity of order is connected directly with the profit distribution to get among member companies. Such as Monden (2009) argued. Thus, in the network formed by loose cooperation, it becomes particularly vital to carry out "profit distribution" fairly. For the smooth operation of joint orders organization, it will enable them to maintain the incentive for participants in network. Furthermore, in order to continue the development of the network and its smooth implementation, it is important to enhance satisfaction among members by appropriate MC. As Tomkins (2001) mentions, trust is key to success for alliances and networks. However, there is not much of previous research focusing on these points.

Therefore, in this chapter, in order to obtain the basic knowledge about the MC of the horizontal inter-organizations, I did interview researchers. Next section shows what kind of information is shared with the network participants and how MC has been done in the analysis based on the interviews.

4.   Three Purposes to Participate in the Network

As current business environment changes rapidly, the formation of the horizontal network is one of the promising alternatives to adapt to. This is because it will help to respond to customer needs quickly and flexibly, which are not realized by one company without investment. Figure 2 shows three types of purposes for making network to SMEs. The purpose of A is to increase the quantity of the product. The purpose of B is to increase the extended process to be managed. The purpose of C is aimed to put together the merit of A and B.

The well-coordinated network which is able to take plural processes on cheaply and quickly is also attractive for the client companies. In order to accomplish the objective, some make voluntary organizations by member companies, the others obtain a legal entity required to contract.

In many cases, the network begins as an unincorporated association (voluntary organization). When the orders increase and/or the business processes to coordinate become complicated, the network attending companies unite as a corporation and tend to share much information quickly by introducing IT. In addition, some divide it for small business processes again and spin out such as Japan Aero Space Part Association (JASPA) and Kyoto Shisaku Net (Kyoto Trial Product).

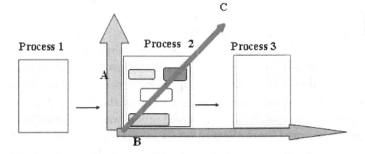

1. Increase in quantity ⇒A

2. Increase in processes to be able to take⇒B

3. A and B plus innovation⇒C

Fig. 2.   Purpose of the formation of the order network.

4.1.   *Migaki-ya (polishing) Syndicate: Type A* (Fig. 2)

(Interview period and Interviewees: January 2007 and June and July 2006, Mr. Masaya Takano who works for Tubame Chamber of Commerce and Industry.)

4.1.1.   *Background and overview*

Migaki-ya Syndicate is an organization of polishing craftsman in Tsubame City, Niigata Prefecture in Japan. Tsubame City is a well-known for premium western tableware such as spoons and kitchenware which are polished to a bright shine. Polishing craftsman used to be a star occupation and was told that they could build a house for three years work in 1980s. At that time, there were SMEs which had many suppliers and customers and served as a nodal point for transaction patterns in the region.

Gradually, the amount of order was reduced to half because many of the demand loading companies in this region were transferred to Asian countries for cheap labor costs. Indeed, the number of the SMEs was about 1,000 and their sales amount was 949,600 million yen in 2000. It was reduced to half with sales amounting to 418,600 million yen and the number of SMEs became fewer than 600 in 2004. In such a circumstance, abrasion suppliers in this region obtained work of mirror surface polishing in large quantities of iPod second generation of Apple Co. Inc., or personal computers of Panasonic. The mass ordering from such domestic and foreign world-famous major home-appliance makers was regarded as an evidence to guarantee height of the quality of the abrasion suppliers. However, it was difficult to continue handling orders in large quantities on short delivery date — the later most of polishing work was allocated to the companies in China.

Craftsmen formed the group called "the Migaki-ya Syndicate (the polishing shop Syndicate)" led by the Tsubame City Chamber of Commerce in January 2003 and started the reclamation of new business fields and new customers that could keep increasing the quantity of order and they could apply their skill for new materials. At the startup of the group, the number of lead manager companies who organized orders was 5, the number of member companies was 15 and the number of supporting members was 2. These lead managers had 3–5 cooperation companies in affiliation. At first, the Syndicate was aimed at increasing orders by appealing marketing their techniques and for securing quantity of orders by utilizing their cooperation in the accumulation area. After the activity of the Syndicate began to get on track, they made use of their techniques for medical care products such as artificial bone, which was an uncultivated field for them. Recently, they have started handling expensive final products for advertising their technical effectiveness and appealing their techniques.

Migaki-ya Syndicate itself is a voluntary organization with no corporate status and performs public relations activities through a website run by the Tsubame City Chamber of Commerce. Managing companies which decide to take an order would bear the legal responsibility for the contract and guarantee of QDC.

4.1.2.   Orders allocation mechanism

Migaki-ya Syndicate has a double network structure in the network. As mentioned earlier, there are five lead manager companies in the network and each lead manager companies has their own co-operation companies like *Keiretsu*. Cooperation companies only work with their lead manager companies. When a request of the work comes through the Tsubame City Chamber of Commerce, an order is distributed, as follows.

Information of order flows to each managing company from the City Chamber. The information is shared, at almost the same time, with the all managing companies. If plural companies hope for an order, there are three procedures for deciding who takes it; first: preliminary talks, second: choice of the ordering company, if the ordering companies do not choose the managing companies, third: bidding. To avoid acute competition among peers, managing companies determine award volume of each. When the amount of orders is quite a lot for one managing company, they share the work and cooperate to guarantee QDC. In case there are not enough workload for applicants, it will carry out a bid., the condition of the order that a managing company gets is almost a market-based order condition. But it is not completely like open market competition because it is a bid by the closed network's participants. From the view point of keeping the network, the participants prefer "talk" to auction in market-base.

On the other hand, as corporation companies are small family-run sized and relies on overall orders from the managing company, so, the managing company is controlling the allocation of orders amounting to them.

4.1.3.   MC in the network

Although there is a competitive environment for lead manager companies as described previously, MC in the networks is MC of the price-base, not that of quantity of order base. On the other hand, the lead manager company has detailed information such as cost, capacity, facilities, quality, and financial information which are related to transaction. Because such information has been accumulated in the close geographical proximity. In addition to long-term relations, its acquisition cost is low, but the precision is quite high. For quality control, each group arranges the opportunity to teach techniques regularly.

Lead managing companies know the business circumstances of each cooperation company. Thus, they try to distribute quantity of order without dissatisfying the members. Naturally the reliability to the network of the constitution company is very high and there is less need to maintain traditional long-term, stable business relations. As a consequence ability and capability such as cost, the level of technology, facilities, and the work load of the cooperation company are shared with a lead manager company. In other words, the MC of profit distribution through the quantity of order distribution is strongly exercised for cooperation companies by the lead manager company.

4.1.4.   *Utilization of IT*

For orders, website of the Tsubame Chamber of Commerce and Industry has played a major role. Although, the web is a powerful tool for introduction and appeal to the network, there is nowhere to know the information for the visualization of the process to perform business process management (BPM) smoothly and grasp the backlogs. Only the lead manager companies know it by the traditional way like visiting or calling cooperation companies frequently.

In the network, there are few roles that IT serves, such as, interstitial information cooperation. Though introduction of IT is necessary as polish companies in other areas join in members of the network, it has not come yet to utilize.

4.2.   *Kyoto Shisaku (prototype production) Net (network): Type B* (Fig. 2)

(Interview period and Interviewees: November 2009 for Mr. Shosaku Yamamoto who was a representative in the network at that time and Ichiro Suzuki who is the previous representative from 2001 to 2007.)

4.2.1.   Background and overview

Kyoto Shisaku Net was formed by the members of Kyoto machinery metal SMEs' youth section. There were 10 member companies at first (as of October 2009, 17 companies have participated in the network), and all the management layer of the 10 companies have participated in a study meeting of Peter F. Drucker, conducted for more than 10 years. All new member companies also have to study his management philosophy before joining the net, to share sense of value on the Net business.

Because major makers of electric apparatus, optical goods, and medical equipment exist in Kyoto-city, the work from trial manufacture to mass production is abundant, and the level of the technical accumulation is high. However, major production companies have kept shifting their manufacturing factories to China or to other countries in which production expense is low. Thus, Kyoto trial manufacture net was formed from a sense of impending crisis to new demand reclamation. They built the Net which was capable of getting an answer within two hours for a purchaser having a difficulty of finding the proper expert for prototype. This unique concept of the Net became so famous that the sales were tens of millions of yen in 2001, which expanded to 250 million yen in 2005. Kyoto Shisaku Net in itself is an arbitrary group without juridical organization, and a lead managing company takes a contract as a juridical organization.

4.2.2.   Orders allocation mechanism

At first, from single order entry point, information is delivered to a member coordinator that keeps rotating every week. The coordinator delivers the information by emails about inquiry contents to all member companies at once, and puts communication to the company regarded as an expert on the case. As every company has different expertise, the principle of market mechanisms does not work yet. The reason why there are many orders even if a competition principle does not act is for the value that a customer demands speed and certainty than cost when manufacturing a prototype is quite difficult. Some need cooperation with multiple companies to make a prototype. In that case, one lead managing company is chosen and the company succeeds all procedures from an original coordinator. The succeeded company requests the member firms or its suppliers for an estimate in order to manufacture a prototype and respond to the ordering company within two hours.[1]

4.2.3. *Management control in the network*

Because a product is specialized in prototype, each company does not share each other's cost and capacity. But facilities, quality, financial information, and the transactional details in the net are shared among members, like Migaki-ya Syndicate we see in sub-Sec. 4.1.3. As such information has been accumulated in the close geographical proximity in addition to long-term relations, its acquisition cost is low, but the precision is quite high. For quality control, each group arranges the opportunity to teach techniques routinely. Implementation of contract is taken by a lead managing company in each contract. At the same time, the member companies have regular meetings for discussion, study, and understanding of each other deeply in order to keep a quality control of the network. Furthermore, they are a tireless promoter of sharing information of customers and sales and marketing force among members. The force performs a study session about the new facilities and technique of members.

As a lead managing company shifts in terms of customer needs in every order, no particular objectives become the organizer. In addition, they do not need to share cost and capacity information of member firms because prototype manufacturing is their main product. Indeed, their clients normally make a priority speed to cost. The prototype order through the Network usually needs the challenge of elemental technology. It is surely a difficult job, but also challenging assignment for members to accomplish together as a team. This will enable the Net participants to keep their motivation to be a member in addition to increase in order.[2]

---

[1]Because area of specialty is so different, the members have almost no competition. Even if they compete, a coordinator arbitrage the trade. There is no complaint among members even in that case because they know each other's skill and specialty.

[2]There is a company who has no job from the net. The reason why the company has been a member of the net is that he owes much inspiration to members' passion for the work and new skills.

4.2.4. *Utilization of IT*

The members use commercially available software and manage all meeting schedules. Most orders and inquiries are accepted on their website. Additionally they share clients' data and transaction information through the internet. However, design information from a client belongs to only an organizer, which is regarded as a trade secret in the viewpoint of the clients. Moreover, they do not have information sharing systems which enables to watch progress situation of business process in each company through IT or website. This information is still shared by telephone, facsimile, and human communication of sales force.

4.3. *NC Network: Type C* (Fig. 2)

(Interview time and interviewees: November and September 2009, Mr. Yasuo Uchihara, who is a president of the Network.)

4.3.1. *Background and overview*

NC network launched to have a joint order site on the Internet by nine manufacturers of mold-related at Katsushika area, Tokyo. At first, they built up Intranet and exchanged Computer Aided Design (CAD) data to derive competitive advantage from speed. However, small linkage of SMEs had only small scale merit. Gradually they tried to make a valued network involving a lot of manufacturing SMEs.

For this purpose, it had to be able to take on a series of jobs from design of a die to manufacturing. In addition, they would like to provide an environment which was capable of easily selecting a proper bidder of an expert from a plural number of the bidders of the experts for a purchaser having difficulty of finding the proper bidder of the expert. Because it was clear that just finding system of an expert manufacture was easy to imitate their competitors, their system had to have some features.

In 1997, the network reopened their membership to all SMEs in Japan and enabled them to find experts in order to complete their valued business process through the websites.

NC Network has membership system and their member companies can obtain information in three level. The first level: members who are free of charge can just register their information on the net. The second level: members who pay 3,240 yen per month can obtain order and ordering party's information through the site, then, contact the company directly. The third level: members who pay 54,000 yen per month can put their packaging movie on the site and ask coordination of their business processes for the net directly in addition to doing it by themselves. Contracts of all business do not belong to the net, though it is a partial exception.[3]

4.3.2. Orders allocation mechanism

This mechanism comes from the closed membership network but many companies join it.[4] Thus, the network seems to provide a competing market environment for member companies. Most order information is put in the websites of NC Network and companies who belong to the second or third level can browse and contact ordering company. Companies who belong to the third level only can ask for NC Network to find a suitable company for order complement and/or coordinate business processes through NC Network's own department of manufacturing.

4.3.3. Management control in the network

For member companies, there are no sharing systems on capacity, capability, and financial information. It can share information on equipment, evaluation from past transaction, deficit balance, names of major clients, and techniques though searching the browser. Most information has been put into the database by member companies themselves, thus, there is a wide range of variation in degree of accuracy even if cost of information is cheap. Basically it works on market mechanism. In other word, there is no MC inter-organization and no trusted partnership with member firms.

On the other hand, NC Network itself has plenty of precise information on member firms because of video recording for PR and building database for them as a routine part of the Network's job. In the end, NC Network accomplishes precise and detailed information which helps making efficient business process and excising transaction. It is very much useful for NC Network to coordinate business processes inexpensively but efficiently.

---

[3]NC Network also becomes a coordinator when their clients ask for them. As they are a stock corporation, they make a contract in that case.

[4]The number of the companies at first level was about more than 16,000, at the second level was about 3,500, and at third level was about 200.

Of course, NC Network needs to keep their first role to keep the network, it just takes order only when clients directly consult the Network.

4.3.4.   *Utilization of IT*

As I described earlier, participating companies can obtain information about participants in three levels via the Internet. NC Network provides a service of matchmaking for SMEs in business field through website. On the other hand, there are no information sharing systems which enables to watch progress situation of business process in each company through IT or website.

4.4.   *Analysis of management control in three type joint-orders organizations*

For Migaki-ya Syndicate, their mission of organization is to increase a volume of order. As members' element technology is quite simple, the mechanism of MC drives from a distribution of amount of order. Although they have a bid system, most orders distribute by fair negotiations among lead managing companies. For participants, to keep the joint orders network is above everything else. It can be said that there is in-direct MC via coordination price.

On the other hand, a lead managing company distributes orders among his group companies by quantity according to his discretion. Of course, there is also some fairness for group members for this distribution. But it clearly works as direct MC by the lead managing company.

Kyoto Shisaku Net has a different order allocation system. Their first mission is to extend members' capability through the Net. It is clear if members can get orders or not, drive from element technologies required clients. Moreover, their clients are less concerned with price and put emphasis on quick delivery and/or technological excellence for making prototypes. Furthermore, a lead managing company is also chosen if he has key technologies or devices for clients. Thus, they have much incentive to extend their own capability with less MC.

In the case of NC Network, it seems like there are no MC among members, as already described. It is a membership organization by paying fee for NC Network and the network plays a role on spot transaction, like auction. Thus, price is a trigger to accept orders. The only difference from auction is that there is plenty of information for member companies and order

Table 1. Features of distribution mechanism in joint order organizations.

		Migakiya Syndicate	Kyoto Shisaku Net	NC Network
Purpose		Capacity	Capability	Both
Order allocation mechanism in the network		Negotiation/ coordination	Element technology	Price
Order allocation mechanism in each group		Quantity	N.A.	N.A.
Shared information in network	Cost	○	×	×
	Capacity	○	△	×
	Facility	○	○	○
	Quality	○	○	○
	Financial climate	○	○	○
	Transaction	○	○	○
Information cost		Cheap	Cheap	Up to the level
Control of QCD	Lead managing company	Lead managing company	Lead managing company	
Use of IT		Order information through the website	Groupware and order information through the website	Database of detailed information on members and order information through the website
Trust in the network		Strong	Strong	Weak

information is available for members only. Especially as over the second and the third level companies share detailed information via video or plenty database on the web, it provides an opportunity to coordinate business partners precisely in addition to price. Moreover, ordering companies check capacity and capability of the candidates as a business partner. These three networks have the following features (see Table 1).

5. Conclusion

This chapter is classified into three types of purposes: joint order network organization and research, what kind of information were shared, and how developing inter-organizational MC systems work. In the case of Migaki-ya Syndicate and Kyoto Shisaku Net, all participants have priority to keep their own network, and allocation of order, in other words, allocation of profit based on convincing among members. Negotiation, coordination, and element technology convince members a mechanism of order allocation because they share enough of each other's information. When there is no consensus among members, coordinator acts as an umpire.

On the other hand, it seems like market based order allocation are implemented in NC Network. However, the market is not perfectly competitive. Order allocation system of NC Network is not only based on price. It is thought to be similar to that of divisional organizations having quasi market mechanism in an enterprise through intra-company transfer price. In the end, it can be argued that order allocation mechanism, in other words, profit allocation of network organizations in SMEs include in a broad sense of MC system.

References

Castells, M. (2000). *The Rise of the Network Society*. Oxford: Blackwell Publishing.

Dekker, H. C. (2008). Partner Selection and Governance Design in Inter-Firm Relationships, *Accounting, Organizations and Society*, 33, January, pp. 915–941.

Davenport, H. T. (2000). *Mission Critical: Realizing the Promise of Enterprise Systems*. Boston: Harvard Business School Press.

Monden, Y. (2009). *Profit Allocation Price for Inter-Firm Cooperation*. Tokyo: Zeimu-Keiri-Kyokai (in Japanese).

Mouritsen, J. (1999). Flexible Firm: Strategies for a Subcontractor's Management Control. *Accounting, Organizations and Society*, 24, pp. 31–55.

Mouritsen, J., Hansen, A., & Hansen, C.Ø. (2001). Inter-Organizational Controls and Organizational Competencies: Episodes Around Target Cost Management/Functional Analysis and Open Book Accounting, *Management Accounting Research*, 12(2), June, pp. 221–244.

Mouritsen, J., Thrane, A., & Thrane, S. (2006). Accounting, Network Complementarities and the Development of Inter-Organizational Relations, *Accounting, Organizations and Society*, 31, pp. 241–275.

Ogushi, Y. (2005). Activation and the Cluster Formation of the Industrial Accumulation Area, *The Operations Research Society of Japan*, 50(9), pp. 27–34 (in Japanese).

Tomkins, C. (2001). Interdependencies, Trust and Information in Relation-ships, Alliances and Networks, *Accounting, Organizations and Society*, 26, pp. 161–191.

van der Meer-Kooistra, J. & Scapens, R. W. (2008). The Governance of Lateral Relations Between and Within Organizations, *Management Accounting Research*, 19(4), December, pp. 365–384.

10

Measuring the Performance of Lean Implementation at a Commercial Printing Company — An Action Research Approach

Khodayar Sadeghi
Tarbiat Modares University

Mohammad Aghdasi
Tarbiat Modares University

1. Introduction

This article aims at introducing an assessment tool to investigate the performance of production in a commercial printing company. This graphical tool can help small and medium-sized enterprises (or SME) commercial print houses to measure and monitor the degree to which implementation of lean discipline is shown to be successful.

Printing industry, the field in which text and image are put together, is highly capital-intensive industry and one of the largest manufacturing industry in the world. This industry has a close relationship with other sectors of the economy including package industry, publishing industry, and advertising industry. As a result, by different type of print houses many print-products such as books, newspapers, magazines, ads, and packaging products are produced everyday all over the world.

According to Smithers Pira's market report on The Future of Print in the Middle East and North Africa to 2018, *"total printing revenues in the Middle East and North Africa (MENA) were $17.6 billion in 2012, and are forecast to grow 7.2% per annum reaching $26 billion by 2018"* (Smithers Pira, 2013). All this is while most of the printing firms are SMEs.

Printing market is mainly categorized based on the type of products such as commercial printing, packaging printing, and publication printing. Commercial printing sector, as the largest sector of the printing business, is responsible for producing paper advertisements and promotional print products such as directories, brochures, posters, and stationaries. This sector, usually produces low-volume, high-mix products based on make-to-order production strategy.

According to official reports, the Iranian printing industry includes more than 5,000 print houses which employ almost 40,000 people. Almost 70% of the printing houses are placed in Tehran, the capital of the country, and more than 2,600 of them do their businesses as commercial printers (based on an offline and official database which is belonging to the Prinitng Department in Ministry of Culture and Islamic Guidance, 2014).

However, printing industry of today, in general, and small and medium printing firms in particular, are facing obvious and ever-growing challenges due to increased competition and the changing environment, including:

(1) Increasing production cost because of increasing cost of labor, material, and energy.
(2) Decreasing commodity and product price imposed by the very competitive environment, many new entrants, and low cost of e-production as a new and very strong competitor of print production.
(3) Decreasing volume of production for most of the commercial print orders.
(4) Growing demand for high quality products from end users and print buyers.
(5) Diversification of products and services as much as possible.
(6) The high cost of ownership of printing machines which are very expensive and not affordable for most small printing firms.

So, for the present and even in the future, competition will be based on price, manufacturing cycle time (order-to-delivery time), quality, and diversity of products. In essence, the big issue we are facing in satisfying the above-mentioned needs and requirements of the customers or print buyers can be best described in this way: What should the printers do to survive in today's highly competitive environment?

Finding an answer to this question is very vital for many of the small and medium printing firms which can go bankrupt and eventually shut down.

To overcome the mentioned challenges and to satisfy the customers, printing firms should adopt the following strategies, to improve the performance of their production systems:

(1) Reducing service or production cycle time as much as possible.
(2) Utilizing the equipment as effectively as possible to get an early return on their investments as well as reducing total production cost.
(3) Reducing any type of waste which is in commercial printing mainly because of low-volume, high-mix, and make-to-order environment of this segment. Besides, lack of skilled labor and leading by traditional style of management are two other reasons for this problem in these type of printing companies.

The implementation of these strategies depends on the improvement of different business processes, which must be monitored and measured. By measuring the performance of production process in any step of the improvement project, the required picture about the situation is taken and decisions about the next steps are made.

Kaydos (1998), defines five major reasons for companies to measure performance:

(1) Improved control, since feedback is essential for any system.
(2) Clear responsibilities and objectives because good performance measures clarify who is responsible for specific results or problems.
(3) Strategic alignment of objectives because performance measures have proven to be a good means of communication for company's strategy throughout an organization.
(4) Understanding business processes since measuring data requires understanding of the manufacturing processes.
(5) Determining process capability because understanding a process also means knowing its capacity.

According to Nakajima (1989), total productive maintenance or TPM was first developed at Nippondenso (one of the automobile part supplier for Toyota) in Japan in 1969 with total employees' participation.

As stated by Ahuja & Khamba (2008), *"TPM is a production-driven improvement methodology that is designed to optimize equipment reliability and ensure efficient management of plant assets through the use of employee involvement, linking manufacturing, maintenance, and engineering."*

As defined by Nakajima (1989), overall equipment effectiveness (OEE) is an important part of this concept. OEE is originally used as a measure for evaluation of utilization effectiveness of manufacturing operation, but it can also be used as an indicator of performance within a manufacturing environment.

Comm & Mathaisel (2000) state that "Industries strive for leanness, because being lean means being competitive by eliminating the non-value-added practices", i.e., wastes. However, the strategy for a generic lean practice implementation, and achieving leanness throughout, lacks strong evidence and is not clear to many.

However, according to our experiences and research results based on implementation of lean production in a printing house conducted on action research (AR) basis, using OEE as a performance indicator is not appropriate for a low-volume, high-mix, make-to-order production environment such as commercial printing industry. This is mainly because OEE is originally developed and used for mass-production environment (de Ron & Rooda, 2006).

So in this chapter in order to clarify the importance and benefits of the implementation of lean discipline in SME commercial printing companies, especially through waste reduction based on an AR methodology, we propose overall equipment deficiency (OED) as a dedicated, simple, and graphical metric to investigate the deficiency of print production. The purpose of OED is trifold: it measures all hidden Type-2 waste in the pressroom (shop-floor) of the production environment, it is used for diagnostic purposes such as finding root causes of waste, and it is used to identify the hidden capacity of production that can be earned.

2. Review of Literature

The concept of lean thinking (Womack & Jones, 1996) originated from the Toyota production system (TPS) developed in 1950s Japan.

Monden (1981) conceptualized what Toyota did in TPS. He then for the first time introduced the concept of Just-in-time (JIT) production system to the United State (Monden, 1998). Monden (2012) explains how to promote the culture and way of thinking needed to settle the TPS across any organization.

For a long time, manufacturing has been trying to optimize operations, supply chains, and capital assets (Pagatheodrou, 2005); and for getting to this aim, elimination of waste has a main role. Recently, achieving this goal has become increasingly complex due to the fast moving global market, budget cuts, and capacity downsizing (Pagatheodrou, 2005). Hence, lean manufacturing has become the key approach to managing this complexity (Liker, 1997). The TPS, the pioneering approach to manufacturing leanness, has become the basis for much of the optimization movement that has dominated manufacturing developments since the last decade (Liker, 1997; Hall, 2004).

While automotive and aerospace industries were the first adopters of lean thinking, its application has spread into other industries (Womack & Jones, 1996).

Comm & Mathaisel (2000) state that "Industries strive for leanness, because being lean means being competitive by eliminating the non-value-added practices", i.e., wastes. However, having a clear idea about leanness in assessing the progress of any lean transformation project is very important. But strategy for a generic lean practice implementation, and achieving leanness throughout, lacks strong evidence and is not clear to many (Comm & Mathaisel, 2000; Chang, 2001).

Waste can be defined as: "Every activity that adds costs but non-value-added for the customer" (Chiarini, 2013).

According to QAD Inc. (2005), eliminating or reducing waste has numerous benefits such as:

(1) Shorter lead times;
(2) Higher throughput;
(3) Reduced costs;
(4) Improved quality;
(5) Better communications;
(6) More efficient collaboration;
(7) Tight integration of production and demand.

Regarding waste, many organizations use the Japanese term *"muda"*, although *muda* in Japanese has a much more restricted definition (Chiarini, 2013). *Muda* is an activity that consumes resources without creating value for the customer. There are two types of *muda*: Type-1 and Type-2 *muda* (Sayer & Williams, 2012):

(1) Type-1 *muda* includes actions that are non-value-added, but are for some other reason deemed necessary for the company. These forms of waste usually cannot be eliminated immediately.
(2) Type-2 *muda* are those activities that are non-value-added and are also not necessary for the company. These are the first targets for elimination.

TPM is a manufacturing program designed primarily to maximize equipment effectiveness throughout its entire life through the participation and motivation of the entire work force (Nakajima, 1989). Nakajima also developed OEE as a measure for assessing the progress of TPM, which is calculated by the multiplication of availability, performance, and quality (Jeong & Philips, 2001). Actually OEE is a key performance measure in mass-production environments (de Ron & Rooda, 2006).

The OEE tool is designed to identify losses that reduce the equipment effectiveness. These losses are activities that absorb resources but create no value. It is a bottom-up approach where an integrated workforce strives to achieve OEE by eliminating six large losses (Nakajima, 1989). According to Muchiri & Pintelon, 2008, in Fig. 1, the six large losses with some examples from a commercial printer are given as follows.

2.1. *Downtime losses*

(1) Breakdown losses are categorized as time losses and quantity losses caused by equipment failure or breakdown. For example, a breakdown of a sheet-fed offset machine.

(2) Set-up and adjustment losses occur when production is changing over from requirement of one item to another. In a commercial printer, this type of loss happens during changing of plates, when switching from one job to another, and fine tuning of inks for color.

2.2. *Speed losses*

(1) Idling and minor stoppage losses occur when production is interrupted by temporary malfunction or when a machine is idling. For example, when some contaminations is found on the printed paper.

(2) Reduced speed losses refer to the difference between equipment design speed, and actual operating speed. In a sheet-fed offset machine, the use of poor quality paper or very low weight paper leads to speed losses.

2.3. *Quality losses*

(1) Quality defects and rework are losses in quality caused by malfunctioning of production equipment. For example, when the printed sheets are not acceptable by the customer because of poor color quality.

(2) Reduced yield during start-up are yield losses that occur from machine start-up to stabilization. For example, in a commercial printer, some start-up paper sheets are wasted because of misregistration of colors.

According to Fig. 1, we can also calculate OEE as,

$$\text{OEE} = \frac{Valuable\ operating\ time}{Available\ production\ time}. \tag{1}$$

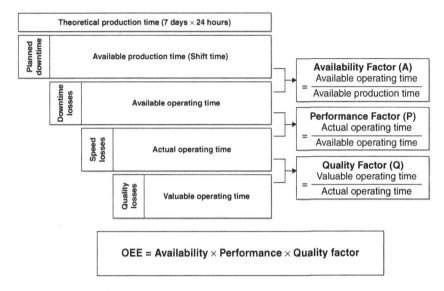

Fig. 1.   OEE measurement tool.

Source: Nakajima (1989).

Jeong & Philips (2001) stated that Eq. (1) can be used to roughly estimate OEE without collecting all six loss categories. Available production time is the total time available for production in a given period and valuable operating time can be estimated by multiplying the theoretical cycle time by the number of products that are successfully completed.

3.   Research Design

This chapter is based on lean transformation project implemented by the first author of this chapter, who used AR in an Iranian commercial printer for his doctoral study under supervision of the second author.

3.1.   *AR at a glance*

Kurt Lewin (1946) is often cited as the founder of AR (soon after World War II) as his research helped the practitioner to generate knowledge about a social system while, at the same time, attempting to change it (Elden & Chisholm, 1993).

AR defined in The Handbook of Action Research as *"a participatory, democratic process concerned with developing practical knowing in the pursuit of worthwhile human purposes, grounded in a participatory world-view which we believe is emerging at this historical moment. It seeks to bring together action and reflection, theory and practice, in participation with others, in the pursuit of practical solutions of pressing concern to people and more generally the flourishing of individual persons and their communities"* (Reason & Bradbury, 2006).

According to O'Brien (2001), in AR, the outside researcher's role is to implement the AR method in such a manner as to produce a mutually agreeable outcome for all participants, with the process being maintained by them afterwards. To accomplish this, it may necessitate the adoption of many different roles at various stages of the process, including: planner, leader, teacher, observer, reporter, designer, and facilitator.

Depending on the type of problem studied and the role of action researcher, there are different approaches to AR including: technical AR, practical AR, emancipatory AR, innovation AR, and participatory AR.

However, in our case we approached AR in participatory manner because of the active engagement of the researcher in helping the commercial printer for implementing the lean thinking in production area.

AR includes some action and research activities which must be repeated in a cyclic manner. According to Müller (2005), we used the special acts as shown in Fig. 2, in the AR cycle.

3.2. AR project in commercial printing company in Iran

This section of the chapter describes an AR study which leads to the development of an assessment tool for investigating the performance of production in a commercial printing company.

Author 1, as a University lecturer in printing field and also a printing industry expert and consultant, wanted to examine the effect of implementing lean production in commercial printing house.

Because in this research we got involved in an implementation project of lean production that was not done before in Iran printing industry, it was a good chance to make use of AR as proper methodology for the research.

As it is shown in Fig. 3, the lean transformation journey includes many phases such as phase 3, i.e., discovering waste, which is implemented through repeating the AR cycles for several times.

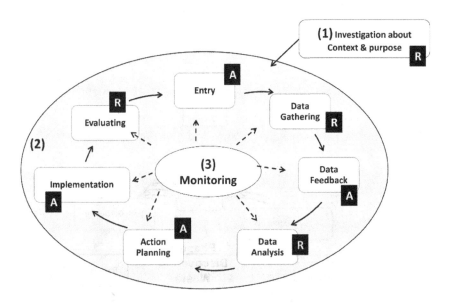

Fig. 2.   AR Cycle.

Source: Müller, M. (2005).

As an example, in Table 1, the activities that were done in the first iteration of the AR cycle of phase 3 are shown in detail.

4.   Proposing Dedicated Deficiency Measure for Commercial Printing

According to lean concepts we know that:

(1) There are two types of non-value-added activities, waste or *muda*[1] which are categorized as: Type-1 and Type-2 *muda*. Type-1 *muda* are actions that are non-value-added, but are for some other reason necessary for the production. Type-2 *muda* are those activities that are non-value-added and are also not necessary for the production.

(2) To move to the destination of lean transformation in production stage of any commercial printing house, we must eliminate Type-2 waste

---

[1]In this chapter we use waste (in narrow sense) instead of *muda*.

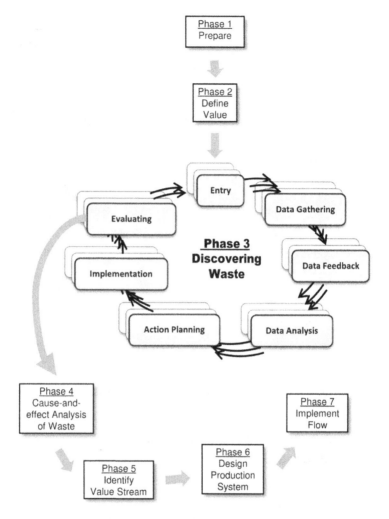

Fig. 3.   The relation between AR cycles and phase 3 of transformation to lean roadmap.

(*muda*) as much as possible, ideally to zero, and reduce Type-1 waste (*muda*) to the minimum level.

(3) For a printing machine, Type-1 waste is mainly because of set-up time and the major part of it is necessary and cannot be totally eliminated. So we can just reduce it to a specific amount (i.e., minimum amount) by some tools such as Single-Minute Exchange of Die (SMED) or standard

Table 1. The activities that were done in the first iteration of the AR cycle of phase 3.

Research step/ Nature of the step	Content of the step
Investigation/Research	1. Identifying the objective of passing this phase (i.e., phase 3) 2. Identifying the main technical terms related to the phase (e.g., waste, Type-1 *muda*, Type-2 *muda*, leanness, OEE, ...) 3. Identifying the type of information we need

Entry/Action	4. Defining research questions as:
	
	  1. investigating on the usefulness of OEE for performance measurement in commercial printing
	
	5. Selecting the method of data collection and feedback such as:
	
	  1. production information written by production operators
	  2. memo written by researcher
	  3. kaizen meeting records
	
	6. Identifying the role of any member of the project team

Data collection/Research	7. Gathering production information
Data feedback/Action	8. Deciding on the adequacy of the data being collected
Data analysis/Research	9. Calculating OEE by data being collected
Action planning/Action	10. Deciding on form and type of more data to be collected 11. Designing the new information form for collecting the production information
Implementation/Action	12. Monitoring and supervising the procedure of collecting data
Evaluation/Research	13. Evaluating the effectiveness/ineffectiveness for measuring of operation performance 14. Deciding on closing the cycle or start the next iteration

work. This minimum amount (Type-1 | min = min T_{setup}) is determined by experience or according to technological and operative restrictions. Therefore, we may conclude:

$$\text{Type-1|actual} = \text{Type-1|min} + \Delta\text{Type-1}. \qquad (2)$$

Since we assume that ΔType-1 is eliminable, it is not inherently necessary and we can take it as Type-2 waste. In other words, the amount of time spent on set-up process which is more than $\min T_{setup}$(= Type-1| min) is included in Type-2 waste by assumption.

(4) From here on wherever we say Type-1 waste or Type-1 *muda* we mean this mentioned minimum amount of Type-1.

(5) So the actual destination in our lean transformation journey, or actual target, is to eliminate total Type-2 *muda* while ignoring to eliminate or reduce Type-1 *muda* beyond the minimum level because it is actually impossible by definition (i.e., non-value-added but necessary).

(6) Afterward, in real situation when we talk about leanness on operating level, e.g., production of a printing machine in a work day, we mean the degree to which Type-2 waste is close to zero and Type-1 waste is close to the minimum level. This is shown in Fig. 4.

(7) From Fig. 4 it is obvious that OEE is a dependent variable and affecting by Type-1 waste, i.e., by decreasing or increasing of Type-1 waste, it changes.

Since Type-1 waste (in minimum level) is usually out of control, therefore its consideration in the process of measuring performance (by some tools such as OEE) prevents us from identification of the major problem i.e., Type-2 waste.

Based on the aforestated logic, while OEE usually is used for indicating how effective the production process is, it will be clear from the following example (see Table 2) that OEE is not appropriate for assessing the leanness of a low-volume, make-to-order production such as commercial printing. This is because in such a production environment, too much time is spend on changeover and set-up operations which result in too much Type-1 waste.

In Table 2, the production information of two days working of a printing machine has been compared to determine the uselessness of OEE in commercial printing industry.

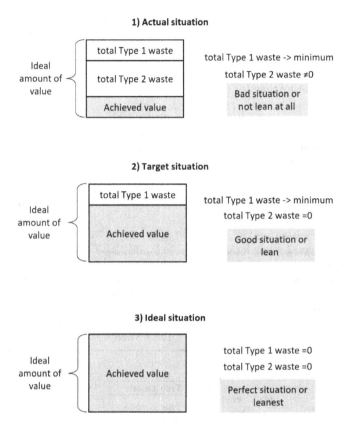

Fig. 4. Possible situations for degree of leanness of a printing machine in an arbitrary time period.

4.1. *Definition of Overall Equipment Deficiency (OED)*

As it is shown in Fig. 5, the new measure proposed as OED, is as follows:

$$\text{OED} = \frac{Type\text{-}2 \ waste}{V_{\text{ideal}}}. \tag{3}$$

This measure directly shows the amount of Type-2 waste and it is independent to Type-1 waste. So in make-to-order production environments as commercial printing industry, where a large number of orders being produced each day and consequently large number of Type-1 waste being recognized, it could be a good measure for justifying about the leanness of the production.

Table 2.   OEE comparison between two working days of a printing machine.

Day	1	2
Number of jobs (n)	1	21
Available operating time or T_{shift} (h)	8	8
Normal print speed or S (sheet per hour)	10,000 (sph)	10,000 (sph)
Minimum amount of T_{setup} for each job (min)	$15'$	$15'$
Actual T_{setup} for each job (min)	$50'$	$20'$
Total time spent for setup	$50'$	$20 \times 21 = 420'$
Other than set-up time waste/ Type-2 waste (min)	$40'$	0
Total Type-2 waste (min)	$40 + (50 - 15) = 75'$	$21 \times (20 - 15) = 105'$
Average of Type-2 waste for each job (min)	$75'$	$5'$
Valuable operating time (h)	$8 - 1.5 = 6.5 \,\mathrm{h}$	$1\,\mathrm{h}$
Total Value earned (number of printed sheets)	65,000 sheets	10,000 sheets
OEE (%)	$(65,000/80,000) \times 100 = 81.25\%$	$(10,000/80,000) \times 100 = 12.5\%$

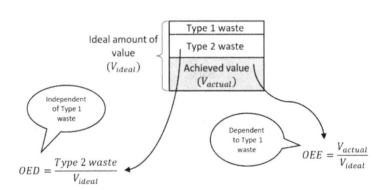

Fig. 5.   The comparison between OED and OEE.

According to Fig. 5, OED is defined as:

$$\text{OED} = \frac{\textit{Type-2 waste}}{V_{\text{ideal}}} = \frac{V_{\text{ideal}} - V_{\text{actual}} - \textit{Type-1 waste}}{V_{\text{ideal}}}, \qquad (4)$$

with:

$$V_{\text{ideal}} = T_{\text{shift}} \times S, \tag{5}$$

$$Type\text{-}1\ waste = nT_{\text{setup}}, \tag{6}$$

$$V_{\text{actual}} = N_T, \tag{7}$$

where:

S: normal printing speed of the machine (sheets per hour).
T_{shift}: standard shift time of the printing house (hours).
T_{setup}: the minimum required make-ready time for the printing machine before each job that is assumed constant and is identified by the experts according to its technological constraints.
n: the number of orders done by a printing machine in a shift time.
N_T: the total number of sheets printed by a printing machine and accepted by the customers during the shift time and through n orders.

Therefore, for a printing machine in each shift time we have:

$$\text{OED}(\%) = \left(1 - \frac{N_T/S}{T_{\text{shift}}} - \frac{nT_{\text{setup}}}{T_{\text{shift}}}\right) \times 100. \tag{8}$$

Example 1: When the minimum set-up time required to have successful press ok for any job is 15 min (T_{setup}), normal speed of printing equals to 11,000 sheets per hour (S), the total number of accepted sheets by the customers equals to 18,000 sheets (N_T), and 16 jobs done in one day (n), then for a 15 hours shift time (T_{shift}) we have:

$$\text{OED}(\%) = \left(1 - \frac{(18{,}000/11{,}000)}{15} - \frac{16 \times (15/60)}{15}\right) \times 100. \tag{9}$$

Then,

$$\text{OED}(\%) = 62.42\%. \tag{10}$$

Example 2: According to the information in the Table 2, for the assumed printing machine in those days we have:

For day 1:

$$\text{OED}(\%) = 1 - \frac{(65{,}000/10{,}000)}{8} - \frac{1 \times (15/60)}{8},$$
$$= 15.625\%, \tag{11}$$

and for day 2:

$$\text{OED}(\%) = 1 - \frac{(10{,}000/10{,}000)}{8} - \frac{(21 \times (15/60))}{8},$$

$$= 21.87\%. \tag{12}$$

By comparing OEDs of day 1 and day 2 with OEEs of these two days, we can see that while the OEE for day1 (i.e., 75%) is very larger than OEE for day 2 (i.e., 12.5%), but this is not the same for OEDs of these two days. In other words their OEDs are not as different as their OEEs.

So if the total Type-1 waste of these two days be neglected, we can say that the leanness of day 2 is almost as much as day1 and it is not so worse.

Remember that the total Type-1 waste, in minimum level, is because of commercial printing business model and it is out of our control.

4.2. OED as a graphical tool

Based on Fig. 5, we can write:

$$V_{\text{actual}} = V_{\text{ideal}} - \textit{Type-1 waste} - \textit{Type-2 waste}, \tag{13}$$

or

$$N_T = S(T_{\text{shift}} - nT_{\text{setup}}) - \textit{Type-2 waste}, \tag{14}$$

if we assume that Type-2 waste equals zero we will have the equation of a line $(N_T = f(n))$ as follows:

$$N_T = S(T_{\text{shift}} - nT_{\text{setup}}). \tag{15}$$

This line has been shown in Fig. 6.

This line is our target for any leanness improvement and it is also the graphical equivalent of the middle situation in Fig. 4.

According to geometric principles, it can be proved that for every operation point A (n, N_T) which is obtained from the production information of a work day, we will have in Fig. 6:

$$\text{OED}_A = \frac{h_A}{H}, \tag{16}$$

and a line, can be sketched parallel to the target line which passes through this point.

As much as the line passing through the operation point be closer to the target line, the related OED is smaller and as much as this line be

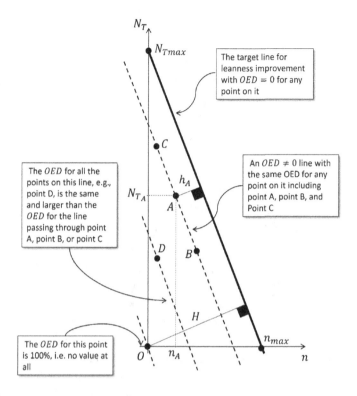

Fig. 6. Graphical model of OED.

away from the target line the related OED is larger and consequently the operation is more inefficient.

Therefore, by putting the points related to the operation of a work center or a printing machine in a specified period of time we can visually have a good idea about the leanness situation of the production. This is shown in Fig. 7, for a printing machines under three days of observation.

4.3. *The comparison of OED and OEE*

The most important difference between these two is that OEE highly depends on Type-1 waste, but OED is independent to Type-1 waste and is a good criteria for measuring the waste which must be observed in implementation of any kind of projects.

Another difference between these two is that OEE differs by a change in the number of orders done in one day; But this is not through about OED;

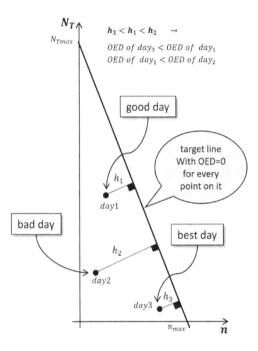

Fig. 7.   Positioning three days of operation on OED graphical model.

it is possible that in two different days with different number of orders have the same OED.

5.   Results and Discussions

The context of this research is a commercial printing company located in Tehran. This printing house is running a project for implementation of lean production in the company, since 2012.

As it is mentioned in Sec. 3.2, in phase 3 of the implementation road map, i.e., the phase of discovering waste, the project team including the researcher investigated on using OEE as a performance metric or progress measure of the project.

But after several running of the AR cycle in this phase, as it is shown in Fig. 3, we came to the following conclusions:

(1) OEE is decreased dramatically because of numerous changeover between productions of orders. So it is useless as a performance

measurement tool for a low-volume, make-to-order environment such as commercial printing business.

(2) Total Type-1 waste (in minimum level which is specified by the number of jobs done and technological constraints) is usually out of the management control, therefore its consideration in measuring performance by any means does not lead us to the main problem in our continuing effort to make the printing operation lean or leaner.

(3) The most important type of waste in operation level is Type-2 waste and can be measured and illustrated by OED very easily and effectively.

In Figs. 8 and 9, the operation points of one of the printing machines (i.e., Sakurai 475SD with $T_{\text{shift}} = 15\,h$, $T_{\text{setup}} = 15'$, and $S = 11{,}000\,\text{sph}$) are shown in two different phases of the lean implementation project:

(1) Firstly, as shown in Fig. 8, at the end of the phase 3 of implementation road map (i.e., phase of discovering waste) on September 2012.

(2) Secondly, as shown in Fig. 9, at the middle of phase 7 (i.e., phase of implement flow) on September 2014.

From these two graphs we can conclude very quickly and easily that:

(1) The overall leanness situation of the production for this Sakurai printing machine is better on September 2014 in relation to the same machine on September 2012. This is because in total the operation points in Fig. 9 are closer to target line than the points on Fig. 8.

(2) As shown in both graphs, identifying the leanest and the most unwanted days of these two months are very simple. These are shown as point A (for the leanest day) and point C (for the day with most Type-2 waste), in Fig. 9 for September 2014.

(3) By OED graphs, we can identify the OED of any point on the graph approximately but very easily. For example, in Fig. 9, point C is positioned between two parallel OED lines 40% and 50%. So its OED should be something about 43%.

(4) By counting the number of points between any two OED lines, i.e., dashed and oblique lines in the graphs, we can figure out which OED interval, i.e., the zone between two parallel OED lines, encompasses the most operation points. For example, as seen in Fig. 8, it is the interval between OED 50% and OED 60% which encompasses eight points. It means that for 8 of 21 days that their operation points have been displayed in the graph, Type-2 waste is more than 50%.

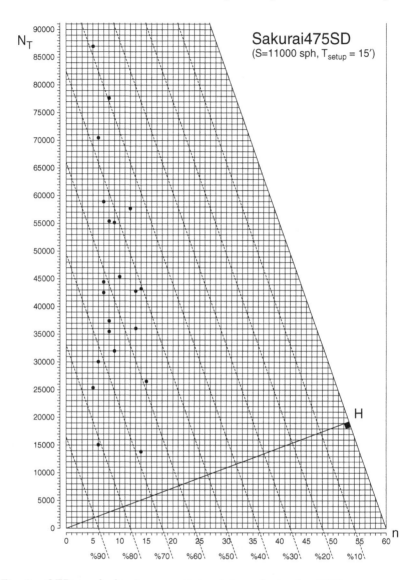

Fig. 8.   OED graph showing operation points on September 2012.

(5) In a commercial printing company, usually many jobs are produced every day and many different printing machines are used. For these reasons, selecting a day of working for cause-and-effect analysis of waste for a printing machine is not a previously specified task. Commonly, this managerial work is done according to the customer's claim or based on

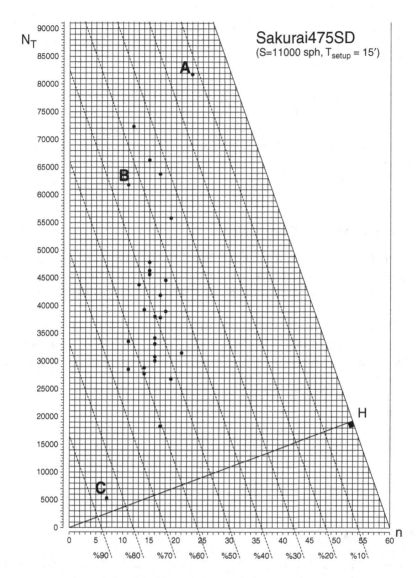

Fig. 9.   OED graph showing operation points on September 2014.

the in-charge manager's desire. By using OED graphs, however, the right days can be selected visually. For example, in Fig. 9, the point C as the worst day or preferably any days on the left side of OED line 70% or OED line 80% can be selected.

Finally, what is most important is that the improvement shown in the OED graph of September 2014 in relation to the OED graph of September 2012 is not accidental. On September 2012 we were at the end of phase 3 (i.e., the phase of discovering waste), but on September 2014 we were nearly at the end of the phase 7 of the lean transformation road map (i.e., the phase of implement flow) as shown in Fig. 3. In other words, after two years of running the lean implementation project in the printing house, we eliminated many causes of the Type-2 waste through establishment of some management systems such as production control and scheduling system, or work standardization.

6. Summary and Conclusions

Although OEE is used in some references for measuring the performance of printing machines, the cases are limited to the mass production in packaging printing and publication printing and do not include commercial printing.

The aim of OED development is to have a measuring tool by which it could be possible to simply and visually indicate the leanness of commercial printing machines which received a large number of orders in daily manners.

In practice, what we need when using the OED graph, for any printing machine in any day, is restricted to the number of orders (n) and total printed sheets accepted by the customers. Obviously, these are simply available in any printing house from usual production or sales records.

The development of OED has been also the successful result at integrating AR cycle with the phase of discovering waste in the lean transformation journey.

References

Ahuja, I. P. S. & Khamba, J. S. (2008). Assessment of Contributions of Successful TPM Initiatives Towards Competitive Manufacturing, *Journal of Quality in Maintenance Engineering*, 14(4), pp. 356–374.

Chang, Y. (2001). Development of the lean manufacturing systems engineering (LMSE) framework. Ph.D. Thesis, School of industrial and manufacturing science, Cranfield University, (UK).

Chiarini, A. (2013). The Seven Wastes of Lean Organization, in *Lean Organization: From the Tools of the Toyota Production System to Lean Office*, Italia: Springer-Verlag, pp. 15–30.

Comm, C. L. & Mathaisel, D. F. (2000). A Paradigm For Benchmarking Lean Initiatives For Quality Improvement, *Benchmarking: An International Journal*, 7(2), pp. 118–128.

De Ron, A. J. & Rooda, J. E. (2006). OEE and Equipment Effectiveness: an Evaluation, *International Journal of Production Research*, 44(23), pp. 4987–5003.

Elden, M. & Chisholm, R. F. (1993). Emerging Varieties of Action Research: Introduction to the Special Issue, *Human Relations*, 46(2), pp. 121–142.

Hall, R. (2004). Lean and the Toyota Production System, *Target*, 20(3), pp. 22–27.

Jeong, K. Y. & Phillips, D. T. (2001). Operational Efficiency and Effectiveness Measurement, *International Journal of Operations and Production Management*, 21(11), pp. 1404–1416.

Kaydos, W. (1998). *Operational Performance Measurement: Increasing Total Productivity*. Boca Raton: CRC Press.

Lewin, K. (1946). Action research and minority problems. *Journal of social issues*, 2(4), 34–46.

Liker, J. K. (ed.) (1997). *Becoming Lean: Inside Stories of US Manufacturers*. Productivity Press.

Monden, Y. (1981). What Makes the Toyota Production System Really Tick, *Industrial Engineering*, 13(1), pp. 36–46.

Monden, Y. (1998). *Toyota Production System* (3rd edn.). Norcross: Industrial Engineering and Management Press.

Monden, Y. (2012). *Toyota Production System: An Integrated Approach to Just-In-Time* (4th edn.). New York: Taylor & Francis Group.

Muchiri, P. & Pintelon, L. (2008). Performance Measurement using Overall Equipment Effectiveness (OEE): Literature Review and Practical Application Discussion, *International Journal of Production Research*, 46(13), pp. 3517–3535.

Müller, M. (2005). Action research in supply chain management — An introduction, in H. Kotzale, S. Scuring, M. Müller, & G. Reiner (eds.), *Research Methodologies in Supply Chain Management*, Heidelberg: Physica-Verlag, pp. 349–364.

Nakajima, S. (1989). *Introduction to Total Productive Maintenance*. Cambridge: Productivity Press.

O'Brien, R. (2001). An overview of the methodological approach of action research. Retrieved from http://web.net/~robrien/papers/arfinal.html (search date October 1, 2014).

Pagatheodrou, Y. (2005). The Price of Leanness, *Industrial Management*, 47(1), pp. 8–13.

QAD Inc. (2005). Empowering the lean value chain. Retrieved from http://www.qad.com/Public/Documents/empowering_lean_value_chain.pdf (search date May 12, 2014).

Reason, P. & Bradbury, H. (eds.) (2006). *Handbook of Action Research: Participative Inquiry and Practice*. London: Sage.

Sayer, N. J. & Williams, B. (2012). *Lean for Dummies*. Hoboken: John Wiley & Sons.

Smithers Pira (2013). *The Future of Print in the Middle East and North Africa to 2018*. Retrieved from https://www.smitherspira.com/market-reports/print/middle-east-north-africa-printing-2018.aspx (search date October 18, 2014).

Womack, J. P. & Jones, D. T. (1996). *Lean Thinking: Banish Waste and Create Wealth in your Corporation*. New York: Simon and Schuster.

Part III

Related Topics in Managerial & Cost Accounting

11

Mechanisms for Lowering Budgetary Slack in Japanese Companies

Ken Lee
Otemon Gakuin University

Naoki Fukuda
University of Hyogo

Satoko Matsugi
Tezukayama University

1. Introduction

The process of budgeting has been criticized by the school of Beyond Budgeting (BB) (Hope & Fraser, 2003). One main ground for criticism is the issue of budgetary slack, which is inevitably created in the process of budget preparation and is difficult to eliminate. Budgetary slack, if created excessively, could have dysfunctional impacts on the organization. Such dysfunctional effects are one of the reasons why many researchers have focused on the causes of budgetary slack (e.g., Onsi, 1973; Merchant, 1985; Young, 1985; Nouri, 1994; Kato, 1999). Japanese companies, however, are said to have less slack in their budgets than Western companies (e.g., Ueno, 1993). What factors underlie this difference in budgetary slack between Western and Japanese companies? This study clarifies the mechanisms for lowering budgetary slack in Japanese companies to provide a new perspective regarding the arguments surrounding the issue of budgetary slack.

In practice, budgeting has long been seen as a useful management system by most Japanese companies, and the criticisms levied against budgeting by BB have rarely been accepted in Japan. Some literature and case studies demonstrate that budgeting works effectively in many Japanese companies.[1] Based on the survey results of Ueno (1993) that Japanese companies build less slack into their budgets than the US companies, he suggests that the low volume of budgetary slack would be one of the outstanding characteristics of Japanese budgeting[2] (Lee, 2006; Lee & Fukuda, 2014).

This study investigates the mechanisms for lowering budgetary slack in Japanese companies.[3] In the Japanese budgeting process, various mechanisms work together to enhance interactions and information sharing at the *ex-ante* and in-process control stages, resulting in less budgetary slack. Similarly, at the *ex-post* control stage, weak linkages between budgetary performance (measured by the degree of budget attainment in each unit) and rewards for unit managers make it possible for stretched targets to be set. Setting stretched goals essentially refers to the practice of formulating budgets with little slack. As far as the budgetary slack is concerned, national culture and employment practices of each country also seem to be important factors in explaining the volume of budgetary slack.

The remainder of this study is organized as follows. First, we review the prior studies on budgetary slack to refine our research questions. Next, we examine the findings from our case studies of four Japanese companies. Finally, we establish a conceptual framework to explain the mechanisms used to achieve lower slack in Japanese companies.

2. Literature Review

Budgetary slack is defined as "the amount by which managers intentionally build excess requirements for resources into the budget, or knowingly understate production capabilities (Young, 1985, pp. 829–830)."[4]

---

[1]For more details, see Sugiyama (2006, pp. 50–56) and Lee *et al.* (2012).

[2]In this study, we refer to "budgeting in Japanese companies" as "Japanese budgeting".

[3]If not excessive, budgetary slack can bring some benefits to companies. A certain amount of slack, for example, often serves as a buffer against uncertainties and eases conflict among units. We, therefore, do not take the position that budgetary slack is always unnecessary but rather recognize the problems of the negative effects that excessive budgetary slack can cause for organizations. Thus, we will examine Japanese companies displaying lower levels of budgetary slack than in Western companies, and explore their mechanisms for lowering budgetary slack.

[4]Van der Stede (2000) operationalizes and measures "budgetary slack" by the following five items: (i) I succeed to submit budgets that are easily attainable, (ii) budget targets induce high productivity in my business unit (reverse coded),

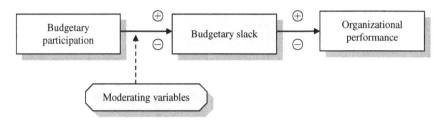

Fig. 1.   A research framework for budgetary slack.
Source: Lee *et al.*, 2008, p. 7.

After being introduced by Argyris (1952) into the management accounting research field (Lukka, 1988, p. 281), the concept of "budgetary slack" has long been studied and still receives attention from many researchers (e.g., Schiff & Lewin, 1968 & 1970; Lowe & Shaw, 1968; Onsi, 1973; Otley, 1978; Merchant, 1985; Young, 1985; Kosuga, 1997; Parker *et al.*, 1989).

Participative budgeting is said to promote managers' commitment and motivation to attaining budget goals, but simultaneously increases the possibility of creating budgetary slack implying that a positive relation exists between budgetary participation by managers and budgetary slack. Meanwhile, some conflicting studies have found that budgetary slack is reduced through budgetary participation (e.g., Dunk, 1993). This dichotomy of views on the relation between budgetary participation and budgetary slack is commonly seen in the literature (Merchant, 1985; Nouri & Parker, 1996). The left half of Fig. 1 illustrates this conflict.

Why does such a discrepancy exist in the results about the relationship between budgetary participation and slack? Given that the extent and/or directions (positive or negative) of budgetary slack have been thought to be influenced by moderating variables, numerous studies have tried to specify these moderating variables. Many factors have been proposed thus far as moderating variables, including information asymmetry (Dunk, 1993; Fisher *et al.*, 2002; Chong & Eggleton, 2007); organizational commitment (Nouri, 1994; Nouri & Parker, 1996); incentive schemes (Chow *et al.*,

---

(iii) budget targets require costs to be managed carefully in my business unit (reverse coded), and (iv) budget targets have not caused me to be particularly concerned with improving efficiency in my business unit, while item (v) is a fully-anchored question asking if the budget is (a) very easy to attain; (b) attainable with reasonable effort; (c) attainable with considerable effort; (d) practically unattainable; or (e) impossible to attain (Van der Stede, 2000, p. 615).

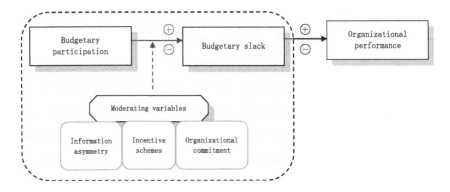

Fig. 2.   The scope of this study.

1988; Chow *et al.*, 1991; Walker & Johnson, 1999); negotiation process
(Fisher *et al.*, 2000; Fisher *et al.*, 2002); budget emphasis (Dunk, 1993;
Merchant 1985; Van der Stede, 2000); risk preference (Waller, 1988; Kim,
1992); and reputation (Stevens, 2002).

Meanwhile, despite numerous studies covering budgetary slack in Western literature, such studies have rarely been conducted in Japan (Lee *et al.*,
2008; Matsugi *et al.*, 2012). Thus, the process of budgetary slack reduction
in Japanese companies has not been apparent yet. This study demonstrates
the mechanisms used by Japanese companies to reduce budgetary slack
by concentrating on three specific moderating variables: (i) information
asymmetry, (ii) incentive schemes, and (iii) organizational commitment,
which are highlighted in the literature as exerting the greatest influence
(Fig. 2).

3.   Findings from Case Studies

3.1.   *Methodology*

We conducted semi-structured interviews with corporate-level managers of
four Japanese companies using interview questions provided in advance.
We adopted the case study method because it seems best suited for the
analysis of process and mechanism of budgetary slack creation. The interview included representatives of company A (rubber product company),
company B (rental company of welfare equipment), company C (chemical
company), and company D (land transportation company), all of which

were selected by accessibility. The interviews had been conducted seven times from February 2009 to November 2011.[5]

The number of employees in the surveyed companies ranges from 400 to over 7,000, and three of the four companies are listed on the First Section of the Tokyo Stock Exchange (TSE), with the other listed on the Second Section of the TSE. All companies have been operating for different amounts of time, with two companies established over 100 years ago and the remaining two established over 50 years and under 20 years ago, respectively.

3.2. *Findings*

Although we did not use the term "budgetary slack" during the interviews, we indirectly asked the managers of each company whether there was any slack in the budgets of the units. Nonetheless, all managers replied that there was very little slack in their budgets. A common element to their answers was an inability to create slack in the budgets because budget targets were stretched.[6] The results confirm very limited slack in the budgets, if any. Closely analyzing each company's budgetary preparation process, this point would become clearer.

First, we identified common features between companies A and D; both first develop medium-term management plans as their stretched targets, and, thereafter, raise their budgets to the stretched level corresponding to their medium-term management plans. Company A formulates its budgets based on its medium-term management plan, which presents very challenging targets. Accordingly, company A does exhibit some divergence between its one-year profit plan based on its medium-term management plan and the division's budget draft as prepared in a bottom-up fashion. In such cases, budget meetings are held to enable negotiations to bridge the gap before senior managers make a final decision. This process indicates that senior management uses the bottom-up budget as a starting point when determining the stretched budget determined by medium-term management plan.

Similarly the budgets in company D are set at stretched levels that correspond to the medium-term management plan. The procedures for

---

[5]For more details about the interviews, see Matsugi *et al.* (2012).

[6]In this study, we use "stretched targets" as a meaning of "tight but achievable targets". For more details about "tight but achievable targets", see Merchant & Manzoni (1989).

formulating the budgets in company D are as follows. First, they embody the long-term vision for the future. Next, they develop a three-year plan containing concrete actions to attain the long-term vision. Based on this plan, they formulate more detailed annual budgets. As far as the long-term vision is concerned, it is considered an extremely high goal imposed in a top-down fashion. In fact, in relation to the consolidated operating revenue set in long-term vision prepared in 2000, the target amount for 2020 is double that for 2005. Such a goal is recognized as unattainable. To achieve this long-term vision, a three-year plan (medium-term management plan) as a concrete action plan is developed by business unit managers in a bottom-up fashion. Surprisingly, the "unattainable" goal gradually becomes a "should-attain" goal as the plan is developed in a bottom-up fashion. This implies that the goals imposed by the top management are changed into their own goals in their minds. Furthermore, budgets are recommended to be set above the level of profit indicated by medium-term management plan. Budgets prepared using this process are recognized as stretched targets (Matsugi *et al.*, 2012).

In contrast, company B follows a process wherein the draft budgets formulated by each unit are already stretched. In company B, these stretched budgets are then lowered to realistic levels through negotiation between each unit and the head office. Specifically, since the figures of initial budget drafts formulated using the bottom-up approach are too high to disclose outside the company, they are decreased to realistic levels for external reporting purposes.

Overall, budget targets in all four companies investigated seem to be set at highly stretched levels.[7] Company B, in particular, exhibits a tendency to engage in some practices contrary to standard practice in budget negotiations wherein the head office requests that unit managers reduce their budget targets instead of increasing them because the initial targets developed by bottom-up approaches are too high. The budget targets of all four companies are stretched as a whole and hence little margin exists for budgetary slack. What factors underlie this lack of budgetary slack? We will explore the answer to this question by focusing on two representative factors: incentive schemes (Chow *et al.*, 1988; Chow *et al.*, 1991;

---

[7] Although we failed to hear about budget preparation processes in company C in detail, we could get some relevant information enough to confirm that their budget targets themselves are as much stretched as those of the other three companies.

Walker & Johnson, 1999) and information asymmetry (Chow *et al.*, 1988; Dunk, 1993; Fisher *et al.*, 2002), both of which moderate the effect of budgetary participation on budgetary slack.

In this study, we found that the effects of budgetary performance upon the total rewards are quite low. Especially in company B, budgetary performance is not reflected in managers' performance evaluations or rewards, which overturns our images of budgeting. Some particularly salient statements regarding incentive schemes are provided in the following paragraphs.

- ○ *In determining middle managers' bonuses, budgetary performance accounts for less than 20% of the criteria* (Company A).
- ○ *Growth rates from last year rather than unit budgetary performance are reflected in bonus payments* (Company B).
- ○ *Quantitative performance evaluation is related to only 10 to 15% of overall annual salaries of the unit managers* (Company C).
- ○ *Even though we evaluate each unit's degree of budget attainment, we subsequently determine the rewards for the unit managers by subjective evaluations* (Company D).

Therefore, it can be seen that incentive schemes strongly linking budgetary performance with rewards are not common in Japan.

Concerning information asymmetry, we also obtained some data that did not strictly follow the literature. Assuming a positive relationship between information asymmetry and budgetary slack (Chow *et al.*, 1988; Dunk, 1993; Fisher *et al.*, 2002), it is notable that the following formal and/or informal interactions exist to reduce information asymmetries in Japanese companies.

- ○ *We conduct two-day and one-night "budgeting camps" (or lodging together to formulate budgets) at training institutes* (Company A).
- ○ *Managers are convinced of the need to follow the budgets because the budgets are formulated during four-day management meetings* (Company B).
- ○ *The president understands our employees best, and spends more time making trips to each business center than sitting in the head office. The president often invites employees for a drink* (Company C).
- ○ *Conversations between the president and general managers motivate the latter to attain the budgets. The current president always asks the*

managers sharp questions and hence it is difficult for managers to create slack in their budgets (Company C).

o *We hold meetings frequently* (Company B, C, and D).

o *We have to report on the progress of budget implementation to top management at frequent meetings* (Company D).

These answers indicate that various types of interactions enable top and middle managers to share information both vertically and horizontally and hence information asymmetries are reduced. The distance between top and bottom at the four case study Japanese companies seems to be quite short, which is in contrast to the US top-down remote-control management (Johnson, 1992).

In sum, the results of these case studies can be summarized in the following three points:

o Since budget targets are stretched in Japanese companies, little scope exists for the slack to be created.

o Through the weak link between unit budgetary performance and the unit managers' compensation and bonuses, Japanese companies have greater scope to set stretched targets with cooperation of unit managers.

o Various types of interactions reduce information asymmetries in Japanese companies, which in turn decrease budgetary slack.

In the next section, we will attempt to establish some conceptual frameworks to explain the observed mechanisms for lowered budgetary slack in Japanese companies.

4. Mechanisms for Lowering Budgetary Slack

We can divide the budgetary control process into three sub-control stages by order of action; *ex-ante* control, in-process control, and *ex-post* control (Ueno, 1993, p. 23). This classification is very effective in explaining the characteristics of Japanese budgeting, which prioritize process control.[8] In this section, we will elucidate the characteristics of Japanese budgeting based on the results of the preceding analyses using this three-type classification.

---

[8]Concerning the process control, refer to Merchant (1982).

4.1. *Ex-ante control stage*

Participative budgeting practices were found to be conducted in all companies that we investigated. According to Sakurai (2009), in Japanese companies it sometimes happens that the accounting department and unit managers interact and share knowledge repeatedly in budgeting process, creating emerging strategies. This practice is called "catch-ball" (that is, communicating with each other as if throwing a ball back and forth) in Japan. Sakurai (2009) suggests that this "catch-ball" practice is representative of Japanese companies' advantage compared to US companies, where less time is spent in budget-related coordination, and budgeting decisions are mostly made from the top-down.[9]

In addition to "catch-ball" practice, we obtained some interesting responses such as *"We conduct two-day and one-night 'budgeting camps' at training institutes* (Company A)." or *"Managers are convinced of the need to follow the budgets because the budgets are formulated during four-day management meetings* (Company B)." Because all these practices involve high levels of interaction, this means that communication and information sharing are enhanced and information asymmetries are greatly alleviated at this stage. Consequently, budgetary slack is likely to be minimized (Chow *et al.*, 1988; Dunk, 1993; Fisher *et al.*, 2002).

According to Hofstede (1980), Japan is categorized as exhibiting relatively high collectivism[10] where superior–subordinate relations are cooperative instead of contractual. In such circumstances, managers' organizational commitment seems to remain high (Lee, 2006; Lee & Cho, 2010; Kato, 1994). Similarly long-term employment practices commonly seen in Japanese companies also enhance not only managers' loyalty to the

---

[9]See Sakurai (2009), pp. 218–219.

[10]The individualism/collectivism dimension is associated with the degree to which individuals are integrated into groups. Individuals from a collectivistic culture are motivated by group interests and emphasize the maintenance of interpersonal harmony (Chow *et al.*, 1994, p. 383). Hofstede (1980) used 6 out of 14 items including individual time, freedom, or work environment to measure this dimension through factor analyses. According to Hofstede (1980), the Japanese Individualism score is 46, which is 32nd out of 69 countries. We cannot say from this position that Japan is outstandingly collective. However, in comparison with US (individualism score is 91, the most individualistic), England (3rd), Netherland (4th), Canada (6th), and Italy (8th), it seems Japanese are surely collectivistic (Iriyama, 2012, pp. 191–202).

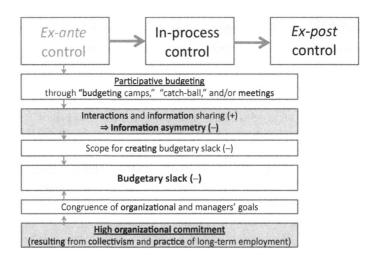

Fig. 3.   *Ex-ante* control and budgetary slack.

organizations but also goal congruence between organization and managers
(Monden, 1985), both of which facilitate the notion of "Organizational benefit is also my own benefit." In addition, in a situation where employment
still tends to be long-term, a naturally long-term orientation tends to be
fostered because certain types of positive short-term performance are not
always good for long-term performance.

In sum, budgetary slack may be lowered by increased organizational
commitment, which can be fostered through collectivism and relatively
long-term employment practices in Japanese companies (Fig. 3). This
relation is also applicable to both in-process control and *ex-post* control
stages.

4.2.   *In-process control stage*

In all four companies that we investigated, high levels of interactions were
found not only in budget preparation but also in the budget implementation process. With formal and/or informal meetings occurring weekly
and monthly, quarterly branch managers' meetings, and semi-annual management meetings, the progress of budget implementation was constantly
monitored and, consequently, milestone management was conducted during in-process control stage. In particular, responses such as *"The president
often invites employees for a drink."* or *"The president spends more time*

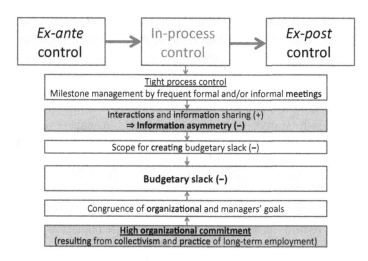

Fig. 4.   In-process control and budgetary slack.

making trips to each business center than sitting in the head office." suggest that not only formal meetings but also informal communications function as important control mechanisms.

Unlike Western companies where results control modes are more popular (Merchant & Van der Stede, 2012), Japanese companies place greater emphasis on process control. Moreover, higher levels of interactions and information sharing by frequent formal and/or informal meetings and communications in Japanese companies reduce information asymmetries and as a result, companies can maintain budgetary slack at a lower level (Fig. 4).

4.3.   *Ex-post control stage*

One important issue that arises following budget implementation is the design of incentive schemes, during which the linkage between budgetary performance and employee rewards has to be determined. According to Yokota (1998 and 2004), Japanese companies do not tend to directly link a unit's budgetary performance to its managers' rewards. Instead, short-term budgetary performance is treated as one of the various determinants of rewards because rewards are thought to be granted from a long-term perspective. Similarly, several survey researches also revealed only weak linkages between budgetary performance and rewards in Japanese companies (Shibata & Kumata, 1988a,b; Mizoguchi *et al.*, 1988; Ueno, 1993;

Asada, 1989a,b; Asada, 1993; Yoshida *et al.*, 2009). Based on the results of these preceding researches, Lee *et al.* (2008 & 2010) hypothesized that budget targets in Japanese companies would be set at relatively stretched levels. When budgetary performance is not strongly linked to rewards, there is less need to set easy-to-attain targets to prevent able managers from leaving (Merchant & Manzoni, 1989).

As previously stated, in Western companies, managers are routinely evaluated by budgetary performance, and their rewards directly reflect the results of these performance evaluations. In contrast, Japanese companies strictly execute process control in the process of budget implementation, whereas results control is not much emphasized.

From our interviews, it became clear that the impact of budgetary performance on rewards as a whole is quite low because managers' rewards are determined by market conditions and subjective evaluations, not only by the unit's success in budget attainment. These findings on the low linkages between performance and rewards are strongly related to the levels of budget targets and budgetary slack. Preceding researches suggested that budget targets are set at different levels according to the degree of linkage between budgetary performance and monetary rewards. For example, Stedry (1960) demonstrated that managers could be motivated to achieve a high performance by setting challenging budget targets. He also insisted that managers should not be blamed for unfavorable variances because such variances tend to be sizeable when facing challenging budget targets. Reflecting budgetary performance in monetary rewards means blaming managers for unfavorable variances, contrary to Stedry's (1960) warning. Similarly, it is easily conceivable that when budgetary performance is directly linked to individual's rewards, managers would be motivated to set their targets at a lower level to enable their budgets to be attained without difficulty.

Merchant and Manzoni (1989) demonstrated that in the companies they investigated, budget targets were not always stretched, but instead were relatively attainable because companies sought to prevent managers from leaving by offering monetary rewards. This result suggests that reflecting budgetary performance in rewards leads to lower target levels. The same logic was also found operating by Hofstede (1968), whose case study discovered that targets tend to be low under schemes offering payment by results but high if not linked to salaries.

We discovered unit budget targets are stretched in all companies we investigated. Clearly, weak linkages between a unit's budgetary performance

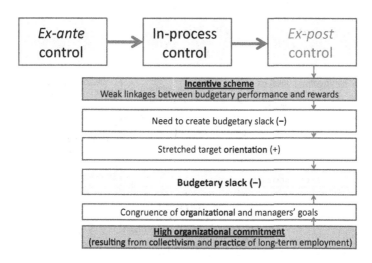

Fig. 5.   *Ex-post* control and budgetary slack.

and its managers' rewards enable stretched targets to be set. Company B is a good example where budgetary performance is not linked to the rewards. In company B, each branch manager sets a stretched budget from bottom-up, and these budgets are then lowered to realistic levels after negotiation with head office. Managers were able to set such a high budget targets because budgetary performance was not linked to rewards. If any linkage existed, the stretch that these managers offered would be lower.

In sum, we can delineate the cause and effect relationships such that weak linkages between units' budgetary performance and the unit managers' rewards promote stretched targets and, as a result, budgetary slack remains low (Fig. 5). Thus, the motivation to lower budgetary slack in Japanese companies results from incentive schemes wherein the linkages between budgetary performance and rewards are relatively weak.

4.4. *Budgeting process and Japanese budgeting*

We have investigated the mechanisms for lower levels of budgetary slack in Japanese companies at each stage of the budgetary control process. In this section, we integrate three stages of budgetary control into one inclusive framework for explaining the characteristics of Japanese budgeting.

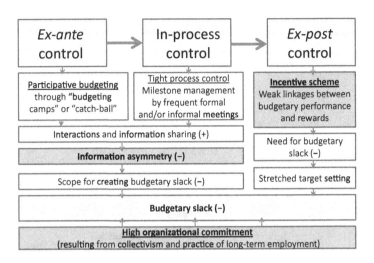

Fig. 6.   Integrated framework for Japanese budgeting.

As Fig. 6 illustrates, Japanese companies reduce information asymmetries through high levels of interaction-producing mechanisms such as "catch-ball" and "budgeting camps" at the *ex-ante* control stage and through milestone management or process control with frequent meetings and informal communications at the in-process control stage. Consequently, little scope remains for budgetary slack to be introduced, therefore keeping it to a minimum. At the *ex-post* stage, on the other hand, the mechanism of weak linkages between unit budgetary performance and unit managers' rewards gives managers incentive to set stretched targets, which in turn minimize budgetary slack.

As Hofstede (1980) and Ueno (1993) suggest, we should not ignore cultural factors and long-held social institutions when investigating budgeting practices in different countries. In this study, our framework incorporated a cultural dimension of collectivism as defined by Hofstede (1980) as well as the institution of long-term employment as two distinctive characteristics of Japanese companies. It is further suggested that collectivism and the practice of long-term employment enhance organizational commitment, by which slack-creating behavior is suppressed (Nouri, 1994; Nouri & Parker, 1996).

In sum, Japanese budgeting is characterized by various mechanisms for lowering budgetary slack not only at *ex-ante* stage but through the overall budgeting processes. Simultaneously, cultural and institutional factors also contribute to minimizing budgetary slack in Japanese companies.

5. Summary and Discussion

This study integrated the mechanisms used by Japanese companies to reduce budgetary slack into a single conceptual framework focusing on three moderating factors: (i) information asymmetry, (ii) incentive schemes, and (iii) organizational commitment. From our interviews, we revealed that *ex-ante* and in-process controls operate much more effectively than *ex-post* control in Japanese companies. These results, however, should be interpreted with care because the target companies were not randomly selected. Rather, target companies were selected by accessibility. Thus, it is possible that these four target companies are not representative of Japanese companies as a whole. With the increased sophistication of research methodology and accumulation of additional related researches, we believe this limitation can be overcome.

As budgetary slack seems to be deeply related to corporate culture and institutions, we need to incorporate these factors into the research context. Concerning the criticism against present budgeting systems by BB, it seems that they implicitly reflect Western culture and institutions, and the same criticism does not necessarily hold under different countries with different cultures. Although management accounting research that incorporates national or corporate cultures into the research framework would be inclined to reach somewhat general conclusions, we do not think it appropriate to draw conclusions without considering the impact of different cultures. As suggested, cultures and institutions are important factors in explaining the organizational phenomenon. Until recently, budgetary slack has been considered a negative influence on organizational performance (e.g., Schiff & Lewin, 1968). However, given that budgetary slack is not inherently detrimental[11] and can in fact, as shown in this study, vary according to cultural factors that do not indicate problems inherent in companies themselves,

---

[11]Budgetary slack does not always have a detrimental impact (Onsi, 1973; Merchant & Manzoni, 1989; Lukka, 1988; Todd & Ramanathan, 1994; Van der Stede, 2000; Davila & Wouters, 2005). For example, Davila & Wouters (2005) confirmed budgetary slack had positive impact of promoting the achievement of multiple goals as well as the budgetary goal (see right half of Fig. 1).

the issue then becomes one of distinguishing between good slack, which should be actively encouraged and bad slack, which hampers corporate performance.

In Japan, performance-based pay systems have become more widely used since the early 1990s. Because a performance-based pay system involving direct linkages between performance and rewards is incompatible with Japanese-style budgeting,[12] there is a possibility that the above-mentioned characteristics of Japanese budgeting could be forced to change. Further research concerning Japanese budgeting in an environment of performance-based pay systems is needed to suggest how the benefits of both systems can be reconciled to work in tandem.

References

Argyris, C. (1952). *The Impact of Budgets on People.* New York: Controllership Foundation.

Asada, T. (1989a). On the Comparison of Budgeting Systems Between Japan and US (1), *Kigyo Kaikei*, 41(4), pp. 603–610 (in Japanese).

Asada, T. (1989b). On the Comparison of Budgeting Systems Between Japan and US (2), *Kigyo Kaikei*, 41(5), pp. 761–769 (in Japanese).

Asada, T. (1993). *Strategy Orientation and Budgeting Systems in Modern Companies: A Comparison of Management Systems between Japan and US.* Tokyo: Dobunkan Shuppan (in Japanese).

Chong, V. K. & Eggleton, I. R. C. (2007). The Impact of Reliance on Incentive-Based Compensation Schemes, Information Asymmetry and Organisational Commitment On Managerial Performance, *Management Accounting Research*, 18, pp. 312–342.

Chow, C., Cooper, J., & Haddad, K. (1991). The Effects of Pay Schemes and Ratchets on Budgetary Slack and Performance: A Multiperiod Experiment, *Accounting, Organizations and Society*, 16(1), pp. 47–60.

---

[12]Various types of negative or dysfunctional consequences of performance-based pay systems in Japanese companies have been reported. Lee & Fukuda (2014) indicate frequent occurrence of back-stepping in performance-based pay systems in many Japanese companies following the introduction of these systems since the early 1990s. As a post-performance-based pay system, they advocate a hybrid system that offers the best aspects of both traditional Japanese management and performance-based pay systems.

Chow, C., Cooper, J., & Waller, W. (1988). Participative Budgeting: Effects of a Truth-Inducing Pay Scheme and Information Asymmetry on Slack and Performance, *The Accounting Review*, 63(1), pp. 111–122.

Chow, C., Kato, Y., & Shields, M. D. (1994). National Culture and the Preference for Management Controls: An Exploratory Study of the Firm-Labor Market Interface, *Accounting, Organizations and Society*, 19(4–5), pp. 381–400.

Davila, T. & Wouters, M. (2005). Managing Budget Emphasis Through the Explicit Design of Conditional Budgetary Slack, *Accounting, Organizations and Society*, 30(7/8), pp. 587–608.

Dunk, A. S. (1993). The Effect of Budget Emphasis and Information Asymmetry on the Relation Between Budgetary Participation and Slack, *The Accounting Review*, 68(2), pp. 400–410.

Fisher, J., Frederickson, J., & Peffer, S. (2000). Budgeting: An Experimental Investigation of the Effects of Negotiation, *The Accounting Review*, 75(1), pp. 93–114.

Fisher, J., Frederickson, J., & Peffer, S. (2002). The Effect of Information Asymmetry on Negotiated Budgets: An Empirical Investigation, *Accounting, Organizations and Society*, 27(1–2), pp. 27–43.

Fisher, J., Maines, L., Peffer, S., & Sprinkle, G. (2002). Using Budgets for Performance Evaluation: Effects of Resource Allocation and Horizontal Information Asymmetry on Budget Proposals, Budget Slack, and Performance, *The Accounting Review*, 77(4), pp. 847–865.

Hofstede, G. (1968). *The Game of Budget Control*. Assen: Van Gorcum.

Hofstede, G. (1980). *Culture's Consequences: International Differences in Work-Related Values*. Beverly Hills: Sage Publications.

Hope, J. & Fraser, R. (2003). *Beyond Budgeting: How Managers Can Break Free from the Annual Performance Trap*. Boston: Harvard Business School Press.

Iriyama, A. (2012). *What are the Managers of the World Thinking About Now?* Tokyo: Eiji Shuppan (in Japanese).

Johnson, H. T. (1992). *Relevance Regained: From Top-Down Control to Bottom-Up Empowerment*. New York: The Free Press.

Kato, Y. (1994). National Culture and Management Control, *Kaikei*, 145(3), pp. 60–75 (in Japanese).

Kato, Y. (1999). *Introduction to Management Accounting*. Tokyo: Nihon Keizai Shinbunsha (in Japanese).

Kim, D. C. (1992). Risk Preferences in Participative Budgeting, *The Accounting Review*, 67(2), pp. 303–318.

Kosuga, M. (1997). *Behavioral Budgeting*. Tokyo: Chuo Keizaisha (in Japanese).

Lee, K. (2006). Reasons-To-Budget and Japanese Budgeting, *Kyoto Gakuen University Keieigakubu Ronshu*, 16(2), pp. 59–78 (in Japanese).

Lee, K. & Cho, M. (2010). National Culture and Budgeting, *Kyoto Gakuen University Keieigakubu Ronshu*, 19(2), pp. 55–73 (in Japanese).

Lee, K. & Fukuda, N. (2014). Research on Cultural Aspects of Budgeting, *Venture Business Review*, 6, pp. 3–11 (in Japanese).

Lee, K., Matsugi, S., & Fukuda, N. (2008). The Retrospect and Prospects of Budgeting Research, *Kokumin Keizai Zasshi*, 198(1), pp. 1–28 (in Japanese).

Lee, K., Matsugi, S., & Fukuda, N. (2010). Budgeting, in Y. Kato, T. Matsuo, & T. Kajiwara (eds.), *The Frontiers of Management Accounting Research*, Tokyo: Chuo Keizaisha, pp. 109–152 (in Japanese).

Lee, K., Matsugi, S., & Fukuda, N. (2012). Budgetary Slack and Japanese Budgeting, *Kyoto Gakuen University Keieigakubu Ronshu*, 21(2), pp. 31–53 (in Japanese).

Lowe, E. A. & Shaw, R. W. (1968). An Analysis of Managerial Biasing: Evidence from a Company's Budgeting Process, *The Journal of Management Studies*, 5(3), pp. 304–315.

Lukka, K. (1988). Budgetary Biasing in Organizations: Theoretical Framework and Empirical Evidence, *Accounting, Organizations and Society*, 13(3), pp. 281–301.

Matsugi, S., Fukuda, N., & Lee, K. (2012). Survey Research on Budget as a Goal: Comparative Case Study of Four Japanese Companies, *Tezukayama Keizai Keiei Ronshu*, 22, pp. 37–56 (in Japanese).

Merchant, K. (1982). The Control Function of Management, *Sloan Management Review*, 23(4), pp. 43–55.

Merchant, K. (1985). Budgeting and the Propensity to Create Budgetary Slack, *Accounting, Organizations and Society*, 10(2), pp. 201–210.

Merchant, K. & Manzoni, J. (1989). The Achievability of Budget Targets in Profit Centers: A Field Study, *The Accounting Review*, 64(3), pp. 539–558.

Merchant, K. & Van der Stede, W. A. (2012). *Management Control Systems: Performance Measurement, Evaluation and Incentives* (3rd edn.). Essex: Pearson Education.

Mizoguchi, K., Kobayashi, T., Tani, T., & Asada, T. (1988). Survey Research on Performance Management and Budgeting Systems, *Kigyo Kaikei*, 40(6), pp. 823–831 (in Japanese).

Monden, Y. (1985). The Characteristics of Performance Management Systems in Japan. *Keiei Jitsumu*, 374, pp. 26–35 (in Japanese).

Nouri, H. (1994). Using Organizational Commitment and Job Involvement to Predict Budgetary Slack: A Research Note, *Accounting, Organizations and Society*, 19(3), pp. 289–295.

Nouri, H. & Parker, R. (1996). The Effect of Organizational Commitment on the Relation Between Budgetary Participation and Budgetary Slack, *Behavioral Research in Accounting*, 8, pp. 74–90.

Onsi, M. (1973). Factor Analysis of Behavioral Variables Affecting Budgetary Slack, *The Accounting Review*, 48(3), pp. 535–548.

Otley, D. (1978). Budget Use and Managerial Performance, *Journal of Accounting Research*, 16(1), pp. 122–149.

Parker, L. D., Ferris, K. R., & Otley, D. T. (1989). *Accounting for the Human Factor*. Sydney: Prentice Hall of Australia.

Sakurai, M. (2009). *Management Accounting* (4th edn.). Tokyo: Dobunkan Shuppan (in Japanese).

Schiff, M. & Lewin, A. Y. (1968). When Traditional Budgeting Fails, *Management Review*, 57(8), pp. 18–23.

Schiff, M. & Lewin, A. Y. (1970). The Impact of People on Budgets, *The Accounting Review*, 45(2), pp. 259–268.

Shibata, N. & Kumata, Y. (1988a). Budgeting Systems in Japanese Companies: Survey Research and Future Challenges, *Kigyo Kaikei*, 40(4), pp. 545–553 (in Japanese).

Shibata, N. & Kumata, Y. (1988b). Budgeting Systems in Japanese Companies: Survey Research and Future Challenges (2), *Kigyo Kaikei*, 40(6), pp. 832–839 (in Japanese).

Stedry, A. (1960). *Budget Control and Cost Behavior*. Englewood Cliffs: Prentice-Hall.

Stevens, D. (2002). The Effects of Reputation and Ethics on Budgetary Slack, *Journal of Management Accounting Research*, 14, pp. 153–171.

Sugiyama, Y. (2006). Breaking Free of the Spell of Budget, *Nikkei Information Strategy*, 165, pp. 50–56 (in Japanese).

Todd, R. & Ramanathan, K. (1994). Perceived Social Needs, Outcomes Measurement, and Budgetary Responsiveness in a Not-For-Profit Setting: Some Empirical Evidence, *The Accounting Review*, 69(1), pp. 122–137.

Ueno, S. (1993). *Budgeting Systems in Japanese and US Companies: Comparative Cultural Approach*. Tokyo: Moriyama Shoten (in Japanese).

Van der Stede, W. A. (2000). The Relationship Between Two Consequences of Budgetary Controls: Budgetary Slack Creation and Managerial Short-Term Orientation, *Accounting, Organizations and Society*, 25(6), pp. 609–622.

Walker, K. & Johnson, E. (1999). The Effects of a Budget-Based Incentive Compensation Scheme on the Budgeting Behavior of Managers and Subordinates, *Journal of Management Accounting Research*, 11, pp. 1–28.

Waller, W. (1988). Slack in Participative Budgeting: The Joint Effect of a Truth-Inducing Pay Scheme and Risk Preferences, *Accounting, Organizations and Society*, 13(1), pp. 87–98.

Yokota, E. (1998). *The Management and Psychology of Flat Organizations: Management Control in the Age of Change*. Tokyo: Keio Gijuku Daigaku Shuppankai (in Japanese).

Yokota, E. (2004). A Discussion About the Context which has Influence on Performance Evaluation Systems in Japanese Companies, *Kanrikaikeigaku*, 13(1–2), pp. 55–66 (in Japanese).

Yoshida, E., Fukushima, K., & Seno, T. (2009). Management Accounting in Japanese Companies (3): A Survey Research in Manufacturing Industry, *Kigyo Kaikei*, 61(11), pp. 1730–1742 (in Japanese).

Young, S. M. (1985). Participative Budgeting: The Effects of Risk Aversion and Asymmetric Information on Budgetary Slack, *Journal of Accounting Research*, 23(2), pp. 829–842.

12

Influence of Decision-Making Goal and Accurate Product-Costing Goal on the Design of Sophisticated Costing Systems: Proposal of Multi-Goal Coordination Approach

Nikhil Chandra Shil
East West University

Mahfuzul Hoque
University of Dhaka

Mahmuda Akter
University of Dhaka

1. Introduction

Cost system design mainly targets to install an ideal mechanism where products/services absorb accurate charges for organizational resources consumed in the process of producing the products or generating the services. "The resources used by a firm is ultimately destined to either producing products or generating services" — is the main rationale of charging products/services for the resources owned by a firm. Thus, making a fair relationship between the products/services and resources in a firm is an important prerequisite of ideal product costing system. A major issue in the design of cost systems is whether the system only assigns direct costs, or whether it also assigns indirect costs to the cost objects of an organization, and if so, how. In order to assign indirect costs, various cost allocation methods have been developed, of which activity-based costing (ABC) is the most recent. In general, these methods consist of two stages. In the first stage, the homogeneous costs of resources are gathered in cost pools. In the second stage, the costs from the cost pools are assigned to the cost objects using cost allocation bases. Both these stages address lot of subjectivity and assumptions which makes it risky of generating distorted cost data at every step. The accuracy of calculated product cost, thus, depends on the way of rationalizing these two stage processes. A system designer should provide enough scope to rationalize the steps at the time of designing the system. Starting from the identification and quantification of resources; numbers and types of cost pools; numbers, nature, and types of cost drivers and other pertinent issues should be resolved objectively to rationalize the costing process that necessitates robust design of product costing system.

The system designer should list and address all potential problems to ensure safeguard to the system at the design stage. Some common problems in product costing system may be like the choice of optimum number of cost pools and cost drivers, formation of cost pools (selection of different costs and fraction in respective cost pools) containing many resources with different consumption patterns, selection of cost driver for cost pools (on the basis of cause and effect, volume or non-volume), etc. Unfortunately, available literatures in the area (see, for example, Cooper, 1988; Turney, 1991) skipped a resourceful discussion and thus, offer limited help. The reasons of such reluctance on part of academicians and practitioners need further research. Some reasons may be pointed out here. *Firstly*, ABC, the most innovative tool in the area of product costing, is a development in academia. Abundant of research papers are available favoring the superiority of ABC over traditional costing on the ground of accuracy of product costing and importance in decision-making. However, most of the papers on the diffusion of ABC result a worrying picture. Low diffusion of ABC in practice is an indication of disperse ideology that exists between academia and practitioners. *Secondly*, the application of contingency approach in management accounting practices exerts another difficulty. The developments in management accounting are not universal and commonly used; rather it should be adjusted with the practitioners' requirements. The empirical research in the social sciences including accounting has less "external validity" because we could not control most of influencing factors unlike the natural sciences. The adoption of the contingency approach helps us to overcome the limitation though the approach still is not a generalized one. *Thirdly*, the complexity and cost of installing innovative tools may not be compensating additional accuracy in product costing and thus practitioners may be happy with their current costing system. In this chapter, we have tried to incorporate all of this in designing sophisticated costing systems.

Sophistication in applying management accounting tools targets to ensure the accuracy of product costing. However, we should not undermine the main goal of sophistication and that is the decision-making capability of information that the system generates. In open market economy where the factors of production can move easily in a fully competitive market, accuracy in product costing becomes a norm of the marketplace. An economy which is led by service industries, where competition is absent, consumers are not aware regarding their rights, inaccuracy in product costing may not be that much problematic. However, the advancement of science and technology brings innovative way of making products, increased earning level expedites the standard of living, globalization rationalizes borderless competition and modern civilization ensures practicable knowledge. All of these forces drive us to move forward to prove wrong what was practiced yesterday. Traditional costing, which reigns product costing literature for centuries, becomes age-old and outdated due to its incapacity of absorbing accurate cost in products. To drive the accuracy in product costing and decision making, ABC has been developed with a generalized prescription of tracing indirect cost with products. However, due to the existence of contingency approach in management accounting research, a holistic approach is required to install sophisticated costing systems. This chapter proposes a scale for measuring sophistication in costing system considering different criteria relating to the multiple goals. A thorough literature review results the main theme of the chapter. The proposed methodology is flexible enough to accommodate any further requirements.

2. Study Design and Rationale

The orientation of the chapter is conceptual and the study is based on reviewing available literature in the area. The study of sophistication in product costing design dates back to the year 2000 with the seminal work of Drury & Tayles (2000) where the authors have measured the level of sophistication on a continuum of 15-point ordinal scale based on number of cost drivers and cost pools. This is the very basic form of sophistication where traditional ABC is used as a proxy to it. The contribution of Drury & Tayles (2000) is great in a sense that they provide an objective definition of sophisticated product costing system based on the basic constructs ABC. Later on, the same authors have tried to bring robustness in measuring sophistication incorporating different nature and types of cost pools and drivers. However, Brierley (2008), through an interview survey, brings criticism to the way how sophistication is defined. The study acknowledges the importance of the earlier definitions of sophistication and, at the same time, proposes that the way sophistication is defined made the scope of sophistication very narrow, which actually is not. Due to the underlying contingency approach in management accounting research, the definition should cover all aspects to bring robustness in it. Here, the study assumes a holistic approach to propose a measurement scale of sophistication which confirms the multiple goals of sophisticated costing systems.

3. Product Costing System

One of the goals of sophisticated costing system is the accuracy of product costing, i.e., how accurately products are being charged for the resources consumed by them. Product costing is a part of overall cost accounting system used in firms. A cost accounting system consists of the techniques, forms, and accounting records used to develop timely information about the cost of manufacturing specific products and of performing specific functions. It requires five parts including an input measurement basis, an inventory valuation method, a cost accumulation method, a cost flow assumption, and a capability of recording inventory cost flows at certain intervals. Out of the five parts, our interest is on inventory valuation or product costing methods. Different costing methods propose different patterns of cost absorption by cost objects. Traditional/conventional view of inventory valuation significantly differs from modern view (Fig. 1). Throughput costing charges products only for direct material (DM) whereas direct costing charges products with DM, direct labor (DL) and variable manufacturing overheads (VMOH). Under absorption costing, products are charged for full manufacturing cost along with fixed manufacturing overheads (FMOH). However, ABC, an innovative development in the area of product costing, charges products not only for manufacturing cost but also for a part of selling and administrative overheads (S&AOH) that can be traced with the products through the identification of activities and respective

Cost Elements					Inventory Valuation	View
DM					Throughput	Traditional / Conventional
DM	DL	VMOH			Variable/Direct	
DM	DL	VMOH	FMOH		Absorption Costing	
DM	DL	VMOH	FMOH	S&AOH	ABC	Modern

Fig. 1.   Elements of product costs across different methods.

drivers.[1] Thus the product costing system has been refined gradually by bringing different elements of cost within the purview of cost as a quest of deriving accurate cost of the resultant products/services from the system. It is a drive towards achieving accuracy in product costing and ensuring sustainability to the firm.

The consensus among the academe and practitioners on traditional product costing systems is that they systematically introduce serious product cost distortions which may lead to inappropriate strategic decisions, and promote and encourage behavior that contradicts corporate strategies with regard to efficient resource allocation and consumption (Cokins, 1998; Drucker, 1990 & 1995; Anthony, 1965; Berliner & Brimson, 1988; Howell & Soucy, 1988, 1987a, 1987b, & 1987c; Kaplan, 1988, 1984, & 1983; Johnson & Kaplan, 1987). The traditional product costing system primarily revolves around a conventional costing theory which makes the following assumptions:

(1) If a cost cannot be associated with a tangible object, then that cost must be expensed.
(2) Costs which are associated and necessary for a product must be allocated to that product.

Therefore, selling and administrative costs are expensed whereas the cost of plant assets is attached to the products' cost. The traditional classification of direct and indirect costs no longer applies. The traditional product costing system emerges with the industrial process during the late 19th and early 20th centuries. During that time, prime costs were the primary components of production costs while product line diversity was less common (Cokins, 1998; Drucker, 1990 & 1988; Berliner & Brimson, 1988; Johnson & Kaplan, 1987; Miller & Vollman, 1985; Chandler, 1977). However, the situation has now been changed significantly due to technology led automation. Indirect cost has caused the true "prime cost" to become the overhead component. The increase in the relative proportion of overhead cost is

---

[1]In case of ABC, fixed manufacturing overhead is *fixed* in terms of volume measure, however, at the same time; it will be *variable* in terms of various cost drivers. The characteristics of ABC lies in its consideration of various cost drivers other than volume to the FMOH. In other words, the concept of fixed costs in the traditional costing appears when the variability of costs depending on the volume only is considered. Since ABC regards the traditional fixed costs as "variable" under various cost drivers other than the volume measure, all costs are regarded as "long-term variable costs".

distorting product costs automatically due to focusing more on prime cost under traditional systems. The significance of DL cost as a component of prime cost has now been reduced which accounts for approximately 10% of a product's cost. Manufacturing overhead now accounts for a significant portion of a product's cost (Peavey, 1990). Considering the current manufacturing environment, it would seem senseless to allocate a significant portion of a product's cost (manufacturing overhead) based on an insignificant activity such as DL hours. Under traditional overhead allocation system, overhead cost is broadly averaged among the products. This simple average is mostly done on a basis not necessarily consistent with the actual resources consumed in the production of the individual product lines. The problem with most cost allocation models (i.e., those based on direct labor, DMs, or machine hours) is that the driving force behind most overhead costs is not unit output or DL (Hicks, 2006; Drucker, 1990; Berliner & Brimson, 1988; Cooper & Kaplan, 1988a & 1988b; Johnson & Kaplan, 1987; Miller & Vollman, 1985; Kaplan, 1987, 1984, & 1983).

The recent management accounting literature provides several case studies of multi-product firms whose product costs are distorted because they allocate overhead costs to products on the basis of a single volume related variable. Johnson & Kaplan (1987) report that most of the firms that they have personally studied use simple cost accounting systems that assign overhead costs to products based on the DL hours expended on each product. Cooper & Kaplan (1987) describe three multi-product firms with complex manufacturing processes that rely mainly on DL hours to allocate overhead costs to products. They document how the apportionment of (long term) variable overhead costs on the basis of a single cost driver led these firms to over-cost some high-volume products and under-cost most low-volume products.

The traditional cost accounting system has not been changed in over 50 years (Haedicke & Feil, 1991) though the environment that it is supposed to support has been changed dramatically. Realizing that the traditional costing system does not accurately support the current manufacturing environment, many companies are beginning to implement other alternatives. ABC, is one alternative. The ABC approach, which is based on a relevant costing theory, emphasizes a cost's economic substance rather than its physical form. The ABC approach assigns direct costs to the product as they are incurred. Unlike the traditional method, ABC does not pool together a company's indirect costs and then spread them out across product lines. Rather, it recognizes that different products incur different costs.

An ABC approach embodies the concept that resources are consumed by activities and that those activity costs determine a products cost. Under this approach, costs are first evaluated to determine whether or not they add value to a product. The value added costs are then assigned to a product based on the activity that incurred the cost. The non-value-added costs are segregated and targeted for elimination (Johansson, 1990). Thus, ABC covers the limitation of traditional costing where overheads are assigned inaccurately to cost objects in most of the cases. And this is done through activity analysis, pooling resources, and using the right drivers on the basis of the pattern of cost consumption by respective cost objects.

4. Sophistication in Costing Systems

Research on sophistication in cost accounting system design attracts a wider community in recent years. Drury & Tayles (2000), for the first time, defined and measured sophistication and their work became a pioneering one for further studies in the field. Most of the works on sophistication so far gets the main idea from the mostly innovative tool in the field of management accounting, that is, ABC. Some papers even measured sophistication as a dichotomous variable considering ABC system as sophisticated one and non-ABC system as unsophisticated one (Ahmadzadeh *et al.*, 2011). However, before presenting any critical evaluation on the way how sophistication is measured, a presentation on sophistication as it is existed in literature is commendable. This section presents a literature on different version of sophistication for the readers' easy understanding and reference.

The seminal work of Drury & Tayles (2000) introduces a new research agenda in management accounting. It is argued that most of the previous surveys have sought to classify costing systems by two discrete alternatives, either traditional or ABC systems. However, Drury & Tayles (2000) adopts a broader perspective and examines cost system design choices that vary along a continuum ranging from very simplistic to highly sophisticated costing systems. The study measured sophistication in 8-point ordinal scales designed on the basis of number of cost pools and the number of different types of second stage cost drivers used by the responding organizations. Number of cost pools and drivers are counted and the study measured sophistication by three subjective categories named as unsophisticated, low sophistication, and sophisticated systems. Unsophisticated systems were described as those having less than 5 cost pools and 2 drivers, or 6 to 10 cost pools, and 1 cost driver. Sophisticated systems were those with more than 10 cost pools and 5 or more cost drivers. Any other combination of cost pools and cost drivers was defined as low sophistication system. Thus, the study measures sophistication combining cost pool and cost driver in a scale. As a company increases number of cost pools and cost drivers to absorb indirect costs by its product or services, it is moving towards achieving more sophisticated cost accounting system.

Abernethy *et al.* (2001) conducted field study in five selected sites to bring new dimension in the study of costing system design choices and brings an obvious improvement of measuring the level of sophistication. To categorize a system as sophisticated one or not, Abernethy *et al.* (2001) brings the qualitative issues relating to drivers and pools which is more important than quantitative issues in achieving sophistication. This study views costing system design choices as varying along three dimensions: nature of the cost pools (i.e., activity cost pools versus responsibility cost pools), number of cost pools (single versus multiple), and type of cost drivers (whether the system had hierarchical cost drivers). Costing system's level of sophistication is evaluated based on where it fitted on a continuum representing these three dimensions. One end of the continuum represented the simple traditional costing system (i.e., with one cost pool and a volume cost driver) and the other end represented a sophisticated costing system. This is a system where costs are grouped into a number of cost pools, there are hierarchical cost pools and there are a variety of hierarchical cost drivers. An ABC system, in its purest form would represent the end of this continuum (Cooper, 1990). Thus, this study also concludes that using ABC system means achieving sophisticated system.

In another study, Drury & Tayles (2005) define cost system sophistication as it is defined in Drury & Tayles (2000) with a slight extension that makes it a robust measure of sophistication. They consider three factors having influence on the level of cost system complexity, i.e., the number of cost pools, the number of different types of second stage cost drivers and the nature of the cost drivers (transaction, duration or intensity). Increasing the number of cost pools bring complexity in system though it captures the variability of resource consumption better. Use of cost drivers at second stage is important to apportion overhead on cost objects properly. An important attribute of a complex costing system is to ensure that cause and effect cost drivers are established for each cost pool so that a link is established between resource consumption and resource spending. Cause and effect cost drivers are more likely to be established by using many different types of cost drivers including different types of drivers within each of the volume-related, batch-related, and product sustaining activities (Drury & Tayles, 2005). Finally, the level of cost system complexity is also influenced by whether transaction, duration, or intensity drivers are used (Kaplan & Cooper, 1998). Transaction drivers are the least complex. Duration drivers represent an increase in the level of complexity since they represent measures based on the amount of time required to perform an activity. Intensity drivers are the most complex drivers since they are based on directly charging for the resources used each time an activity is performed. Costing system design choices varies along a continuum according to their level of complexity and measures a firm's costing system's level of complexity based on where it is located on the continuum. At one end of the continuum, the lowest level of complexity (described as simplistic systems) is represented by a single cost pool and a single volume-based cost driver. Such costing systems are commonly classified as systems involving plant-wide or blanket overhead rates. Higher levels of complexity are assumed to be associated with increasing the number of cost pools in the first stage of the two-stage overhead allocation process and/or the number of different types of second stage cost drivers. Interestingly, the third criteria of cost system complexity (nature of cost drivers) is defined theoretically, but the paper is silent regarding its use in defining cost system complexity which is based on 15-point scale as it is done in Drury & Tayles (2000).

Al-Omiri & Drury (2007) view product costing design choices as varying along four dimensions: the number of cost pools, the number of different types of cost drivers used in the second stage of the two-stage overhead assignment process, the types of second stage drivers used, and the extent to which direct assignments or resource drivers are used in the first stage of the allocation process. Costing systems are classified according to their level of sophistication based on where they fit on a continuum representing the four dimensions for assigning indirect costs. The most simplistic system is a direct costing system with single plant-wide cost pools. The second dimension influencing the level of sophistication relates to the number of different types of second stage cost drivers that are used. Using a greater variety of cost drivers that are the significant determinants of costs enables cause and effect drivers to be established for each cost pool that more accurately measure the resources consumed by cost objects. The level of cost system sophistication in respect of the third dimension relates to the extent to which transaction or duration drivers are used in the second stage of the allocation process (Kaplan & Cooper, 1998). Transaction drivers are less sophisticated since they assume that the same quantity of resources is required each time an activity is performed. In contrast, duration drivers are more sophisticated since they represent measures based on the amount of time required to perform an activity. Finally, higher levels of sophistication are also achieved by relying more extensively in the first stage of the allocation process on directly assigning costs to each cost pool or using cause and effect first stage drivers (i.e., resource drivers).

The study uses four different measures as a proxy to the dependent variable for determining the level of cost system sophistication. First, ABC adopters and non-ABC adopters are used as a dichotomous variable. ABC adopters were categorized as having sophisticated systems and non-ABC adopters were categorized as having non-sophisticated systems. Second, the number of cost pools (centers) used is considered in an ordinal scale to measure cost system sophistication and the third measure used the number of different types of second stage cost drivers as it was in case of Drury & Tayles (2000 and 2005). Finally, another dichotomous variable represented by direct costing or absorption costing systems was used. To ascertain whether absorption or direct costing systems were used respondents were asked to indicate whether or not their costing systems assigned indirect costs to products or services.

Brierley (2008), for the first time, brings criticisms to the way of defining sophistication. He believes that prior researches have conceptualized sophistication too narrowly by imposing a definition of sophistication in terms of the assignment of indirect overhead costs to product costs. If the word 'sophistication' is not defined broadly considering the wider spectrum of product costing and its use, researchers run the risk of theoretical sterility and tunnel vision in their research methods. Even, Drury & Tayles (2006) mention that sophistication could cover other areas, though they do not discuss what this might entail. Searching for a new definition of sophistication, Brierley (2008) has initiated a research in interview method which results 16 different definitions of sophistication summarized into three categories: the calculation of product costs, the use of product costs, and the combination of both of these. The study reveals three most popular definitions as, (i) the assignment of indirect overhead costs to product costs, (ii) the inclusion of all costs in product costs, and (iii) the understandability of product costs by non-accountants. Frequency count of the 16 definitions results that most (31 out of 45) of the interviewees vote for the definitions categorized as calculation of product costs. Thus, the study also concludes that sophistication is defined mainly on the basis of how costs are absorbed by the products or services. Though the work sought for an inclusive definition of sophistication, it remains silent regarding the measurement of sophistication.

To measure sophistication, Wallace (2009) attempted to capture the number of cost pools, resource drivers, cost drivers, as well as the type of cost drivers and resource drivers used within the organization's cost accounting system. The measures employed within this study use, refine, and extend the Drury & Tayles (2005) measures of cost accounting system sophistication. It captures the components of cost accounting system which has been neglected by academic researchers (Anderson *et al.*, 2002; Kaplan & Cooper, 1998).

The measure of cost accounting sophistication used within the analysis is a weighted composite (percentage) scale. Consistent with the Drury & Tayles (2005) measure, the product of the cost drivers and cost pools were obtained. The types of cost drivers were then categorized into cost hierarchy dimensions and relevant percentages calculated for each. Only two cost hierarchy dimensions were identified i.e., unit related and batch related drivers. These dimensions were weighted: the unit-related and batch-related dimensions with a weight of 1 and 2, respectively. This allowed for the cost accounting sophistication measure to be calculated as the sum of the number of cost centers and the number of cost drivers multiplied by the relevant weighted percentage of unit-related cost drivers and batch-related cost drivers. This resulted in an applied ranking scheme within the scale for cost accounting sophistication measure to incorporate the dimensions of the cost hierarchy. That is, unit and batch related cost pools and drivers are no longer considered equal. Therefore, two cost accounting systems with the same number of cost pools and cost drivers will be distinguished by their inclusion of unit and batch related activities i.e., a system that includes batch related activities will have a higher ranking than a unit only based system. Given only two hierarchy levels therefore the potential range of this measure is 2 to 32. In reviewing the variability in the sophistication of the cost accounting systems, minimal variation was found for the resource drivers and therefore this sub-component was not included in the analysis.

Schoute (2009) measures cost system sophistication by using two questions like Drury & Tayles (2005). Respondents were asked to indicate the number of cost pools and cost allocation bases used in respective firm's cost systems. Both were measured using a $\log_2 N$ scale, where N is the number of cost pools and cost allocation bases. It is assumed that their nature is best reflected by a base 2 logarithmic function. The justification of using the logarithmic function is that the author posits the influence of both the number of cost pools and the number of cost allocation bases on cost system sophistication is non-linear. A composite scale was constructed by adding the two $\log_2 N$ scores for each firm.

As an additional robustness check, all analyses have also been conducted using a second, more comprehensive measure for cost system sophistication which was not only based on the two questions as discussed previously, but also on two additional ones in which respondents were asked to indicate the nature of cost pools and cost allocation bases used in their firm's cost system. Specifically, the respondents were first asked which type of cost pools are used in their firms cost system: functionally oriented (e.g., departmental) cost pools, functionally and process oriented cost pools, or process (e.g., activity) oriented cost pools. Next, they were asked which type of cost allocation bases are used in their firm's cost system: only unit-level allocation bases, both unit-level and batch level allocation bases, or both unit-level, batch-level, and product-sustaining allocation bases. For both characteristics, three options were coded as 1, 2, and 3. A composite scale was constructed for this measure by standardizing the scores for each of the four cost system design characteristics and taking the average of the resulting Z-scores. Thus, the study also considers similar type of parameters to measure cost system sophistication. However, the methodology applied by Schoute (2009) is more robust than other studies.

The study conducted by Mgbame & Osamuyimen (2010) followed the framework of Al-Omiri & Drury (2007) and applied in Nigerian manufacturing companies whose shares are quoted in the floor of the Nigerian Stock Exchange. Thus, the work does not generate anything new in defining or measuring sophistication. Ahmadzadeh et al. (2011) conducted a similar study on the listed companies of the Tehran Stock Exchange. It measures sophistication as a dichotomous variable. Companies adopted ABC system is considered having sophisticated system and coded as 1 whereas, companies without ABC system is considered as having unsophisticated system and coded as 0. This chapter, similarly, added nothing new in defining sophistication rather used a very generic form of measuring sophistication.

Ismail & Mahmoud (2012) used three different proxy measures for determining the level of cost system sophistication. First, a dichotomous variable was used to measure the level of cost system sophistication. ABC adopters were categorized as sophisticated systems and non-ABC adopters were categorized as non-sophisticated systems. Respondents were asked to express the stage in which ABC systems are implemented to define whether firms

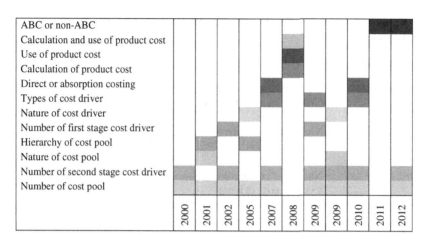

Fig. 2.   Gradual refinement of measuring and defining sophistication.

are ABC adopters or non-adopters. Second, respondents are requested to state the number of cost centers or cost pools used within the cost systems to assign indirect costs to products or services. Third, respondents were requested to identify how many different types of overhead allocation bases were used in the allocation process. This study also uses common measures of sophistication without any new dimensions.

On the basis of this discussion, we may conclude that the word sophistication is used in different terms in different researches and some common parameters are used to measure sophistication. The figure (Fig. 2) presents the gradual improvement of measuring and defining sophistication which is based on the studies of Drury & Tayles, 2000; Abernethy *et al.*, 2001; Anderson *et al.*, 2002; Drury & Tayles, 2005; Al-Omiri & Drury, 2007; Brierley, 2008; Wallace, 2009; Schoute, 2009; Mgbame & Osamuyimen, 2010; Ahmadzadeh *et al.*, 2011, and Ismail & Mahmoud, 2012.

A careful look at Fig. 2 reveals that the addition of new parameters in defining sophistication has reached its peak in 2007 with the work of Al-Omiri & Drury. Brierley (2008) criticized the way it is defined in 2008 and calls for widening the scope. Other papers simply replicate the established parameters in different time, country, and population. A frequency distribution table is presented in the following paragraph to identify the parameters those are mostly used. It is important to know the significance level of different parameters as established in literature. This may be helpful for the researchers to choose mostly accepted parameters for their own

Table 1. Frequency distribution of parameters used in measuring sophistication.

Category	Parameters	Frequency	Scale
Quantitative	Number of cost pools	9	Ordinal
	Number of cost drivers — First stage	4	Ordinal
	Number of cost drivers — Second stage	7	Ordinal
Qualitative	Nature of cost pools	2	Categorical
	Nature of cost drivers	3	Categorical
	Type of cost drivers	4	Categorical
Dichotomous	ABC or non-ABC	2	Dichotomous
	Direct or absorption	2	Dichotomous
Others	Calculation of product costs	1	Subjective
	Use of product costs	1	Subjective
	Calculation and use of product costs	1	Subjective

study relating to the measurement of the level of sophistication of product costing. In that case, content validity cannot be questioned.

Table 1 shows that number of cost pool is the mostly used parameter in measuring product costing sophistication followed by number of second stage cost driver. In few studies, some qualitative issues relating to cost pools and cost drivers are also used although an estimation of availability of data is warranted before choosing such parameters. Very few other papers used dichotomous variables to measure sophistication and one paper used some objective measure claiming that the sophistication is defined broadly with wider scope.

5. Goals of Sophisticated Costing Systems

At the time of designing the sophisticated costing systems, it is important to be very specific with the requirements expected from the system so designed. Thus, identification of the goals is the most important step for the system designer. So far, two broad goals are identified from available literature, viz., costing system targets to calculate accurate cost of the products and costing system leading to accuracy in the decision that management

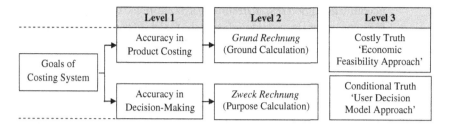

Fig. 3. Goals of sophisticated costing systems.

take regularly. These goals are presented in the figure (Fig. 3) at different levels.

Level 1: At this level, the very basic (core) level of goals is cited for the easy interpretation of the readers. For long, cost accounting system design targets to provide accurate product costing data. Many renowned management accounting researchers (Drury & Tayles, 2000; Abernethy *et al.*, 2001; Anderson *et al.*, 2002; Drury & Tayles, 2005; Al-Omiri & Drury, 2007) voted for this straight forward purpose of cost accounting system design. Due to ensuring extra accuracy in product costing, ABC receives extra attention and publicity over traditional product costing system. And the journey of sophistication of product costing system begins with the introduction of ABC in product costing literature. However, Brierley (2008) extends the goal of sophisticated system design and brings criticisms to the way how sophistication is perceived and defined. He said that the most important goal that we are missing behind the sophisticated costing system is the extra accuracy level that the system ensures in taking day to day managerial decisions. If we relate the goal of sophisticated cost accounting system with the accuracy of product costing only, we are narrowing down the scope and bringing theoretical sterility to the research. This criticism is timely and frees the research from tunnel version with widening the scope.

Level 2: At this level, the goals of sophisticated costing system are made operational, based on the idea of Eugen Schmalenbach, old German professor of accounting, who proposed the *"Grund Rechnung"* (ground calculation) and the *"Zweck Rechnung"* (purpose calculation) relating to the application of cost and management accounting. The *Grund Rechnung* system must be established first for measuring the common data base for various measurement purposes, and the *Zweck Rechnung* will be done for producing the accounting information for various purposes based on the data of *Grund Rechnung*. Here the first goal, calculating accurate product costing data, falls under the category of *Grund Rechnung* where cost accounting system generates product cost across different elements that may be based on actual or standard costing. And the second goal, taking accurate decision, falls under *Zweck Rechnung* where management may need to take various decisions like pricing, transfer pricing, product profitability, discontinuation of product lines, cost cutting initiatives, cost re-engineering, etc. accurately.

Level 3: At this level, goals of costing system design are aligned with the established approaches that exist in cost accounting system design literature. The costing system should be selected considering the cost-benefit of the alternative costing systems. This approach is called the information evaluation approach or economic feasibility or "costly truth" approach. We cannot exert pressure on our customers by implementing costly costing system with the excuse of revealing truth that is not much worthy to them. Under the current popularity of IT technology the costs of information systems may become reduced, but still total cost of ownership (TCO) of computer systems is much higher. Although the cost of information systems is measurable, it is still hard to measure of its benefits. Thus, in the study of sophisticated costing system design, we should bring some parameters that is related to accuracy in product costing and represents the cost of the system. Regarding the second goal, we can purposively bring the famous phrase of the economist J. Maurice Clark, "Different Costs for Different Purposes". This means the so-called "conditional truth approach". The conditional truth implies that the costing system should be as relevant to the user's purpose in question. This is also called the "user decision model approach", which was once used by the American Accounting Association (AAA's) Report of the committee on Managerial Decision Models (1969) published in the Accounting review.

These "Costly Truth" and "Conditional Truth" paradox is intuitively addressed by Horngren in one of his papers published in

1989 (Horngren, 1989). Bringing two alternatives (System A and System B) in product costing situation, where system A allocates total factory overhead to products based on DL costs and system B does the same thing based on multiple overhead rates (considering three different denominators as DM costs, DL hours, and machine hours), he shows that System B perform better than System A in terms of accuracy in product costing. Now the question is, if a firm currently deploys system A, will system B be a good buy? The answer, of course, depends on the buyer's assessment of costs and benefits. This theme is not doctrinaire, it is almost a truism. It does not say that multiple overhead rates are better; rather it depends on the specific circumstances facing a specific organization at a specific time in its life. The challenge to researchers and writers is to provide guidance regarding whether a system is cost-effective (Horngren, 1989).

6. A Proposed Framework of Measuring Sophistication

Discussion on the definitions or measurements of sophistication concludes that there is no single way to consider it. Most of the researchers used a mixture of cost pools and cost drivers related information to measure it. Brierley (2008) tried to introduce a new dimension in defining sophistication, however, it will be very subjective in measurement and, in fact, Brierley (2008) remained silent regarding the measurement of different definitions of sophistication. However, the surveys confirm the existence of contingency theory underlying the research. The research and application of contingency approach is not abundant in recent studies which may restrict it to be a generalized theory. Still, empirical research in the social sciences including accounting has less "external validity" unlike natural sciences. Adoption of contingency approach may be a solution to overcome the limitation.

Initial researches like Drury & Tayles, 2000; Abernethy *et al.*, 2001; Anderson *et al.*, 2002; Drury & Tayles, 2005; Al-Omiri & Drury, 2007; Brierley, 2008; Schoute, 2009; and Wallace, 2009 are conducted in economically advanced countries (e.g., UK, Australia, etc.) where a level of sophistication has already been achieved. Some researchers (Mgbame & Osamuyimen, 2010; Ahmadzadeh *et al.*, 2011; Ismail & Mahmoud, 2012) in developing countries (e.g., Iran, Egypt, Nigeria) have tried to replicate such research considering the core parameters of sophistication. But the main theme of contingency framework is that there is nothing universally applicable rather depends on some social, economic, political, environmental, and alike factors. Thus, the definition and measurement of sophistication also depends on some parameters which may vary in terms of its importance in different situations. For example, the way sophistication is measured in economically advanced countries should be different than the way it is measured in a developing or less developed countries. It will be irrational to say that developing or less developing countries do not have sophistication in costing system. Keeping contingency framework under consideration, it would be very difficult to develop and propose any model that will be universally applicable. However, it is an honest effort of the authors to propose and promote a scale of measuring sophistication of costing system that addresses most of the diversity in management accounting practices across different countries. Literature review on the topic and the wisdom of the researchers identified the following parameters of measuring sophistication in line with the respective goals (Fig. 4).

6.1. Accuracy of product costing

These criteria confirm the sophistication leading to the accuracy of product costing. The superiority of ABC over traditional costing is on this single ground where traditional costing traces indirect cost with cost objects by using a pre-determined overhead rate (grossly aggregated) leading to distortion in product costing. However, ABC goes for cause and effect relationship with the identification of cost pools and respective cost drivers for product costing. Thus, the study assumes that cost pools and drivers related information will be the appropriate criteria if

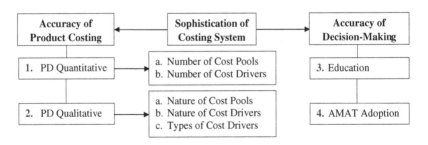

Fig. 4.   Parameters of sophistication of product costing.

the goal of sophisticated costing system is ensuring accuracy in product costing.

6.1.1. PD quantitative

This parameter includes the numbers of cost pools and cost drivers. This is very common and becomes core parameter used in most of the studies related to sophistication (Drury & Tayles, 2000; Anderson *et al.*, 2002; Al-Omiri & Drury, 2007; Schoute, 2009; and Wallace, 2009). Respondents may be asked to write the number of cost pools and cost drivers they used. Other way, respondents may be given a scale with pre-set number of cost pools and drivers so that they may choose the respective category where they fall.

6.1.2. PD qualitative

To bring robustness in measuring sophistication, some studies (Abernethy *et al.*, 2001; Drury & Tayles, 2005; Wallace, 2009) address some qualitative characteristics of pools and drivers like types and nature. Nature of cost pools indicate whether they are resource based or activity based and whether there exists any hierarchy. Types of cost drivers means transaction, duration, or intensity based drivers whereas nature identifies any hierarchy exists in identifying the drivers. These are some advanced considerations relating to the measure of sophistication which requires more sophisticated systems.

6.2. Accuracy of decision-making

It is very difficult to measure sophistication of costing system with regard to this very important objective. However, the study identified two proxy criteria, education, and adoption of advanced management accounting techniques (AMAT), to measure sophistication. Practitioners' skill and experience are very important to apply sophisticated costing system successfully. To quantify the skill and experience, we may consider the educational profile of the practitioners, years of experience of the practitioner, etc. At the same time, we may develop a composite scale based on the extent of applying different management accounting techniques to measure the second criteria. This is directly related to objective under consideration as different management accounting techniques are applied to take different type of decision.

6.2.1. *Education*

Bringing education in measuring the sophistication of product costing system is an obvious addition of the study to the current state of knowledge on the area. Neither of the studies done so far considered the level of education of practitioners as a parameter of attaining sophistication in costing system design. There should not be any doubt that without the proper knowledge and strong integration between academia and practitioners, it is not possible to bring innovation in practice. Some studies already identified that accounting education and practices are not properly integrated that is detrimental to the development of the discipline. Sterling (1973) observed a lack of congruence between research in accounting, classroom instruction in accounting, and professional accounting practice. He also noted that some educators/researchers had advocated different stances on issues in the classroom than they recommended in their own research publications.

The differences among the parties involved in accounting research, education, and practice arose more from isolation than from harmony, more specifically the isolation of research from the education–practice alliance. Sterling (1973) asserted that the absence of conflict between education and practice was due to harmony engendered mainly by "educators' predilection to prepare students for practice. We educators teach our students acceptable practices so that they can get jobs." He represented the process as presented in Fig. 5. According to this view it is practice, not education or research that brings about change. That is, practitioners add to their store of accepted practices and then educators observe, codify, and teach these additional accepted practices. Bringing education in measuring sophistication may be difficult; however, a proxy measure may be used like the existence of professionals working in costing issues. The importance of professionals in implementing sophisticated system cannot be undermined as

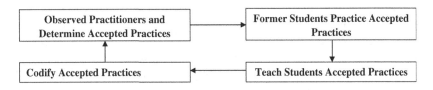

Fig. 5.   Integration of practice, class room discussion, and research.

the professionals are guided by the rules set by the institutes and learn continuously as a requirement of their membership to the institutes.

6.2.2. *AMAT adoption*

Adoption of AMAT itself may be a proxy to the measure of sophistication in designing costing systems. For example, some studies (Ahmadzadeh *et al.*, 2011 and Ismail & Mahmoud, 2012) consider the practice of ABC as sophisticated system and non-use of ABC as unsophisticated system. Similarly, some management accounting techniques relating to costing may be identified and used as a parameter of measuring sophistication. Due to the highest level of subjectivity to the degree of adoption, a Likert scale may be developed to capture the responses easily and later on different data management techniques may be used to calculate respective values.

7. Designing the Scale

Different criteria of sophistication of costing systems as identified earlier needs to measure independently that will be aggregated later on to form a generalized scale of sophistication. Measurement of the criteria may be done as Table 2.

The scale designed to measure the level of sophistication of costing system will carry a total of 100 marks. Each of the four criteria will receive a mark out of 100 and later on the marks will be weighted so that the value

Table 2.   Measurement scale of criteria used in sophistication study.

Criteria	Notation	Questions	Measurement
Education	EDUN 1	Number of professional accountants working	Ratio
PD quantitative	PDQN 1	Number of cost pools	Ratio
	PDQN 2	Number of cost driver — First stage	Ratio
	PDQN 3	Number of cost driver — Second stage	Ratio
PD qualitative	PDQL 1	Nature of cost pools	Categorical
	PDQL 2	Nature of cost drivers	Categorical
	PDQL 3	Types of cost drivers	Categorical
AMAT adoption	AMTA 1	Average score on a 5-point Likert scale	Ratio

of sophistication comes out as maximum 100. Each parameter will receive a point on 100 just to generalize the scale without any biasness considering each component having similar impact. Later on, the introduction of weight is made to bring contingency approach in calculation where the researchers are free to consider different organizational and environmental factors with appropriate significance. We believe that the parameters are not same in significance and the level of significance depends on lot of contextual factors. To address this contingency in designing the scale, we propose to use different weights for different parameters, i.e., higher weight for the more important parameter and lower weight for less important parameter. The scale value for measuring the sophistication level may be computed by using the following equation.

$$\text{SOP}_i = \sum_{i=1}^{4} W_i X_i \in \sum_{i=1}^{4} W_i = 1. \tag{1}$$

Here, we are applying a methodology like multi-attribute utility theory to find out the value for sophistication across different alternatives. Let us assume that $X_1, \ldots, X_n, n \supseteq 2$ be a set of attributes associated with the decision. We need to estimate n conditional utilities $u_i(x_i)$ for the given values of all n attributes. Then we can calculate $u(x_1, \ldots, x_n)$ by combining the $u_i(x_i)$ of all attributes: $u(x_1, \ldots, x_n) = f[u_1(x_1), \ldots, u_n(x_n)]$.

Assuming four attributes (edun, pdqn, pdql, amta, $n \supseteq 2$) we may revise Eq. (1) in the form of a utility function in additive form as given:

$$\text{SOP} = w_{\text{edun}} \cdot u_{\text{edun}}(\text{edun}) + w_{\text{pdqn}} \cdot u_{\text{pdqn}}(\text{pdqn}) + w_{\text{pdql}} \cdot u_{\text{pdql}}(\text{pdql})$$

$$+ w_{\text{amta}} \cdot u_{\text{amta}}(\text{amta}). \tag{2}$$

For solving Eq. (2), we need the respective weights and utility value of four criteria we have considered in the study.

7.1. *Determining weights*

It is important to determine the weights for each criterion since the method deals with multi-goals. Under the multi-goal seeking the optimal solution will usually be multiple as the "Pareto Optimal" solutions, some utility function or weights, or trade-off among goals of the decision maker must be applied. For such determination of weights the democratic method (for example, plurality rule or majority rule) is hardly applied as

Kenneth J. Arrow's "impossibility theorem" says. In 1950, Arrow (1950 and 1963) provided a striking answer to a basic abstract problem of democracy: how can the preferences of many individuals be aggregated into social preferences? The answer, which has come to be known as Arrow's impossibility theorem, was that every conceivable aggregation method has some flaw. In his book, "Social Choice and Individual Values", he proved that it would be impossible to integrate the subjective value criterion of various persons in a society into single value criteria via the democratic procedure. Thus, the "decision by majority" as the democratic procedure cannot make any unique priority order (unique solution) in the society. Arrow's conclusion was that only single dictator's priority order can decide the policy of the society as a whole. He focused only on the logical aspect of deriving the social selection.

Our objective is to determine criteria weights $(w_1, \ldots, w_n)$ for all multi-attribute utility theory contexts in which Eq. (2) is applicable. As dictatorship has limitations in itself, we can apply weighing based on the ranks as given by some influential respondents just to incorporate social preference to some extent. Each respondent $(R_i, i = 1, 2, \ldots, n)$ may select and rank a subset of n_i criteria $(n_i \subseteq n)$ that he or she seems to be relevant, giving each criterion j a rank r_{ij}. Given the ranks of criteria as provided by all respondents, we aim to develop aggregate (group) weights for all n criteria.

In order to develop aggregate criteria weights, we utilize the empirical rank–weight relationship of Alfares & Duffuaa (2006). This linear relationship specifies the average weight for each rank for an individual respondent, assuming a weight of 100% for the first-ranked (most important) factor. For any set of n ranked factors, the percentage weight of a factor ranked as r is given by:

$$w_{rn} = 100 - s_n(r - 1), \tag{3}$$

where,

$$s_n = 3.19514 + \frac{37.75756}{n} \quad \text{and} \quad 1 \subseteq n \subseteq 21,$$

$$1 \subseteq r \subseteq n \text{ and } r \text{ and } n \text{ are integer.} \tag{4}$$

Let us assume that we have m respondents and n criteria that are common to all respondents $(n_1 = n_2 = \cdots = n_m = n)$. We also assume that each respondent i assigns a rank of r_{ij} to factor j.

In this method we first convert individual ranks into individual weights for each criterion, and then calculate the average weight for each criterion among all individuals. The two steps are given as follows:

(1) For each respondent i, use Eq. (3) to convert ranks r_{ij} into individual weights w_{ij} for all n criteria.

$$w_{ij} = 100 - s_n(r_{ij} - 1), \quad i = 1, \ldots, m; \quad j = 1, \ldots, n. \quad (5)$$

(2) However, in the second step, the geometric mean of individual weights is used to determine aggregate weights as proposed by Barzilai & Lootsma (1997).

$$W_j = \sqrt[m]{w_{1,j} \times w_{2,j} \times \cdots \times w_{m,j}} \quad \text{where,} \quad j = 1, \ldots, n. \quad (6)$$

Table 3 shows a solved example for aggregation of weights when the same set (number) of criteria is ranked by all respondents. The example involves three respondents and four decision criteria (PD Quantitative, PD Qualitative, Education, and AMAT Adoption).

Table 3. Determination of weights based on the ranks chosen by respondents.

Criterion	PD quantitative	PD qualitative	Education	AMAT adoption
Rank chosen by respondent 1	1	2	3	4
Rank chosen by respondent 2	2	1	3	4
Rank chosen by respondent 3	1	2	4	3
Weight for respondent 1	100	87.37	74.73	62.10
Weight for respondent 2	87.37	100	74.73	62.10
Weight for respondent 3	100	87.37	62.10	74.73
Geometric average weight	95.60	91.39	70.26	66.05
Percent weight	29.57	28.27	21.73	20.43

7.2. *Measurement of parameters*

Out of four criteria, three uses a ratio scale and one is categorical. This pose a threat to the researcher as the scale is heterogeneous with different scales, values, and ranges. To ensure proper justice to the data used in the study and validity to the methods applied, it is important to reduce the diversity among the criteria used in the study. To bring all parameters into a same scale, a process of normalization is applied here as proposed by Chuang-Stein (1992) which actually results the utility value of different criteria as required in Eq. (2). The procedure selects a set of reference ranges against which to normalize all values. To be specific, let X represents an assay value with a corresponding reference range of (L_x, U_x). Furthermore, let (L_s, U_s) be the reference range chosen to be the standard range for the assay under discussion. Chuang-Stein (1992) proposed normalizing X relative to (L_s, U_s) through the following expression:

$$X_s = L_s + (X - L_x)\frac{(U_s - L_s)}{(U_x - L_x)}. \tag{7}$$

In (7), X_s represents the normalized value of X. This normalized value satisfies:

$$\frac{X_s - L_s}{U_s - L_s} = \frac{X - L_x}{U_x - L_x}. \tag{8}$$

In other words, X and X_s are of the same unit distance from L_x and L_s, respectively, where a unit distance is defined by $U_x - L_x$ and $U_s - L_s$ under the two sets of reference ranges. All of the four criteria we are using to measure sophistication have respective scales with ranges that may be normalized in a common scale of 0–100 by using the Eq. (7).

8. A Hypothetical Example

To apply the rule of normalization across parameters with heterogeneous scale and ranges, let us assume a hypothetical example with all the parameters used in measuring sophistication (Table 4). The table presents the example data.

The range is very important in Table 4, where contingency is operationalized. For example, EDUN 1 shows a range of 15 to 0. It means maximum number of professionals working in sampled firms is 15 and minimum is 0. Thus, the respective value of this parameter depends on this range.

Table 4.　Hypothetical data across parameters used in measuring sophistication.

Notation	Questions	Answer (X)	Range U_x	L_x	Reference range
EDUN 1	Number of professional accountants working	3	15	0	
PDQN 1	Number of cost pools	7	9	1	
PDQN 2	Number of cost driver — First stage	4	5	1	
PDQN 3	Number of cost driver — Second stage	6	14	1	0–100
PDQL 1	Nature of cost pools	2	3	1	
PDQL 2	Nature of cost drivers	2	3	1	
PDQL 3	Types of cost drivers	3	3	1	
AMTA 1	Average score on a 5-point Likert scale	3.4	5	1	

For a different country of different research, the range may be changed and the scale automatically addresses the difference with different values. We have four criteria to measure sophistication. Criteria education (EDUN) has no sub-criteria. However, criteria number of cost pools and drivers (PDQN); and nature and types of cost pools and cost drivers (PDQL) have sub-criteria that required an extended form of computation to measure the respective normalized points in the final scale value. Finally, the last criteria, adoption of AMAT, may have some sub-criteria which have been averaged to form only one scale value in a 5-point Likert scale just to avoid too much complexity in calculation. We have explained a method of calculating weights in Sec. 7.1 based on Arrow's impossibility theorem where we tried to bring social preference. Based on the hypothetical data and normalization formula Eq. (7), we may compute the scale value as given in Table 5.

The analysis reveals that a firm with the values as mentioned in Table 4 will have a total point equal to 50.452 out of 100. Criteria EDUN and AMAT have no sub-criteria and thus the calculations were direct. However, PDQN and PDQL have sub-criteria and the scale value for each sub-criteria (X_{ss}) has been computed which is then multiplied by the respective sub-weights (W_{si}) to compute the scale value for the criteria (X_s). The benefit of this

Table 5.   Scale value computation.

Notation	X	U_x	L_x	U_s	L_s	X_{ss}	W_{si}	X_s	W_i	$\sum W_i X_i$
EDUN 1	3	15	0	100	0					
EDUN								20	0.2957	5.914
PDQN 1	7	9	1	100	0	75	0.4	30		
PDQN 2	4	5	1	100	0	75	0.2	15		
PDQN 3	6	14	1	100	0	38.46	0.4	15.38		
PDQN								60.38	0.2827	17.069
PDQL 1	2	3	1	100	0	50	0.3	15		
PDQL 2	2	3	1	100	0	50	0.3	15		
PDQL 3	3	3	1	100	0	100	0.4	40		
PDQL								70	0.2173	15.211
AMTA 1	3.4	5	1	100	0					
AMTA								60	0.2043	12.258
Total Point									1.0	50.452

analysis is that depending on the requirement of the methodology applied in respective studies, sophistication scale may be ratio, ordinal, interval, and categorical.

9. Scope of Further Research

This chapter opens a good number of avenues to carry out further researches. Firstly, the chapter is a proposal that may be applied in practice to confirm its robustness. Secondly, different multi-criteria decision-making tools like analytic hierarchy process (AHP) may be applied to compute the weights for respective criteria and sub-criteria. Thirdly, a methodology is proposed to absorb contingency framework in explicating sophistication which may depend on some contextual variables relating to specific firm (internal) or business environment (external). It may be possible to work on any expectancy gap in practice. Finally, the research may be extended to put a comment of the current level of sophistication achieved by a firm and probable ways of attaining more sophistication. In this chapter, the authors have tried to put focus on existing literature to innovate something and bring some new areas where further studies may be carried out.

10. Conclusion

Dramatic change of management accounting practices in recent years is caused by the use of advanced technologies in production, cut-throat competition among competitors, integrated global market, and a change in cost structure. As modern technology took over the manual production process, the command of prime cost has been reduced greatly giving its way to the manufacturing overheads. Apparently, practitioners of management accounting come from heterogeneous background due to increased significance of overheads. Costing products accurately becomes a challenge to manufacturer due to the dominance of indirect cost over direct cost where tracing becomes very critical. At the same time, managerial decision-making based on cost accounting data receives new dimensions where accuracy left no other alternatives. Thus, sophistication of costing system becomes a norm in costing system design literature now-a-days.

The main tenet of sophistication in product costing centered on the core concept of identifying the cost with the product for the right portion of organizational resources consumed by the respective products. However, traditional product costing seriously distort the product cost due to the impact of gross aggregation of overheads whereby high-volume products are undercosted and low-volume products are overcosted resulting a cross-subsidized situation. This is an unethical practice and goes against professionalism where a group of customers gains at the cost of others due to the wrong practice of firms. In a sophisticated product costing system, practitioners try to charge the products accurately for the physical resources consumed by them through an activity analysis under cause and effect manner. ABC is a method developed so far to address these issues where products are being charged via activities following the basic principle of product costing — "it is not the product rather activities that consume cost." However, it does not mean that ABC and sophistication is synonymous though some studies use ABC as a proxy to sophistication. Most of the studies used cost pools and cost drivers to define and measure sophistication. This chapter proposes a holistic approach of measuring sophistication considering underlying contingency framework in management accounting research. The new definition of sophistication covers multi-goals of sophisticated costing system which is ensuring accuracy in product costing and taking the accurate decision in time.

To bring accuracy in decision-making in defining sophistication, we have used the level of education of practitioners and level of adoption of different management accounting tools relating to managerial decision-making. Education is an important criterion to measure sophistication which none of the papers considers. Practitioners' philosophy is codified in text from where young learners learn practice in class room and when they come to practice, they enjoy ample opportunity to innovate something and this reciprocity continues until some further developments are coming in the field. At the same time, a score come from the level of application of different management accounting tools as for example some papers used direct costing (Al-Omiri & Drury, 2007; Mgbame & Osamuyimen, 2010), ABC (Ahmadzadeh *et al.*, 2011 and Ismail & Mahmoud, 2012), etc. This consideration acknowledges the call of Brierley (2008) for a wider definition of sophistication addressing the use of cost accounting information. Cost drivers and cost pools are also used as independent parameters to measure sophistication as done in mostly all of the studies.

Finally, an integrated scale is proposed here to measure the level of sophistication attained by a firm in a holistic manner. Here we have tried to make a balanced scale covering both "conditional truth" and "costly truth" approaches. Weighted method leaves enough scope of flexibility to the researchers and practitioners to consider underlying contingency in research. The work of Brierley (2008) is the motivation of the chapter, where he acknowledges candidly that the way sophistication is defined in earlier papers made the scope of a wider concept very narrow. The proposal of Brierley (2008) is operationalized here by bringing different definitions into a single scale.

References

Abernethy, M. A., Lillis, A. M., Brownell, P., & Carter, P. (2001). Product Diversity and Costing Design: Field Study Evidence, *Management Accounting Research*, 12(3), pp. 261–280.

Ahmadzadeh, T., Etemadi, H., & Pifeh, A. (2011). Exploration of Factors Influencing on Choice the Activity-Based Costing System in Iranian Organizations, *International Journal of Business Administration*, 2(1), pp. 61–70.

Alfares, H. K. & Duffuaa, S. O. (2006). Assigning Cardinal Weights in Multi-Criteria Decision Making Based on Ordinal Ranking, *Journal of Multi-Criteria Decision Analysis*, 15, pp. 123–133.

Al-Omiri, M. & Drury, C. (2007). A Survey of Factors Influencing the Choice of Product Costing Systems in UK Organizations, *Management Accounting Research*, 18(4), pp. 399–424.

American Accounting Association (1969). Report of Committee on Managerial Decision Models, *The Accounting Review*, Supplement to *XLIV* pp. 43–46.

Anderson, S. W., Hesford, J. W., & Young, S. M. (2002). Factors Influencing the Performance of Activity Based Costing Teams: A Field Study of Abc Model Development Time in the Automobile Industry, *Accounting, Organizations and Society*, 27(3), pp. 195–211.

Anthony, R. (1965). *Planning and Control Systems: A Framework for Analysis*. Boston: The Harvard Business School.

Arrow, K. (1950). A Difficulty in the Concept of Social Welfare, *Journal of Political Economy*, 58, pp. 328–346.

Arrow, K. (1963). *Social Choice and Individual Values* (2nd edn.). New York: John Wiley & Sons.

Barzilai, J. & Lootsma, F. A. (1997). Power Relations and Group Aggregation in the Multiplicative AHP and SMART, *Journal of Multi-Criteria Decision Analysis*, 6(3), pp. 155–165.

Berliner, C. & Brimson, J. (1988). *Cost Management for Today's Advanced Manufacturing: The CAM-I Conceptual Design*. Boston: Harvard Business School Press.

Brierley, J. A. (2008). Toward an Understanding of the Sophistication of Product Costing Systems, *Journal of Management Accounting Research*, 20(Special Issue), pp. 61–78.

Chandler, A., Jr. (1977). *The Visible Hand: The Managerial Revolution in American Business*. Cambridge: Belknap Press of Harvard University Press.

Chuang-Stein, C. (1992). Summarizing Laboratory Data with Different Reference Ranges in Multicenter Clinical Trials, *Drug Information Journal*, 26, pp. 77–84.

Cokins, G. (1998). Why is Traditional Accounting Failing Managers? *Hospital Material Management Quarterly*, 20(2), pp. 72–80.

Cooper, R. (1990). Cost Classifications in Unit-Based and Activity-Based Manufacturing Cost Systems, *Journal of Cost Management*, Fall, 4(3), pp. 4–14.

Cooper, R. (1988). The Rise of Activity-Based Costing — Part II: When Do I Need An Activity-Based Cost System? *Journal of Cost Management for the Manufacturing Industry*, 2(3), pp. 41–48.

Cooper, R. & Kaplan, R. S. (1987). How cost accounting systematically Distorts Product Costs? in W. Burns & R. S. Kaplan (eds.), *Accounting and Management: Field Study Perspectives*, Boston: Harvard Business School Press, pp. 204–228.

Cooper, R. & Kaplan, R. S. (1988a). How Cost Accounting Distorts Product Costs, *Management Accounting*, 69(10), April, pp. 20–27.

Cooper, R. & Kaplan, R. S. (1988b). Measure Costs Right: Make Decisions Right, *Harvard Business Review*, 66(5), pp. 96–103.

Drucker, P. (1988). The Coming of the New Organization. *Harvard Business Review*, January–February, 66(1), pp. 45–55.

Drucker, P. (1990). The Emerging Theory of Manufacturing. *Harvard Business Review*, May–June, 68(3), pp. 94–102.

Drucker, P. (1995). The Information Executives Truly Need, *Harvard Business Review*, 73(1), pp. 54–62.

Drury, C. & Tayles, M. (2000). *Cost System Design and Profitability Analysis in UK Companies.* London: Chartered Institute of Management Accountants.

Drury, C. & Tayles, M. (2005). Explicating the Design of Overhead Absorption Procedures in UK Organizations, *The British Accounting Review*, 37, pp. 47–84.

Drury, C. & Tayles, M. (2006). Profitability Analysis in UK Organizations: An Exploratory Study, *The British Accounting Review*, 38(4), pp. 405–425.

Haedicke, J. & Feil, D. (1991). In a DOD Environment: Hughes Aircraft Sets the Standard for ABC, *Management Accounting*, 72(7), pp. 29–33.

Hicks, D. T. (2006). Good Decisions Require Good Models: Developing Activity-Based Solutions that Work for Decision Makers, *Cost Management*, 19(3), pp. 32–40.

Horngren, C. T. (1989). Cost and Management Accounting: Yesterday and Today, *Journal of Management Accounting Research*, 1(Fall), pp. 21–32.

Howell, R. & Soucy, S. (1987a). Operating Controls in the Manufacturing Environment, *Management Accounting*, 69(4), pp. 25–31.

Howell, R. & Soucy, S. (1987b). The New Manufacturing Environment: Major Trends for Management Accounting, *Management Accounting*, 69(1), pp. 21–27.

Howell, R. & Soucy, S. (1987c). Capital Investment in the New Manufacturing Environment, *Management Accounting*, 69(5), pp. 26–32.

Howell, R. & Soucy, S. (1988). Management Reporting in the Manufacturing Environment, *Management Accounting*, February, pp. 22–29.

Ismail, T. H. & Mahmoud, N. M. (2012). The Influence of Organizational and Environmental Factors on Cost Systems Design in Egypt, *British Journal of Economics,Finance and Management Sciences*, 4(2), pp. 31–51.

Johansson, H. J. (1990). Preparing for Accounting Systems Changes, *Management Accounting*, 72(July), 37–41.

Johnson, H. & Kaplan, R. S. (1987). *Relevance Lost: The Rise And Fall Of Management Accounting.* Boston: Harvard Business School Press.

Kaplan, R. S. (1983). Measuring Manufacturing Performance: A New Challenge for Managerial Accounting Research, *The Accounting Review*, 58(4), 686–705.

Kaplan, R. S. (1984). Yesterday's Accounting Undermines Production, *Harvard Business Review*, 62(4), 95–101.

Kaplan, R. S. (1987). How Cost Accounting Systematically Distorts Product Costs, in W. Bruns & R. S. Kaplan (eds.), *Accounting and Management Field Study Perspectives*, Boston: Harvard Business School Press, pp. 204–228.

Kaplan, R. S. (1988). One Cost System Isn't Enough, *Harvard Business Review*, 66(1), pp. 61–66.

Kaplan, R. S. & Cooper, R. (1998). *Cost & Effect — Using Integrated Cost Systems to Drive Profitability and Performance*. Boston: Harvard Business School Press, p. 357.

Mgbame, C. O. & Osamuyimen, E. (2010). Product Costing Systems in Nigerian Companies, Journal of Research in National Development, 8(2), pp. 344–351.

Miller, J. & Vollman, T. (1985). The Hidden Factory, *Harvard Business Review*, 63(5), pp. 142–150.

Peavey, D. E. (1990). Battle at the GAAP? - It's Time for a Change, *Management Accounting*, 71, February, pp. 31–35.

Schoute, M. (2009). The Relationship between Cost System Complexity, Purposes of Use, and Cost System Effectiveness, *The British Accounting Review*, 41, pp. 208–226.

Sterling, R. R. (1973). Accounting Research, Education and Practice, *Journal of Accountancy*, 136(3), pp. 44–52.

Turney, P. B. B. (1991). *Common Cents: The ABC Performance Breakthrough*, Cost Technology, Hillsboro, Oregon.

Wallace, S. (2009). Non-linear influences of price competition on cost accounting system sophistication. *PMA Conference Online Proceedings*. Dunedin, New Zealand: University of Otago.

Index

ABC, 256
Abeggren, 41
Abernathy, 41, 102
accuracy of decision-making, 269
accuracy of product costing, 268
Acer, 23
activity map, 66
Adam Smith, 122, 123
advance pricing agreement (APA),
    87, 89–91
advanced countries, 14
adverse selection, 49
aggressive market price, 79
air pollution, 103
air/fuel ratio, 103
alliance between Toyota and BMW,
    118
alliances with the new partners, 111
allocation of joint profit, 127
Allow, 113
almost fabless, 65
alternative energies, 108
"Ambidexterity" management, 111
Android 4.4, 32
Android OS, 26
animism, 124
App Store, 26
Apple Operational International
    (AOI), 28
Apple Sales International (ASI), 26
"Apple-Pay", 20
Appli, 25
Applies providers, 26
AR, 212
arm's length method, 88
arm's length price, 87, 89, 91

artificial products, 125
"asset-light" strategy, 20
Asura, 128
au, 25
automobile industry, 133–136, 138,
    142, 143

bad slack, 246
Baldwin, 23
Base Erosion and Profit Shifting
    (BEPS), 26, 27, 83, 86, 88, 89
bench-mark, 77
benefits of fuel economy, 110
best buy, 72
Beyond Budgeting, 231
big-data of automobiles, 26
biological "re-programing", 102
biological analogy, 102
bipolarization of markets, 31
blue ocean strategy, 42
Bosch, 37
bottle neck resources, 172
brand makers, 29
break-even time (BET), 51
breakdown losses, 210
Broadcom, 22
budgetary performance, 232
budgetary slack, 231, 232
budgeting, 231
business ecosystem, 25, 26
Business innovation, 6
business model, 6, 68
business model of the cost minimum
    combination, 42
business-value creation model, 43

calibrated design, 71
carbon dioxide (CO_2), 104
carbon fiber, 119
carbon monoxide (CO), 103
Carlos Ghosn, 114
carriers, 24
Cash Conversion Cycle (CCC), 21
cash on hand, 42
cash-rich company, 42
catch-ball, 239
"cell-stack" of FCV, 119
Chandler, 32
chaos, 115
Check-the-box Classification
   Regulations, 27
"China + Taiwan" network, 30
Chinese mobile-phone makers, 31
chip size, 22
Christensen, 14
chrystal panel, 24
circulating life-cycles, 112
clinical departments, 174
"closed" modularization, 116
CO_2 emissions, 107
Coase, 7
code of conduct, 70
collectivism, 239
commercial printing, 205
commission agent, 93, 94
commissionaire, 93, 94
commissioned company, 96
common modular components, 35
Common Module Family (CMF), 35
common parts, 9
common platform, 35
commons, 123
communization strategy, 134,
   137–139, 143
compact cars, 106
competency trap, 110
competition among oligopoly, 118
competitive patterns, 69
complementarities, 115
complementarity, 118
conditional truth, 266

configuration, 68
consigned manufacturers of
   automobile, 35
consignment manufacturing, 94
consignment sales, 92–94, 96, 97
consolidated operating cash flows,
   156
contents providers, 26
Continental AG, 37
contingency framework, 268
continuous process improvement, 161
contract manufacturer, 38, 92
contract manufacturing, 92, 96, 97
cooperative behaviors, 123
cooperative game theory, 127
core competence, 66
core concept of the network
   organization, 115
corporate social responsibility (CSR),
   70
cost centers, 134, 140, 141, 143
cost crisis, 161
cost drivers, 165, 258
cost hierarchy, 261
cost plus methods, 88
cost sharing, 92
cost-center, 141
costly truth, 266
costs are distorted, 256
creating shared value (CSV), 66
creation of value-added product, 41
cultural controls, 164
culture, 245
custom-made parts, 9
customer-value, 42
cybernetic controls, 164

"*de facto*" standard, 116
de-maturity, 41, 102
decision by majority, 114
definition of OED, 217
democratic procedure, 114
design architecture of the purchased
   parts, 16
design blueprint, 29

development of iPhone, 20
diagnosis, 167
Diagnosis Procedure Combination
  (DCP), 161
dictator's priority order, 114
direct costs, 174
divine apparatuses, 121
divisional profit and loss statement
  (P/L), 174
DNA, 125
dominant design concept, 108
double taxation, 91
"double-brands" strategy, 31
downtime losses, 210

earth, 128
eco-car subsidy, 108
ecology, 124
economies of scale, 133, 137–141, 143
economy of scope, 17
egoism (selfishness) based value, 122
egoistic greed, 121
Electronic Fuel Injection, 103
electronics manufacturing services
  (EMSs), 11, 48
emerging countries, 14
emission trading, 123
emissions, 73
emitted CO_2 per 1kWh, 107
empowered, 170
energy thermal efficiency, 107
energy-efficient gasoline cars, 107
enlarged wafer, 22
Euro 6, 119
even out, 163
ex-ante control, 238
ex-post control, 238
exploitation of knowledge, 110
exploration of knowledge, 110

fabless auto-makers, 35
fabless design houses, 18
fabless firms, 48
fabless production, 65
fabless supply chain, 11, 66

FDK of Fujitsu, 7
financial measures, 148, 150, 156,
  177
flash memory, 24
floods and landslides, 122
Ford system, 133, 137
fossil fuel, 108
foundry, 12
Foxconn, 21
free cash flow, 21
"frontier" curve, 112
fuel consumption, 105
Fujifilm, 112
full-fledged manufacturer, 93
full-lineup strategy, 37
functional shiftability, 61

gas-guzzler car, 105
general proposition, 3, 39
(general) impossibility theorem, 113
global, 126
global operational alliances, 112
global supply chain, 68
global supply chain of Apple's
  iPhone, 17
Go to Gemba, 166
goals of the environmental needs, 103
God of creatures, 125
God of earth, 125
God of fire, 127
God of rain, 128
God of river, 125
God of sun, 125, 127
God of water, 125
God of wind, 125
good slack, 246
Google, 26, 32
governance costs, 7
government structure, 164

Hardin, 123
hierarchical vertical-integration, 4
high-end market, 13
high-end market cars, 40
Hinduism, 124

Hon Hai, 11, 21
Horizontal Network Organizations, 189
horizontal combination of firms, 118
human-motivation, 102
hybrid, 69
hybrid architecture product, 10
"hybrid network of *keiretsu* and market", 116
hybrid of hierarchy and inter-firm network, 34
hybrid of market and inter-firm network, 11
hybrid supply chain, 11
"hybrid" strategy, 32
hybrid-type exploration of development knowledge, 112
hydro carbon, 103
hydroelectricity, 107
hydrogen-storage-tank, 119

iBooks, 26
ideology (value system) of the famous "invisible hand", 122
idling and minor stoppage losses, 210
impossibility theorem, 273
in-process control, 238
incentive schemes, 234
individualism, 239
industry life-cycle, 13
information asymmetry, 234
innovation, 42, 101
insourced, 66
institutional theory, 164
institutions, 245
integral architectures, 133, 135, 136, 142
integral type product, 9
Integrated Device Manufacturer, 18, 24
Intel, 22
inter-firm network, 10
interfaces, 20, 21
Intergovernmental Panel on Climate Change (IPCC), 104

Internal Revenue Service (IRS), 27
international taxation problem, 27
intra-company transfer price, 97
intra-company transfer pricing, 87
intricate pattern, 74
iOS, 26
iPad, 26
iPhone 5c, 32
iPhone 5s, 32
iPhone 6, 20
ISO 9001, 173
iTunes Store, 26
IWAY, 76

Japan Display, 24
Japanese automobile network, 33
Japanese budgeting, 232
JIT Cash Flows, 150, 151, 154, 156, 157
JIT Residual Income, 152, 153, 155, 157
joint development, 118
joint profit allocation, 58
just-in-time, 74

Kaizen, 173
Kazuo Inamori, 114
Keiretsu, 10
Kim, 42
Kindle Appli, 26
"Kindle" terminal, 26
Kindle-store, 26
knowledge portfolio, 111
Kodak, 112
Kuhn–Tucker condition, 127
Kyoto Protocol, 104

laboratory, 77
Lavie & Rosenkopf, 111
lean (cost-efficient) business model, 41
lean accounting, 162
lean patient flow, 162
lean production systems (LPS), 147, 161

"lean" management in the global
supply chain, 20
level out, 167
LG Display, 24
LIB, 116
light trucks, 105
limited production, 133, 134, 138–141
limited-risk distributor, 93
lithium-ion battery, 116
local management, 147, 149
location savings, 83, 84, 89, 90, 97
Location Specific Advantage, 89
longer product life-cycle, 32
low-end market cars, 40
low-end products, 13, 31
low-price smartphone, 29

Magna International, 38
make of buy decision, 7
management by the ambidexterity,
110
management control, 189
Management Control Package
(MCP), 65, 164
Management control systems (MCS),
161
MAP, 90, 91
March, 110
market needs or wants, 12, 15
market network, 116
market premium, 90
market price method, 88
market price-based transfer pricing,
58
market-based transaction, 17
mass production, 133, 137–139, 141,
143
mathematical optimization algorism,
127
Mauborgne, 42
measuring the performance, 207
Media Tek, 29
medical expenses, 174
medical insurance system, 161
medical treatment fee, 176

mega-platforms, 37
mega-suppliers, 37
Michelin, 37
middle management, 147
mini-car, 106
Mitsubishi Motors, 39
Mobile Virtual Network Operation,
25
moderating variables, 233
modular and integral architectures,
143
modular architectures, 133–135, 137,
142, 143
modular design architecture in the
auto-industry, 35
modular type product, 9
modularization of EV components,
115
modularization of Volkswagen, 36
modularization strategies, 133, 135,
139
moral hazard, 49
Moral Sentiment, 123
MPG, 105
MQB, 36
Muda, 209
multi-attribute utility theory, 273
multi-layer strategy, 25
multiple Pareto optimum points, 112
mutual agreement procedures, 90
mutual sympathy among the egoistic
individuals, 124
MVNO, 25
"nature-centered" philosophy, 125

need for changing our way of living,
121
network organization, 19, 126
new sales ratio, 51
NHI point system, 176
nitrogen oxides, 103
NO, 103
non-financial measuring systems, 164
non-value activities, 172
nonconformity errors, 167

NTT DoCoMo, 25
nuclear electricity, 107

OECD transfer pricing guidelines, 88, 89
OEE, 207
OEM manufactures, 38
oil-engine cars, 107
open custom-parts, 19
"open" custom-parts suppliers, 11
"open" modularization, 116
operating cash flows, 154, 155, 157
operating profit ratio on sales, 22
opportunity cost, 57
optimal balancing problem, 111
optimal combination points, 5
optimal point, 126
order of universe, 128
"ordinal" preference priority for the policies, 113
Organization Model of Lean Strategy, 134, 141, 143
organizational commitment, 234
organizational learning, 110
outsourced, 66
overall equipment effectiveness, 207
overhead costs, 175

paradigm of "ideology", 122
Pareto improvement, 112
"Pareto optimal solution", 111
Pareto Optimum, 11
participative budgeting, 233
particulates (PM), 119
patient care cycles, 163
patient flow, 165
PDCA, 179
peaceful coexistence of individuals, 124
People & Planet Positive, 76
performance indicators, 175
performance management, 133, 134, 138, 139, 141, 143, 144
performance-based pay systems, 246
philosophy for living, 121

photochemical oxidants, 103
photovoltaics, 107
physical measures, 147–149
Pity or Compassion, 123
planet, 122
platform leaders, 26
platforms, 133, 136–139, 141, 143
PLC, 13, 15
post-fabrication services, 24
power-train function, 108
power-train mix, 118
pre-fabrication stage of smile curve, 23
price shock, 74
primary energy, 106, 107
primary residual income, 155
primary sources of electricity energy, 107
prime energy, 108
printing industry, 205
process control, 238
process innovation, 162
product costing system, 254
product design architectures, 8, 133–135 142, 143
production or purchase costs per unit, 7
profit centers, 133, 134, 138, 140, 141
profitability, 174
prototypes, 162
purchasing matrix, 72
pure market network, 4

Qualcomm, 11
quality defects and rework, 210
quality deviations, 167
quality losses, 210

rain, wind, storm, and thunder, 128
re-birth, 101
re-incarnation, 41
re-incarnation cycle, 112
reconfiguration, 66
reconstruct, 161
redesigned, 161

reduced speed losses, 210
reduced yield, 210
regeneration, 41
regenerative energy, 108
regional headquarter, 94
relationship-specific investment, 52
Renesas, 24
repetitive alliances with the same
   companies, 111
residual income, 155, 157
resource exhaust, 122
resource-based strategy, 66
resource-based view, 110
responsibility, 177
results control, 241
Retina display, 24
Retina-panel, 19
rewards, 164
Rig-Veda, 124, 127
rightsourcing, 73
risks of poverty, food, 105
rita, 128
rolling horizon, 73
root cause, 167
routing, 72

sales channel of iPhone, 28
Samsung, 22, 24
Scandinavian style, 72
Schumpeter, 101, 110
secondary energy, 109
semiconductor, 22
Sequential Seeking Approach, 126,
   127
Sequential Seeking Approach to the
   Global Optimum, 127
set-up and adjustment losses, 210
shared information highway, 68
Sharp, 24
Shibata, 115
Shimokawa, 106
Shoichiro Toyoda, 104
shrunk chip, 22
SIM cards, 31
Simon, 16

smartphone for high-end market, 40
smartphone for low-end market, 40
SMEs, 189
smile curve, 23
social contract, 128
social responsibility, 65
social welfare function, 113
SoftBank, 25
solar, 107
Sony, 31
Sophistication in Costing Systems,
   257
sourcing, 70
specialized parts, 9
speed losses, 210
Sport Utility Truck (SUT), 39
Spring of Order, 128
Stan Shi, 23
standardization, 178
stem cell, 125
"stimulus" for Innovations, 102
stimulus, 101
strategic flexibility, 55
strategic planning, 164
stretched goals, 232
subjective value criterion, 113
supply chain structures, 9
sustainability, 43, 76
sustainable mobility, 125
sustainable world, 125
Swedwood, 72
switching cost, 54
symbiosis, 123, 124
symbiosis (coexistence) with natural
   world, 124
sympathy, 123
sympathy (altruism) based value,
   123
synergy effect, 115
system LSI, 22

Tablet PC, 26
target costing, 70
target price, 70
targets to prevent able, 242

TDABM, 165
teaching of Buddha, 124
technology portfolio, 113
telecommunication service, 24
Tesla Motors, 117
theory of the complex systems, 115
Three Way Catalyst, 103
Throughput costing, 254
tier 1 group, 32
tier 2 group, 33
tier 3 firms, 33
Time-Driven Activity-Based Costing
    (TD-ABC), 162
time-to-market (TTM), 51
TNGA, 35
toll manufacturer, 92
top management, 147, 154, 156
top management's spirit, 114
Toshiba, 7
Toyota, 133, 134, 138–140, 142, 143
Toyota Business group, 32
Toyota group, 34
Toyota New Global Architecture, 35
Toyota Production System (TPS),
    133, 134, 138–141, 143, 173
TPM, 209
trade-off ratio, 113
traditional financial measures, 148,
    154
traditional product costing system,
    255
tragedy of the commons, 123
transaction costs, 7
Transfer Pricing Taxation, 83
transmigration, 41, 102, 114
transmigration of the PLC, 41
"transmigration" between the parent
    and the child, 125

"transmigration" of nature and
    energy, 125
triple bottom line, 65
TSMC, 12, 18, 22
turbo-charger, 107
turnover, 41
Type-1 *muda*, 209
Type-2 *muda*, 209

unit manufacturing costs, 16, 17
unit purchase cost, 16
United Nations Environment
    Programme (UNEP), 104

Valeo, 37
value adding, 163
value chain, 66, 163
value constellation, 67
value engineering, 70
value for patients, 163
value premises, 101
value streams, 163
value system, 66
value-based pricing, 56
VDL Nedcar, 38
Vernon, 14, 41
vertically divided network, 20
vertical combination of firms,
    118
Vietnamese people, 121

wafer foundries, 18
waste, 73, 209
waters, 128
Wearable Watch, 21
Williamson, 7
woods, 128
working conditions, 76

Printed in the United States
By Bookmasters